Rhetoric Reclaimed

Rhetoric & Society

General Editor: Wayne A. Rebhorn

Rhetoric Reclaimed

Aristotle and the
Liberal Arts Tradition

JANET M. ATWILL

CORNELL UNIVERSITY PRESS

ITHACA AND LONDON

First published 1998 by Cornell University Press.

Cornell University Press strives to utilize environmentally responsible suppliers and
materials to the fullest extent possible in the publishing of its books. Such materials
include vegetable-based, low-VOC inks and acid-free papers that are also either
recycled, totally chlorine-free, or partly composed of nonwood fibers.

Printed in the United States of America

Library of Congress Cataloging-in-Publication Data

Atwill, Janet, 1955–
  Rhetoric reclaimed : Aristotle and the liberal arts tradition /
Janet Atwill.
       p.   cm. — (Rhetoric & society)
  Includes bibliographical references and index.
  ISBN 0-8014-3263-4 (alk. paper)
    1. Education, Humanistic.   2. Techne (Philosophy)   3. Rhetoric, Ancient.   I. Title.
II. Series.
LC1011.A89   1997
370.11′2—dc21   97-35244

Cloth printing 10 9 8 7 6 5 4 3 2 1

For my family

my parents, Joan Bland and Harold Wagner

my son, Peter Nathan Foltz

Contents

Foreword

Stated simply, the purpose of this series is to study rhetoric in all the varied forms it has taken in human civilizations by situating it in the social and political contexts to which it is inextricably bound. The series Rhetoric and Society rests on the assumptions that rhetoric is both an important intellectual discipline and a necessary cultural practice and that it is profoundly implicated in a large array of other disciplines and practices, from politics to literature to religion. Interdisciplinary by definition and unrestricted in range either historically or geographically, the series investigates a wide variety of questions; among them, how rhetoric constitutes a response to historical developments in a given society, how it crystalizes cultural tensions and conflicts and defines key concepts, and how it affects and shapes the social order in its turn. The series includes books that approach rhetoric as a form of signification, as a discipline that makes meaning out of other cultural practices, and as a central and defining intellectual and social activity deeply rooted in its milieu. In essence, the books in the series seek to demonstrate just how important rhetoric really is to human beings in society.

Janet M. Atwill's *Rhetoric Reclaimed: Aristotle and the Liberal Arts Tradition* is an important study of ancient rhetoric which has significant implications for our contemporary understanding of the discipline and for its crucial role in education. Its particular aim is to reexamine what Aristotle called productive knowledge, a category that includes rhetoric as well as such arts as medicine and navigation, and that is distinguished from theoretical and practical knowledge, both of which assume the existence of a fixed self, a stable worldview, and a determined set of values. By contrast, productive knowledge is situational and relational; representing the realm of human invention and intervention, it is a power rather than a body of principles or information, and it creates new subjectivities and produces new possibilities and lines of power in every exchange. In this rich and richly informed book, Atwill shows how Aristotle's concept of productive knowledge is in turn derived from a centuries-old tradition in ancient Greece and is an equivalent for the key term *techne*. That term, which can be translated as "art," was a model of knowledge and was associated with trickery, with the disruption of received wisdom, and with challenging and redefining the boundaries separating things and beings in the world. It was this art that Prometheus brought to human beings and that was identified as the source of human culture in a variety of ancient Greek myths. Atwill shows conclusively that medicine and navigation were designated *technai*, that is, human interventions in unstable situations designed to exploit the indeterminacies involved, and that the techne of the sophists, namely rhetoric, should be understood as deriving from this conceptual context. Atwill then goes on to explain how Plato denigrated this art because of his commitment to theoretical knowledge, a knowledge that transcends the contingencies of time, space, and the individuals who possess it. Plato did accept the notion of techne, however, but defined it as a form of "professional knowledge," which made it a principle of social organization and thus took the art of politics out of the hands of rhetors and placed it firmly, instead, in the hands of philosophers. By contrast, Aristotle, although sharing something of Plato's preference for theory, preserved the sophists' notion of rhetoric as a techne, as productive knowledge, in his *Rhetoric*. What has happened after Aristotle, however, according to Atwill, is the progressive obscuring of this category and its replacement by the dualism of theory and practice, a dualism that permits only timeless, context-independent knowledge to pass for true knowledge. Such a vision of knowledge informs the tradition of the liberal arts and the various humanisms associated with them; it has also guided later interpretations of Aristotle and has led to serious misunderstandings of his thinking on rhetoric. Taking a decidedly postmodern perspective, which is informed by a judicious understanding of thinkers such as Derrida and Bourdieu, Deleuze and Guattari, Atwill urges a renewed understanding of rhetoric as a form of productive knowledge, a restoration with social and political consequences, for it would require a pedagogy based on diversity and dialogue and would entail a profound democratization of the educational process.

WAYNE A. REBHORN

Acknowledgments

Research for this book was generously supported by grants from the Graduate School of the University of Tennessee and the Hodges Better English Fund.

This book is the product of a personal journey and a community of inquiry and support. With kindness, patience, and good humor, Bernhard Kendler guided me through Cornell's publication process. Carol Betsch and Nancy Malone provided meticulous editing. Frederick Antczak's generous responses to the manuscript helped me view my project in a new light. An anonymous reader for Cornell University Press pushed me to make what I am confident are significant improvements in the book's argument. At the University of Tennessee, Trent Eades provided invaluable research assistance; Susan North's intellectual and moral support carried me through the final stages of this project; and my students, Debra Hawhee and Carter Mathes in particular, gave me a teacher's best gift of letting me learn from them. I am especially indebted to David Tandy, who performed the most generous of collegial acts—that of actually reading the manuscript. I owe special thanks to Virgil Lokke, for his gift of theory; Michael Leff, for his abiding love of rhetoric; Kenneth Jobson, for his own art of redrawing the boundaries of nature; Ronald Hopson, for the wisdom that invention is impossible without hope; Alfhild Ingberg, for her enactment and articulation of an art of listening; La Vinia Jennings, for her faith in and expression of the bonds of *philia*; and two special families who opened their homes and hearts to my son and me:

Hope, Bernard, and Max Gulker, and Donna, David, Charlotte, Carolyn, and Andrew Walker.

I would believe this project to be a success if in some way it keeps alive the wisdom shared with me by my teacher, colleague, and friend James Berlin and my grandparents William and Noval Dawes Bland, from whom I received a vision of civic virtue. Finally, no thanks are adequate to those who knew the details of my journey and refused to give up on me. William Berez shared with me his art of redrawing the boundaries of fate; in no small sense he is the coauthor of Chapter 5. Don and Andrea Cox demonstrated the miracle of the human ties that are chosen rather than inherited; friendship does not seem like an adequate word for their faithfulness. This book only continues an argument concerning the significance of *technē* begun by Janice Lauer; her own determined journey created a path that gave me the luxury of my scholarly inquiry. My family, to whom this book is dedicated, demonstrated their love in their patience with this project. Joan Bland and Harold Wagner provided the emotional and financial support that made the book possible. My son, Peter Nathan Foltz, has taught me what is at stake in an art of the invention of the possible. In him I see its power; he has been my best teacher of the art of hope.

J. M. A.

Note on Texts

Unless otherwise indicated, the following editions have been used:

Aristotle
The Complete Works of Aristotle, ed. Jonathan Barnes, 2 vols. (Princeton: Princeton University Press, 1984). Parenthetical citations refer to Bekker line numbers from Oxford Classical Texts. References to the *Rhetoric* are taken from George Kennedy's translation, *On Rhetoric: A Theory of Civic Discourse* (New York: Oxford University Press, 1991).

Plato
The Collected Dialogues of Plato, ed. Edith Hamilton and Huntington Cairns (Princeton: Princeton University Press, 1961).

Sophistic Fragments
The Older Sophists, ed. Rosamond Kent (Columbia: University of South Carolina Press, 1972). Parenthetical citations refer to Greek texts in Hermann Deils and Walther Kranz, eds., *Die Fragmente der Vorsokratiker,* 11th ed., 3 vols. (1952; reprint, Zurick/Berlin: Weidmann, 1964).

See appropriate volume of Loeb Classical Library for texts of Aeschylus, Cicero, Hesiod, Hippocrates, Homer, Isocrates, Quintilian, and Solon.

Abbreviations

DK	*Die Fragmente der Vorsokratiker*
LSJ	*A Greek-Englsih Lexicon*, ed. Henry George Liddell, Robert Scott, and Henry Stuart Jones.
OCD	*Oxford Classical Dictionary*

Aeschylus

Pr.	*Prometheus Bound*

Aristotle

De An.	*De Anima (On the Soul)*
EN	*Nicomachean Ethics*
Phys.	*Physics*
Pol.	*Politics*
Rhet.	*Rhetoric*
Met.	*Metaphysics*
Top.	*Topics*

Hesiod

Theog.	*Theogony*
WD	*Works and Days*

Isocrates

Antid.	*Antidosis*
Areop.	*Areopagiticus*

Plato

Rep.	*Republic*
Protag.	*Protagoras*

Quintilian

Inst.	*Institutio Oratoria*

Bourdieu, Pierre
LP   *The Logic of Practice*
OTP   *Outline of a Theory of Practice*

Detienne, Marcel and Jean-Pierre Vernant
CI   *Cunning Intelligence in Greek Culture and Society*

Vernant, Jean-Pierre
MT   *Myth and Thought among the Greeks*

Rhetoric Reclaimed

Introduction

This book is both a response and an investigation. It is a response to the challenges posed by cultural diversity to the aims and methods of a humanist, liberal arts education; and it is an investigation of a neglected tradition of rhetoric, embodied, as I argue, in Protagoras's political *technē* and Isocrates' *logōn technē* and preserved, in a somewhat modified form, in Aristotle's *Rhetoric*.

Historically, the aim of a liberal arts education, in the most general terms, has been to inculcate a set of cultural values through texts and traditions believed to exemplify those values. In other words, the purpose of such an education has been to pass on "culture"—to transmit the values, practices, and institutions a culture believes to be its fabric and framework. The product of such an education would be the individual, a kind of normative subject, whose values and expectations conformed to those of the exemplars and traditions protected by the liberal arts. Few precepts could have a more august history or seem at first glance less problematic. The problem arises, however, at the point we are forced to define "culture." What does "culture" in the singular mean? Whose culture? And if we endeavor to bring other cultures into a liberal arts education, is the goal of producing a normative subject either feasible or desirable? These questions were not raised as long as the constituency of the liberal arts was stable and homogeneous. The notion that reading heroic epics was ennobling (particularly if read in Greek) was "commonsensical" as long as those who read the text held heroic adventures in similar regard. However, if common sense is the product of a fit between expectations and perceived reality, such epics would not necessarily embody timeless virtues for those who valued stable communities over valiant quests. Put another way, the time-lessness of a set of values is largely the product of the homogeneity of the community holding those values. This is essentially the crux of the encounter of the liberal arts with cultural diversity at the end of the twentieth century. New constituencies are no longer willing to be evaluated against a normative subject that seldom embodies their val-ues and experiences—let alone their best interests. This is not to say that traditional exemplars of Western culture have no value for the new constituencies that enter the academy. These exemplars, how-ever, can no longer be the last word on culture and value.

My purpose in this book is to set the ancient logōn technē tradition against the normalizing tendencies of the Western humanist tradition of the liberal arts. As I interpret it, this ancient rhetorical tradition was far more concerned with challenging and recalculating standards of value than with protecting a specific set of values from the forces of time and circumstance. My sources for this portrait of technē include Western medical, technical, and rhetorical treatises and mythical ac-counts, particularly the Prometheus narratives depicted by Hesiod, Aeschylus, Protagoras, and Isocrates. These accounts are examined in most detail in Chapters 2, 3, and 4.

As I insist throughout the book, this depiction of technē is as heuris-tic as it is descriptive. There is little support for an argument that the technē tradition championed a kind of cultural democracy. For the most part, such rhetors as Protagoras and Isocrates only helped the al-ready advantaged seize even more. Rather, the importance of the technē tradition lies in its distinctive differences from liberal arts tra-ditions on three specific points:

(1) A technē is never a representational body of knowledge.

(2) A technē resists identification with a static, normative subject.

(3) Technē marks a domain of human intervention and invention.

What is at stake in a technē is neither subjectivity nor virtue. In con-trast to philosophical or disciplinary models of knowledge, a technē is defined by its contingency on time and situation. In sum, a technē is knowledge as production, not product, and as intervention and artic-ulation rather than representation.

Because technē is persistently implicated in the transgression of boundaries, its story is tied to the construction of limits at a number of points—limits of knowledge and subjectivity, as well as social, political, and economic limits. Thus technē's story is interwoven in complex ways with the story of Athenian democracy. For those who met democracy's admission requirements, citizenship ensured a new equality before the law. But the price of equality before the law was the legitimation of the unequal distribution of resources. In other words, the "equality" of democracy's citizen was created by excising "him" from the conditions in which he was embedded and of which he was the product. As ancient historians have argued, democratic law signaled a historic shift in the Greek conception of equality and justice away from *isomoiria*, "equality of portion," to *isonomia*, "equality only with regard to the law." One part of my argument is that the Athenian citizen, extricated from time and circumstance, served as a model for the humanist subject. Just as the Athenian citizen was the product of historically specific requirements of gender and birth, the normative subject of the liberal arts was also a historically specific product—the universalization of a particular class, race, and gendered subject. This discussion occurs in its most explicit form in Chapters 2 and 5.

In taking on this subject, I do not want to trivialize either difference or tradition. The questions at issue are complex, and the stakes are high. At issue are the character of the social identities of gender, race, and class and the nature of the social ties by which we are bound as families, communities, states, and nations. Thus, the feminist critique embedded in my argument is part of my examination of the very construction of difference. Indeed, one of the primary purposes of this book is to point to new ways of recalculating the value of difference and identity. It is my hope that this argument will serve as a heuristic that will enable us to take the same pleasure in the differences of the social world that Aristotle took in the differences of the natural world:

> All men [*anthrōpoi*] by nature desire to know. An indication of this is the delight we take in our senses; for even apart from their usefulness they are loved for themselves; and above all others the sense of sight. For not only with a view to action, but even when we are not going to do anything, we prefer sight to almost everything else. The reason is that this, most of all senses, makes us know and brings to light many differences between things. (*Met.* 980a21–27)

1 Rhetoric, Humanism, and the Liberal Arts

What is important is to try to show how 'Man" has been produced in modern times, how the 'human' subject—that is, the bearer of a human identity without distinctions—appears in certain religious discourses, is embodied in juridical practices and is diversely constructed in other spheres. An understanding of this dispersion can help us to grasp the fragility of 'humanist' values themselves, the possibility of their perversion through equivalential articulation with other values, and their restriction to certain categories of the population—the property-owning class, for example, or the male population. . . . [S]uch an analysis can show us the historical conditions of its emergence and the reasons for its current vulnerability, thus enabling us to struggle more efficiently, and without illusions, in defence of humanist values.

—Ernesto Laclau and Chantal Mouffe, *Hegemony and Socialist Strategy*

The very idea of a subject . . . prior to its values, goals, desires, talents, and possessions seems not so much suspect as unimaginable. What is clear . . . is that such a self has more to do with solving a philosophical problem . . . than it does with grounding a theory of justice in the needs of real individuals.

—C. Fred Alford, *The Self in Social Theory*

In first-century imperial Rome, while Quintilian was crafting his program of rhetorical education based on the premise that "perfect eloquence, the noblest of human attainments," could never be "united with a vicious character of mind,"[1] Tacitus offered the following description of the art of rhetoric:

---

[1] See Quintilian, *Inst.*XII.i.32.

The art which is the subject of our discourse is not a quiet and peaceable art, or one that finds satisfaction in moral worth and good behavior; no, really great and famous oratory is a foster-child of licence, which foolish men called liberty, an associate of sedition, a goad for the unbridled populace. It owes no allegiance to any. Devoid of reverence, it is insulting, off-hand, and overbearing. It is a plant that does not grow under a well-regulated constitution. (*Dialogue on Oratory*, 40)

In the context of the dialogue, Tacitus's description of rhetoric is neither disparaging nor simply ironic. Though he admits that the conditions that left Roman eloquence "degraded, like a discrowned queen" (32), are the same conditions that secure the stability of the commonwealth in his own time (36), the dialogue as a whole is a hymn to the "power of eloquence" and a lament to its decline (35).

There is little question that Tacitus's *Dialogue on Oratory* is, in part, a critique of an empire that had sharply restricted rhetoric's domain. The deliberative rhetoric of Athens had been displaced by forensic addresses centered largely on property and inheritance disputes and by two new genres: the *actio gratiarum*, a speech of thanks addressed to the emperor and the gods given by the emperor's appointees to the consul,[2] and the art of *delatio*, a speech of accusation, given by professional *delatores* in the political service of the emperors.[3] First-century Rome might have confirmed Plato's portrait of rhetoric in the *Gorgias* as an art of flattery and force. Still, how could Tacitus give such a definition to an art that Quintilian had defined succinctly as the "vir bonus dicendi peritus" (the good man speaking well)?

This book is an attempt to answer that question. My argument in its most general terms is that Tacitus and Quintilian were referring to not only two different rhetorical traditions but also two different—and virtually incommensurable—epistemological traditions: a humanist-liberal arts tradition, illustrated by Quintilian, which was grounded in normative conceptions of knowledge and subjectivity; and an older model of knowledge identified with *technē* (commonly translated as "art"), which appears in the rhetorical traditions of Protagoras, Isocrates, and Aristotle.

---

[2] In *Rhetoric in the Roman World*, Kennedy notes that a kind of deliberative oratory persisted in the addresses of military commanders. Oratory as a means of "promoting unity throughout the empire" was generally replaced, according to Kennedy, by the "rhetoric of public works and coins, of bread and circuses" (431).

[3] See Winterbottom, "Quintilian and the *Vir Bonus*."

Technē played an important thematic role in mythological accounts as early as the eighth century B.C.E.; it is at the heart of the Prometheus narratives of both Hesiod and Aeschylus. In fifth-century B.C.E. medical treatises attributed to Hippocrates, technē is carefully described as a distinct model of knowledge, while Thucydides depicted sea navigation, warfare, and politics as technai. The early sophists used technē to describe the knowledge they purveyed; Protagoras described his instruction as a political technē; Isocrates, Aristotle's contemporary, also referred to his instruction as a *logōn technē*, or art of discourse. After Plato's bifurcation of technē into the true and the sham, however, Aristotle's classification of art in the domain of productive knowledge was one of the last and most serious treatments of technē as a model of knowledge.

Aristotle refused to accept Plato's distinction between true and false arts. For Aristotle, technē was not bound by the measures of value and knowledge that govern the other two categories of Aristotle's epistemological taxonomy—theoretical knowledge and practical knowledge.[4] Theoretical knowledge encompassed philosophy, mathematics, and the natural sciences; practical knowledge subsumed ethics and politics. Productive knowledge, however, included a wide range of arts: medicine, military strategy, architecture, poetics, and—as I argue—rhetoric.[5] Aristotle did not treat technē as a rhetorician might in defense of the legitimacy of the art. Instead, as a philosopher, Aristotle provided coherent theoretical accounts of both productive knowledge and rhetoric. Though rhetoric's status as a productive art was debated by Quintilian—a debate that continued for generations to come—the dispute was increasingly framed in the terms of philosophy. Rhetoric as a technē became identified largely with the handbook tradition—a neutral tool in service to the higher causes of ethics, politics, or philosophy, whereas productive knowledge largely disappeared as an epistemological category, emerging primarily as it became identified with arts and crafts that produce a material "product."[6]

In the period on which I focus, roughly the seventh century B.C.E. through the fourth century B.C.E., the concept of technē goes through several transformations. Three defining characteristics, however, remain relatively stable:

---

[4] See Aristotle, *Met.* 982ia, 982b10, and EN 1139b25–30, 1139b1, 1140a1–20.

[5] A similar argument could be made for poetics.

[6] For one of very few treatments of the demise of productive knowledge, see Lobkowicz, *Theory and Practice.*

(1) A technē is never a static, normative body of knowledge.[7] A technē is described as a *dynamis* (or power) and a set of transferable strategies, both contingent on situation and purpose. A technē neither represents reality nor encompasses a set of deductive postulates.

(2) A technē resists identification with a normative subject. In Hesiod's Prometheus narratives, every exchange of a technē creates a different order of power—different subjectivities. As such, there are no well-defined boundaries between the subject and knowledge. Consequently, it is difficult, if not impossible, to make technē conform to either Plato's equation of knowledge and virtue or to Quintilian's vir bonus.

(3) Technē marks a domain of human intervention and invention. What is at stake in a technē is neither subjectivity nor virtue. In both ancient literary and technical treatments, technē is defined against the forces of necessity, spontaneity, experience, chance, compulsion, and force; it is often associated with the transgression of an existing boundary—a desire for "more" that challenges or redefines relations of power. In contrast to philosophical knowledge, a technē is defined by its relation to situation and time. A technē is knowledge as production, not product; intervention and articulation, rather than representation.

The Institution of Humanism

The Humanist Paradigm and the Tradition of *Technē*

If productive knowledge disappeared soon after Aristotle, it was not without good reason, for it is defined against virtually every distinguishing feature of traditional Western humanism. Obviously, defining the humanist paradigm is hardly a simple task. Paul Oskar Kristeller contends that Renaissance humanism, for example, *cannot* really be defined, because it was not a unified "philosophical tendency or system, but rather a cultural and educational program" (*Renaissance Thought*, 22). In other words, humanism is "institutions" more than a coherent philosophy; it is books, methodologies, curricula, departmental divisions, funding programs, professional organizations, and methods of evaluating professional competence. It is precisely for this reason that humanism *is* so difficult to define, for when we talk

---

[7] Norms, of course, are the fabric of any conception of knowledge and character. I use "normative" here to refer to "standardizing" processes that obscure their contingent character.

about the humanities as both institution and ideology, we are trying to discuss what by definition cannot be brought before us as an object of analysis. In other words, it is the very character of institutions to be invisible—to be our constitutive condition rather than our objects of analysis. This does not mean that treatises aiming to provide conceptual coherence for humanism are not expressions of its values. But humanism as a coherent perspective is always something constituted "after the fact," a construction of the past in the rhetorical present.[8]

The definition that guides this analysis is drawn primarily from twentieth-century accounts of humanism and postmodern critiques of knowledge and subjectivity; to many this definition of humanism will frequently sound reductive, if not altogether false. Admittedly, I use the term "humanism" as a label for a very heterogeneous set of precepts and practices. For example, Werner Jaeger's *Paideia: The Ideals of Greek Culture*, which will be examined in some detail, outlines one version of "classical humanism" that frames itself in the culture of antiquity. At the same time, proponents of various traditions of scientific humanism have argued, as did Harvard's nineteenth-century president C. W. Eliot, that "liberal studies" are "pursued in the scientific spirit for truth's sake."[9] What these diverse treatises hold in common, however, is the faith that one model of subjectivity can guide descriptions of knowledge and attributions of value. Indeed, it is humanism's tendency to place knowledge, value, and subjectivity in a chain of equivalences, and this relationship of equivalence ob-

[8] The notion of "civic humanism" is a case in point. Although several generations of historians have argued over the character of "civic humanism" in the Renaissance, Albert Rabil notes that the term was first used in the 1920s by the Renaissance scholar Hans Baron. Moreover, Rabil observes that Baron's thesis that "political democracy and cultural pluralism" were the "hallmarks" of the true spirit of Renaissance was formulated as Baron himself fled Hitler's Germany in the 1930s ("Significance of 'Civic Humanism,'" 152). Rabil goes on to suggest that "the way in which he [Baron] finally formulated his thesis has an intrinsic relation to the rise of tyranny before his eyes" (152). While the singular nature of Nazi Germany's crimes may suggest that Baron's circumstances were unique, Baron's interpretive situation is the given case in which all scholars write. The present always determines our construction of the past. Critical interpretations, historical narratives, and humanist manifestos are always to some extent responses to the rhetorical exigencies of the present.

[9] See Kimball, *Orators and Philosophers*, chaps. 5 and 6, for other versions of the "liberal free" ideal, which attempted to accommodate classical humanist values to the spirit of scientific inquiry. The quotation from C. W. Eliot is taken from page 167. See also Feinberg, *Reason and Rhetoric*, and Kate Soper's treatment of technological humanism in *Humanism and Anti-Humanism*.

scures the inadequacy of a single model of the subject to accommodate human difference. For our purposes, humanism will refer to the following restricted set of terms and precepts.[10]

Human. The "human," generally translated "man," can be defined by common, essential features that transcend gender, culture, and history. This assumption is tacitly expressed in Goethe's familiar aphorism that "man carries within himself not only his own individuality but all of humanity"; in other words, the historical individual is an expression of the ahistorical "human." At the same time, many humanist treatises insist that this generic subject found its full expression in a particular historical moment—the culture of Greece or Rome, for example. Consequently, these versions of humanism effectively "universalize" a specific model of subjectivity. Though this model is defined by its proposed universality, the ideal features by which it is characterized are not present in every subject. The humanities are a means of inculcating or actualizing these features in "the individual."

Knowledge. Knowledge can be extricated both from the subject and from relations of power and economic exchange. Like the humanist subject, humanist knowledge can transcend the specificities of time, place, and gender. This kind of knowledge can be characterized in one of two ways. Classical humanism frequently depicts knowledge as an attribute of the knowing subject, the "actualization" of knowledge in the mind. Consequently, this version of humanism is centrally concerned with the construction of character. Scientific or philosophical humanism generally depicts knowledge as a coherent description of an object or a practice. Consequently, scientific humanism is centrally concerned with demarcating an object of study and securing conditions under which one might claim that objective description is possible.

Value. "Value" is a rather unproblematic term that can be assessed by a single measure. That scale, for the most part, has been calibrated simply by the terms "man" and "knowledge." In other words,

---

[10] These characteristics clearly do not account for such varieties of humanism as socialist and marxist humanism. See Sher, ed., *Marxist Humanism and Praxis,* and Fromm, ed., *Socialist Humanism.*

knowledge is conceived as valuable either as a means to the end of human fulfillment or as an end in itself. Both alternatives, however, yield a similar model of subjectivity. When knowledge is a means to an end, that end is generally the realization of "man's" potential; when knowledge is an end in itself, the search for knowledge becomes "man's" highest distinguishing feature. Thus, the humanist scale of value takes the form of a chain of equivalences between "man," knowledge, and value; this scale of value generally excludes other, more specific and temporal strategies for calculating value—situated and flexible measures in a wide range of spheres, such as the domains of economic exchange and of community and family relationships.[11]

Because institutions of learning have been largely guided by humanist precepts, we are left with numerous accounts of humanism's forms, aims, and values. This is clearly not the case for the paradigm of productive knowledge. Although one of the most extensive treatments of technē as an epistemological model is found in Aristotle's discussion of productive knowledge, the definition of technē that guides this analysis is drawn from a variety of genres—literary, historical, technical, and philosophical. Consequently, this definition will often be as heuristic as it is descriptive. In other words, productive knowledge is neither embodied in an institution that can be described nor defended in a wide range of academic accounts that can be analyzed. What we can investigate are points of incommensurability between humanism and the paradigm of technē.

This treatment of technē and humanism is guided by several assumptions. My primary assumption is that a model of knowledge always brings with it a corresponding model of subjectivity—and, therefore, social relations. Put more simply, orders of knowledge are invariably tied to social, political, and economic orders.[12] This discussion also assumes that the stable subject of humanist discourse is a specific historical construct; its generic nature is contingent on restricting alternative models of subjectivity. Finally, despite the fact that many traditions of Western humanism reject Plato's aims and methods, humanism, as a whole, has retained the Platonic distinctions between knowledge, the subject, and value. Consequently, to a great extent, the lexicon of the humanities is the lexicon of philoso-

[11] See Barbara Herrnstein Smith, *Contingencies of Value*, for a careful discussion of situated calculations of value.

[12] The equation of social to epistemological order is present throughout the work of Bourdieu. See especially *Outline of a Theory of Practice* and *Distinction*.

phy.[13] In this context, the scholarly neglect of Aristotle's domain of productive knowledge bears witness to the power of the philosophical paradigm to obscure alternative, situated standards of knowledge and value.

Critiquing Humanism from Within the Humanities

Rhetoric's propensity to challenge static disciplinary models of knowledge has been explored in different ways by a number of scholars in rhetoric: James Berlin, Janice Lauer, Michael Leff, and Richard Young, to name a few. Postmodern theory as a whole, however, has been a large-scale assault on Western conceptions of knowledge and value, ranging from Richard Rorty's *Philosophy and the Mirror of Nature* to Michel Foucault's *Archaeology of Knowledge*—from Pierre Bourdieu, Jacques Derrida, and Jean-François Lyotard to Gilles Deleuze and Félix Guattari.[14] Contemporary political theorists, like Iris Marion Young, have increasingly included critiques of the political

---

[13] To a degree, these terms simply describe the building blocks of Western epistemological foundationalism. For the classic treatment of this perspective, see Rorty, *Philosophy and the Mirror of Nature.*

[14] See Berlin, *Writing Instruction in Nineteenth-Century American Colleges* and *Rhetoric and Reality;* Lauer, "Issues in Rhetorical Invention"; Leff, "Genre and Paradigm in the Second Book of *De Oratore*" and "The Habitation of Rhetoric"; and Richard Young, "Arts, Crafts, Gifts, and Knacks." Edward Schiappa and Thomas Cole have outlined revisionist treatments of rhetoric's disciplinary history. For specifically postmodern approaches to rhetoric's disciplinary status, see the work of Victor Vitanza. The past two decades have also yielded a number of revisionist approaches to the classical tradition and the history of rhetoric. A representative sample would include Detienne and Vernant, *Cunning Intelligence in Greek Culture and Society;* Vernant, *Myth and Society in Ancient Greece* and *Myth and Thought among the Greeks;* Vidal-Naquet, *Black Hunter;* Catherine Osborne, *Rethinking Early Greek Philosophy;* Jarratt, *Rereading the Sophists;* du Bois, *Sowing the Body* and *Torture and Truth;* and Bernal, *Black Athena.* Bourdieu's work is centrally concerned with the inextricability of subjectivity from social, political, and economic orders; see especially *Outline of a Theory of Practice, Distinction, Logic of Practice,* and *Language and Symbolic Power.* For specific Derridean critiques of humanism, see "The Ends of Man," "Principle of Reason,"and "The Age of Hegel." Lyotard's *Postmodern Condition* is one of the earliest revisions of epistemological paradigms; see also *The Inhuman* and *The Differend.* Deleuze and Guattari's *Anti-Oedipus* and *Thousand Plateaus* are two of the most radical postmodern critiques of subjectivity. A similarly radical critique is embedded in Lacanian psychology. For a broad treatment of postmodern approaches to problems of the subject, see Paul Smith, *Discerning the Subject.* For other critiques of humanist institutions, see Paul Bové, *Intellectuals in Power;* Graff, *Professing Literature;* and Weber, *Institution and Interpretation.*

"individual," or the "generic citizen." Feminist discourse has issued some of the most serious challenges to the gender specificity of dominant humanist models, while the work of cultural critics such as Gayatri Chakravorty Spivak, Cornel West, Edward Said, Henry Louis Gates Jr., and Seyla Benhabib has raised similar questions concerning humanism's cultural, political, and racial specificity.[15]

Challenges to the humanist paradigm, however, have not been confined to the university. From the late 1960s on, humanities departments have turned into battlegrounds for conflicts concerning the values and exemplars of the humanist tradition. In the late 1980s and early 1990s those conflicts became the subject of wide media attention in debates over cultural diversity, political correctness, and revisionist literary canons and historical accounts. Just what is at stake in these culture wars is succinctly expressed in a 1991 editorial in the *New Republic* that responds to a multicultural curriculum in the New York public school system:

> At issue . . . is the nature of the pedagogy that will install these cultures in the minds of our children—the replacement of any notion of a factual account of our country's history or geography with a curriculum geared

---

[15] For specific critiques of political subjectivity, see Dallmayr, *Twilight of Subjectivity* and *Polis and Praxis*, and Alford, *Self in Social Theory*. More traditional examinations of "individualist" political structures and theories are implicit in any examination of liberal theory. M. M. Taylor's *Men versus the State* is a careful examination of nineteenth-century liberal theory that situates itself in the resurgence of conservative politics in the 1970s and the development of communitarianism in the 1980s and 1990s. Defenses of liberal theory similarly confront the concept of the "generic individual"; see Sandel, *Liberalism and the Limits of Justice*. For postmodern/postmarxist approaches to political subjectivity, see especially Iris Marion Young, *Justice and the Politics of Difference*, and Laclau and Mouffe, *Hegemony and Socialist Strategy*. Other postmodern analyses of political theory include Arac, ed., *Postmodernism and Politics*, and Kramer, *Legal Theory, Political Theory, and Deconstruction*. For communitarian critiques, see especially, Glendon, *Rights Talk*, and Bellah, *Habits of the Heart* and *The Good Society*. For critiques of liberal theory, see especially Arblaster, *Western Liberalism*; Lefort, *Democracy and Political Theory*; and Bowles and Gintis, *Democracy and Capitalism*. A representative sample from the feminist discourse might include Julia Kristeva, Gayatri Chakravorty Spivak, Hélène Cixous, and Catherine Clement. See especially Spivak, *In Other Worlds*; Kristeva, *Revolution in Poetic Language*; and Cixous and Clement, *The Newly Born Woman*. For humanism's cultural and racial specificity, see West, *Keeping Faith* and *Race Matters*; Said, *Orientalism* and *The World, the Text, and the Critic*; Gates, *Loose Canons*; and Benhabib, *Critique, Norm, and Utopia* and *Feminism as Critique*. Though not originating in cultural studies, the work of Martin Bernal could be included as well.

primarily to attack the notion of objectivity itself, to delegitimate the idea of critical distance and replace it with an ideal of knowledge acquired through participation, through the unmediated illuminations that are conferred by ethnicity, which is the highest intellectual authority.[16]

"At issue," indeed, is the type of subjectivity produced by the "paideia" of a multicultural curriculum—that subject's values, views of reality, and relationships to cultural and political authority. The editorial writer underscores the extent to which current revaluations of the humanities are much more than territorial skirmishes within the academy; rather, they involve a matrix of intangible cultural boundaries, which—as the writer notes—secures not only orders of knowledge but also social, political, and economic orders. What happens when the once supposedly secure standard of "man" is put into question? What is at stake are both the ability of the humanist paradigm to represent social difference and its very role in securing specific social, political, and economic orders.

Though the editorial writer betrays what is now generally viewed as a naïve faith that "critical distance" can create objective knowledge, the problem of critical perspective persists, particularly when one attempts to critique a "tradition." Such attempts invariably create a conceptual, institutional, and historical unity that exists only in the present.[17] The problem of perspective is even more acute when we attempt to analyze our own traditions, for the only lenses we have for examining the humanist paradigm are those largely bequeathed by it. The extent to which we remain prisoners of its terms is underscored in definitions of both humanism and the humanities, which tend to be either obvious tautologies, on the one hand, or simple descriptions of institutions or curricula, on the other. For example, the best definition that the 1980 Rockefeller Commission Report on the Humanities could offer was that "the essence of the humanities is a spirit or attitude toward humanity" (Lanham, "Extraordinary Convergence," 34). Jacob Burckhardt characterized Renaissance humanism as

[16] *New Republic*, July 15 and 22, 1991, 5. For a treatment of the widely publicized Stanford debate, see Pratt, "Humanities for the Future."

[17] For example, the Western culture curriculum at Columbia, the model for Western culture courses across the country—including the Stanford curriculum that largely initiated the canon debate of the 1980s—was instituted only in 1919.

a perspective that took "humanity as its source, center, and end."[18] In "The Idea of the Humanities," R. S. Crane defined the humanities as those *"arts* or *disciplines"* with the "peculiar capacity to deal with those aspects of human experience that differentiate man most completely from the animals, to the end that individual men may actualize as fully as possible their potentialities as men" (1:7–8). In other words, the humanities are concerned with being human; humanism simply is "what is."

The Historical Search for "Humanism"

The term "humanism" is generally attributed to the German educator F. J. Niethammer, who first used it in 1808 to describe a curriculum that emphasized Greek and Latin classics in secondary education to counter an educational program that was increasingly utilitarian, technical, and scientific (Kristeller, *Renaissance Thought*, 22). Twentieth-century treatments of the humanist perspective frequently cite—without seriously exploring—the use of the Latin *humanitas* in Varro and Cicero (Crane, "Idea," 1:23).[19] Cicero uses "humanitas" in a number of ways: to describe human nature, human feeling, and humane character or kindness. In the Loeb edition of book II of *De Oratore*, translated by E. W. Sutton and H. Rackham, "humanitas" refers to good breeding (II x.40) and polished manners (II.xxxvii. 154).[20] One of its most explicit uses of "humanitas" to describe what the translators call "polite education" is found in book II, where Antonius argues that all that is required for the orator to speak on any topic is that he is "no dullard and has had some training and is not unacquainted with general literature and a tolerably polite education" (II.xvii.72).[21]

---

[18] For standard treatments of the sources and shapes of Renaissance humanism, see Burckhardt, *Civilization of the Renaissance in Italy* (1860); Trinkaus, *In Our Image and Likeness*; Kristeller, *Renaissance Thought*. For a bibliography on materials in English, see Kohl, *Renaissance Humanism*. For a discussion and critique of Burckhardt's position, see Coates, White, and Shapiro, *The Emergence of Liberal Humanism*, 1:3.

[19] See also Campana, "The Origin of the Word 'Humanist.'" Campana's analysis largely seconds the notion that the word "humanist" was used to describe concrete institutions and curricula.

[20] See also Cicero, *De Oratore* II.xvii.270, and Lewis and Short, *Oxford Latin Dictionary*, 869.

[21] For more on "humanitas" in Cicero, see Barbu, "De Ciceronis humanitate."

The extent to which humanitas can be simply identified with the liberal arts is a complicated question, frequently avoided by scholars. As Crane notes, the second-century C.E. Roman grammarian Aulus Gellius argues that the Latin humanitas is equivalent to the Greek paideia, which he defines as "education and training in the good arts" (quoted in Crane, "Idea," 1:23).[22] His argument for the identification of humanitas with a particular Greek curriculum echoes a familiar tautology. Gellius acknowledges that, in Latin, humanitas is frequently identified with the Greek *philanthropia*, "signifying a kind of friendly spirit and good-feeling towards all men"; he goes on to insist, however, that the humanities are closely tied to philanthropia because "those who earnestly desire and seek after these are the most highly humanized *(maximi humanissimi)*" (quoted in Crane, "Shifting Definitions," 1:23).

Those who attempt to make a simple bridge from the Greek concept of a common, general, or regular learning *(enkuklios paideia)* to Roman humanitas and finally the *artes liberales* generally do so with little historical or philological support.[23] John H. Randall Jr., for example, argues that what all three bear in common is that they refer to knowledge that "liberates man, which releases the freedom of the mind."[24] Though such associations as Randall's often underwrite our easy identification of paideia, humanitas, and artes liberales, there is little textual or historical evidence for a simple synonymous relationship among these terms. Thus, while it is relatively easy to trace the *septem artes liberales* beginning with Martianus Capella in the fifth

[22] In Marrou's explication of Greek paideia, he notes that classical education militated against the racial, political, and geographical disunity of Hellenistic Greece after the death of Alexander. It was "an initiation into the Greek way of life, moulding the child and the adolescent in accordance with the national customs and submitting him to a particular style of living—the style that distinguished man from the brutes, Greeks from barbarians" *(Education in Antiquity,* 99).

[23] See Kimball, *Orators and Philosophers,* for a discussion of the source of Greek paideia in the notion of enkuklios paideia, or "common," "regular," or "general education," which he argues appears as early as the fifth century B.C.E.. For more on enkuklios paideia, see Marrou, *Education in Antiquity,* 176–77. The most thorough examination is offered by L. M. de Rijk in *"Enkuklios Paideia:* A Study of Its Original Meaning."

[24] Kimball, *Orators and Philosophers,* raises Randall's argument on page 8. Randall begins his argument by situating himself in a philosophical paradigm: "It is sometimes claimed that only the true philosopher is adequately equipped to deal with the fundamental problems of education" ("Which Are the Liberating Arts?" 135).

century C.E.,[25] the task is not so easy for "humanitas." Kristeller maintains that by the late fourteenth century the *studia humanitas* refers to increasingly well-defined curricula; it is used, for example, by Italian scholars to refer to the "liberal or literary education" they found represented by Cicero and Quintilian (Kristeller, *Renaissance Thought*, 22).[26] By the second half of the fifteenth century, according to Kristeller, *studia humanitatis* designates a specific curriculum of grammar, rhetoric, history, poetry, and moral philosophy (22), a curriculum which overlaps with but which certainly is not identical to the seven liberal arts of grammar, dialectic, rhetoric, geometry, arithmetic, astronomy, and music.[27]

Protagoras's familiar dictum that "man is the measure of all things" is often invoked as an origin of the humanist perspective—a concise expression of the faith that "man" can serve as the normative standard of knowledge and value.[28] Traditional interpretations of the doctrine cite it as a sign of a movement away from archaic debates in early science and toward issues of culture.[29] The Italian Renaissance humanist

[25] See Kimball, *Orators and Philosophers*, 22–23, and Murphy, *Rhetoric in the Middle Ages*, 44. Marrou suggests that the seven liberal arts were "definitively formulated" by the first century B.C.E. (*Education in Antiquity*, 177).

[26] Though Cicero's paideia—"broad, cultural education"—is invoked as a Renaissance ideal, Renaissance curricula were far more influenced by Quintilian's pedagogical program than by Cicero's goals for the training of an orator. For several treatments that attempt to distinguish the influences of Cicero and Quintilian on Renaissance ideals and curricula, see Grafton and Jardine, *From Humanism to the Humanities*; Seigel, *Rhetoric and Philosophy in Renaissance Humanism*; and Kimball *Orators and Philosophers*. The debate concerning these influences generally centers on the character of Ciceronian rhetoric; see also Struever, *Language of History*; Kahn, *Rhetoric, Prudence, and Skepticism*; and Grafton and Jardine, *From Humanism to the Humanities*, 210.

[27] See also Kimball, *Orators and Philosophers*, chap. 4.

[28] For specific treatments of the man/measure doctrine, see Untersteiner, *Sophists*; Farrar, *Origins of Democratic Thinking*; and Versenyi, *Man's Measure*. For discussions of the sophistic sources of Italian Renaissance humanism, see Jaeger, *Paideia*, vol. 1; Marrou, *Education in Antiquity*; Seigel, *Rhetoric and Philosophy in Renaissance Humanism*; Struever, *Language of History*; and Guthrie, *History of Greek Philosophy*, vol. 3.

[29] Cynthia Farrar suggests the doctrine was a reaction against the contemporary Eleatic tradition, which had so divorced rational speculation from the world of experience as virtually to annul moral and intellectual investigation. For discussions of this opposition, see Kerferd, *The Sophistic Movement*, chap. 10. For a discussion of the sophists and the fifth-century enlightenment, see Guthrie, *History of Greek Philosophy*, vol. 3; and Versenyi, *Man's Measure*. Farrar examines the conflict between the epistemology of Parmenides of Elea and Protagoras, concluding that the Eleatics

Leon Battista Alberti refers to the doctrine in *Libri della famiglia* as an expression of the humanist focus on the "dignity of man."[30] In a more recent humanist treatise, Moses Hadas uses the *homo mensura* dictum to describe the classical ideals that endowed men with "individual responsibility and the incentive to realize such excellence as they were capable of" (*Humanism*, 84). Again, these definitions of humanism and the humanities are better characterized as a set of equivalences: "man" is culture's highest value, "man" comes to know and experience that value in the pursuit of humanistic knowledge, and the distinctive features of "man" are the object of that pursuit, the subject of knowledge.

This chain of equivalences appears in some form in virtually every description of the humanist perspective. In *The Emergence of Liberal Humanism*, Willson H. Coates, Hayden V. White, and J. Salwyn Schapiro describe modern humanism as "an attitude of mind which takes man as the effective qualitative center of the universe and as sole responsible agent for the creation of order in the world of human affairs" (5). The institutional expression of this attitude of mind is the humanities, a "world-view which rearranges the medieval order of the disciplines and places the *studia humanitatis* at the apex" (5). Just what this means for our conceptions of knowledge, subjectivity, and value is summarized in their depiction of "true humanism":

> For a true humanism, such subjects as science, theology, and philosophy are less important for what they tell us about their specifically designated objects of study than for what they tell us about man and his creative capacities. For modern humanism particularly, all attempts at knowledge are essentially efforts at human self-understanding, and they are valuable ultimately only insofar as they contribute to man's effort to know himself. (5)

Crane echoes the humanist equation when he defines the humanities as subjects that allow us to "actualize as fully as possible" our

---

constructed "a cosmos which resembled the world men experience but whose unity and stability existed only at the cosmic level, and one which was stable and unified but in every respect alien to human life, a world without change" (*Origins of Democratic Thinking*, 40).

[30] See Trinkaus, "Protagoras in the Renaissance," 195. Trinkaus also notes that the doctrine was used as a point of conflict for Christian humanists such as Cardinal Nicholas of Cusa and Marsilio Ficino, who argued that God rather than man was the "true" measure.

"potentialities as men" ("Idea," 8) and also "fix our attention upon those characteristics of any subject matter that reflect any of the possibilities of unusual excellence, beyond the necessities of nature and of the mass mind in which we all share" (15).

These scholars all agree that the business of the humanities is not so much the dissemination of knowledge or competencies as it is the production of a particular "kind" of subject. Indeed, most classic treatments of the humanist perspective place the humanist subject and the humanities in a mutually reflective, mutually constitutive relationship: the humanities reflect human value; human value is inculcated through the humanities.

That Protagoras's dictum should be seen as an expression of the humanist equation is ironic on several counts.[31] In Plato's *Protagoras*, the sophist's educational practice is specifically set against the "liberal" course of studies advocated by the philosopher. Moreover, though contemporary scholars invoke the doctrine to authorize humanist values, they also agree that Protagoras was referring to "man" in particular rather than "man" in general, "each individual man, . . . not the human race or mankind taken as a single entity."[32] This interpretation of the doctrine echoes the second-century C.E. assessment of Sextus Empiricus, who noted that the *homo mensura* doctrine was a radically relativist conception of both subjectivity and knowledge: "Protagoras, too, will have it that of all things the measure is man, of things that are that they are, and of things that are not that they are not. . . . And for this reason he posits only what appears to the individual, thus introducing relativity" (Sprague, 10–11; DK, 80. A 14). Sextus Empiricus goes on to explain that, according to Protagoras, what appears to man is governed by a number of contingencies: men "apprehend different things at different times according to their various dispositions" (11). These contingencies include "differences in age, the question whether one is asleep or awake, and every type of variation in one's condition" (11). Rather than constituting "man" as

---

[31] The sophistic concern with *nomos* ("culture" or "custom") challenged the scientific and philosophical focus on *physis* ("nature"). Nomos and physis marked two different intellectual and even social traditions: the ancient, aristocratic sages and poets, on the one hand, whose learning was rooted in wisdom traditions, religious cults, Homeric chivalry, and knightly culture, and the sophists, on the other, as itinerant heralds and exploiters of the democratic reforms of the fifth century.

[32] Kerferd, *Sophistic Movement*, 86. See also Farrar, *Origins of Democratic Thinking*, 47–53.

an objective yardstick of value and knowledge, the doctrine maintained that subjectivity is contingent on incalculable specificities, encompassing physical perception itself. The dictum challenged static models of both subjectivity and "reality."

Arts of Virtue, Sedition, and Advantage

If Tacitus was, indeed, referring to a tradition of rhetoric that was relatively unconcerned with either Quintilian's vir bonus or Plato's conceptions of knowledge and virtue, many controversies over rhetoric's ethical, epistemological, and disciplinary character are placed in a new light. Perhaps more important, such a reevaluation forces us to examine the constituent terms of these controversies. Even a cursory look at the conflicting characterizations of rhetoric by Plato, Protagoras, and Isocrates suggests that what is at stake is less the virtue of either rhetoric or the rhetorician than the terms in which virtue, rhetoric, and knowledge are cast. For Protagoras and Isocrates, a well-marked boundary between subjects and objects of knowledge is difficult to find, and virtue is neither a private attribute nor an external standard. For example, by Plato's accounts, the sophist Protagoras was willing to engage debates concerning rhetoric's relationship to knowledge and virtue. Unlike Plato, however, Protagoras insists that virtue can be taught, and he steadfastly refuses to frame his art of discourse according to Plato's conceptions of philosophical knowledge (*epistēmē*) and virtue (*aretē*).[33] Whereas Plato insists his epistēmē gives birth to virtue in the individual soul, Protagoras gives the following description of the knowledge he would impart to his student: "The proper care of his personal affairs, so that he may best manage his own household, and also of the state's affairs, so as to become a real power in the city, both as a speaker and man of action" (*Protag.* 318e–19).[34] It is not that Protagoras offers amoral, utilitarian knowledge, whereas Plato offers moral, ideal knowledge; rather, the sophist and the philosopher look at knowledge, the knowing subject, and virtue in very different ways.

Though Isocrates is hardly a proponent of democratic principles, his view of a rhetorical education shares many characteristics with that

[33] See *Protagoras* 361a–c.

[34] What is translated here as "influence," *dunatōtatos,* also connotes power and might; see Liddell and Scott, *A Greek-English Lexicon,* 453.

of Protagoras. Like the sophist, Isocrates refuses simply to dismiss questions of knowledge and virtue in his rhetorical education. The teacher and orator calls his instruction "philosophy," and he insists that the student who follows the "true precepts" of his discipline will be "helped more speedily towards honesty of character than towards facility in oratory."[35] Isocrates appears to agree with Plato that virtue cannot be taught: "The kind of art which can implant honesty and justice in depraved natures has never existed and does not now exist" (*Antid.* 275). But Isocrates' judgment does not bring him to Plato's conclusions. While Isocrates does not promise to impart virtue, he does claim to help his students "become better and worthier," provided they conceive an "ambition to speak well" (275).[36] Speaking well can be taught, he insists, as long as his students "set their hearts on seizing their advantage" (275).

Isocrates explains that he means "advantage" not "in the sense given to that word by the empty-minded, but advantage in the true meaning of that term" (275–76). We are made well aware, however, that the Greek conception of advantage is something of a double-edged sword. In some cases, the word for "advantage," *pleonexia*, simply connotes excess or gain. But, for the most part, it signifies a kind of overreaching—even greediness; it is identified with going "beyond bounds," claiming "more than one's due."[37] When Isocrates enjoins his students to "seize the advantage," he is not instructing them in the use of what Plato might call an instrumental technē. For Isocrates, neither the rhetor nor his acts of seizing the advantage are subject to transcendent standards of virtue. Only knowledge that enables acts of social and political intervention earns the title of "philosophy." Other

[35] Isocrates, *Against the Sophists*, 21. As George Kennedy notes in his 1991 translation of Aristotle's *Rhetoric,* Aristotle carefully distinguishes his conception of philosophy and rhetoric from that of Isocrates. For Aristotle, rhetoric is *not* equivalent to philosophy. "Philosophy" remains Aristotle's privileged term (39 n. 46).

[36] Isocrates' conception of "better and worthier" is in keeping with sophistic epistemology and axiology. There are no decontextualized standards of knowledge and virtue, only situated appraisals of the relative. Thus, sophistic rhetoric never aimed to "represent" true knowledge but rather to manipulate perceptions of what is relatively better or worse.

[37] Liddell, Scott, and Jones detail three primary senses of pleonexia: (1) greediness, assumption, arrogance; (2) advantage; and (3) excess (LSJ, 1416). For one dimension of pleonexia's complex relationship to justice, see Gregory Vlastos, "*Isonomia Politikē,*" especially 19–21 and 19 n. 1.

study is only mental exercise, "a gymnastic of the mind and a preparation for philosophy" (266).

Neither Protagoras nor Isocrates goes so far as Tacitus in identifying rhetoric with impiety and sedition; however, all three depictions
of rhetoric clearly contrast with that of Plato's. The distinctions between the subject, knowledge, and value that guide Plato's equation
of knowledge to virtue simply do not hold for these rhetors. The instruction of Protagoras and Isocrates is neither disinterested knowledge nor a specific political and ethical ideal. Moreover, though both
Protagoras and Isocrates acknowledge that their instruction is tied to
the production of character, *ēthos* is not guided by a single model of
the subject or judged by a single model of virtue. Their instruction has
more to do with the polis than the individual soul, and it is far more
likely to disrupt standards of value than to secure them. Within the
terms of Plato's philosophy, however, the logōn technē of Protagoras
and Isocrates can be only a morally neutral technē or an immoral art.

Paradoxes of the Humanist Paradigm

Naturalizing the Contingent

Humanist treatises frequently obscure the relative nature of humanist values by securing a specific model of subjectivity in something outside or beyond humankind. These propensities toward naturalizing the contingent and universalizing the particular frequently
lead the humanist perspective into a very problematic relationship to
specific historical and cultural exigencies.

Though Protagoras's doctrine is invoked to illustrate the transition
from philosophical speculation on nature to deliberation on culture,
in humanist treatises "man" frequently serves as a measure of knowledge and value only to the extent that his defining characteristics are
rooted in something beyond "the human."[38] Renaissance humanism,
for example, was instrumental in reviving secular learning and challenging religious authority, but it was also used to reinforce Christian
doctrine. Charles Trinkaus offers one example in his description of the

[38] See Kerferd, *The Sophistic Movement*, chap. 10, on the "*nomos-physis* controversy." Standard treatments of early Greek science and mathematics may be found in
Burnet, *Greek Philosophy*, and Lloyd, *Early Greek Science*.

Renaissance attitude toward creativity: "The capacity of man to command and shape his world was regarded as an emulation of divinity, since it was in this respect that man was created in the image and likeness of God." According to Trinkaus, though Renaissance humanism heralded new faith in man's creative powers, in the end those powers had their source in God.[39] Thus, in the Christian humanist equation, when man most fully actualizes his distinctive features, he will be acting most like God.

When humanism does not explicitly invoke a divine origin, it frequently posits a "suprahuman" end. Crane's description of the "nature and basic terms" of humanism from Roman "humanitas" to Renaissance humanism echoes Trinkaus's description in a somewhat more ecumenical spirit:

> Throughout this long period the various statements of the humanities we have encountered have normally involved the assertion of some human, or "more human," end or of some broad social utility, with respect to which the subject matters and the arts thought to be humanistic have been selected and their pursuit justified or urged. The humanities, thus, have been in the modern period, no less than for the Romans, means to the realization of some ideal or use over and above the understanding and appreciation of the peculiarly human achievements in art or philosophy or science which have been their subject matter.[40]

Both permutations of humanist doctrine prevent "man" from becoming a relative measure of knowledge and value by extricating subjectivity from history and culture. Man can serve as a final measure either because what is "most human" partakes of the atemporal divine or because man's humanity is expressed in a process that transcends individual human history.

[39] Trinkaus, *In Our Image*, xx–xxi. Howard Mumford Jones in *American Humanism: Its Meaning for World Survival* also asserts that while the very term "humanitas" was intended to distinguish the secular from the theological, it never precluded a rapprochement with religious traditions—thus the "honorable history of Christian humanism" (10–11).

[40] Crane elaborates: "They have been recommended or defended (as in Vives) on the ground that they restore man to humanity and raise him toward God, or (as in Sidney) that they lead to the knowledge of a man's self, with the end of well-doing and not of well-knowing only, or (as in Newman) that they induce a philosophic habit of mind, or (as in Arnold) that they lead to a harmonious expansion and interrelation of all the powers which make the beauty and worth of human nature" ("Shifting Definitions," 158).

Universalizing the Particular

One of the most critical paradoxes of the humanist paradigm is the transformation of a specific, historical subject into a universal form. Despite their claims to universality, humanist treatises frequently locate that subject in a particular historical moment and in a specific gender, class structure, and race. The result is the paradoxical claim that the humanist subject both embodies and transcends the values of a specific cultural milieu.

Jaeger's three-volume *Paideia* is a classic example of humanism's reconstruction of Greek antiquity. The treatise in no way reflects the current state of classical scholarship. But it provides a uniquely detailed picture of the aims and values of a humanist education; those values, for the most part, continue to influence our conceptions of the liberal arts. Jaeger's humanist subject is unambiguously modeled after the Homeric hero. His "ideal man" is characterized by aretē, which he defines as "a combination of proud and courtly morality with warlike valor" (1:5). *Aretē* unites the military virtue of "valor" with the aristocratic virtues of "honor," "highmindedness," a "sense of duty," and excellence (*"aristeia"*)—demonstrated in the hero's "race for the first prize, an unceasing strife for supremacy over his peers." This "new ideal of human perfection," according to Jaeger, "united nobility of action with nobility of mind" (1:7–11).

Despite the gender, race, and class specificity of this "new ideal," it is precisely this form of "human perfection" that the humanist paideia aims to produce. According to Jaeger, the humanitas of Varro and Cicero referred to "the process of educating man into his true form, the real and genuine human nature" (1:xxiii). Jaeger insists that this form *does* transcend history; it is a "universally valid model of humanity which all individuals are bound to imitate" (1:xxiv). At the same time, that form is not an "empty abstract pattern, existing outside time and space"; rather, it is "the living ideal which had grown up in the very soil of Greece" (1:xxiv). How does one reconcile the universality of this subject with its cultural and historical origins? Jaeger does it primarily through his conception of race. Though the defining characteristics of this "new ideal" are situated in a specific moment of Greek history, they are not themselves the product of history; instead, these features are the expression of the "peculiar character of the Greek mind" (1:xix). The traits that gave birth to the Greek ideal were inherent: "The variety, spontaneity, versatility, and freedom of individual character . . . were not deliberately cultivated subjective qualities in the modern sense. They were natural, inborn" (1:xix–xx).[41]

According to Jaeger, what is most significant about these "inborn" characteristics is that they led to the realization of the value of the individual. His description of the significance of this Greek achievement is an almost canonical description of the humanist perspective on subjectivity and value:

> The beginning of Greek history appears to be the beginning of a new conception of the value of the individual. And it is difficult to refrain from identifying that new conception with the belief—which Christianity did most to spread—that each soul is in itself an end of infinite value, and with the ideal proclaimed during and after the Renaissance, that every individual is a law to himself. (1:xix)

Jaeger contrasts the individuality of the Greek ideal with the human image of other races, particularly "the self-abnegation of the pre-Hellenic Orient" and the "exaltation of one God-king far above all natural proportions" (1:xix).

For Jaeger, the "classical" is, indeed, the "timeless": "The Greek critics who lived at the beginning of the Roman empire were the first to describe the masterpieces of the great age of Greece as 'classical' in the timeless sense—partly as formal patterns for subsequent artists to imitate, partly as ethical models for posterity to follow" (1:xxv). Jaeger explicitly rejects the historical perspective, offering the "permanent values of classical antiquity" as a corrective to "a century of historical research," driven by "a boundless and aimless passion for viewing everything as history, a night in which all cats are grey" (1:xxv). Jaeger's analogy underscores the threat that temporality holds for his perspective, for the most dangerous adversary of his "ideal man" is the relativizing force of history.

Privatizing the Public

Immediately after he criticizes the historical perspective, however, Jaeger insists that the "permanent values" of Greece cannot be set up

---

[41] The Greek sense of the individual is specifically set against the "Oriental" propensity to see "man as a member of a horde" (Jaeger, *Paideia*, 1:xxiv). Jaeger insists: "There could be no sharper contrast than that between the modern man's keen sense of his own individuality, and the self-abnegation of the pre-Hellenic Orient, made manifest in the sombre majesty of Egypt's pyramids and the royal tombs and monuments of the East" (1:xix).

as "timeless idols" (1:xxv); his explanation of this apparent contradiction points to the social and political character of his humanist ideals. Jaeger explains that these "permanent values . . . cannot display the standards implicit in their meaning, and their irresistible power to transform and mould our lives, except as forces working within a definite historical milieu—just as they did in the era when they were created" (1:xxv). In other words, these ideals have a "directive impetus" (1:xxix); they must be used daily in that process of transformation and molding. Greece's special contribution to that process is the recognition that "education means deliberately moulding human character in accordance with an ideal" (1:xxii).[42] Jaeger argues that the artist, educator, and legislator hold similar functions: the Greeks' "greatest work of art . . . was Man" (1: xxii). Only the legislator has a similar formative function.

> The true representatives of paideia were not, the Greeks believed, the voiceless artists—sculptor, painter, architect—but the poets and musicians, orators (which means statesmen) and philosophers. They felt that the legislator was in a certain respect more akin to the poet than was the plastic artist; for both the poet and the legislator had an educational mission. The legislator alone could claim the title of sculptor, for he alone shaped living men. (1:xxvii).

If, as Jaeger argues, the beginning of Greek history was the genesis of the notion that "each soul is in itself an end of infinite value" and a "law to himself" (1:xix), then the educator functions to oversee and enforce that law.

How will the subject constructed by paideia relate to "his" own social and political milieu? Though Jaeger insists that Greek ideals were "deeply rooted in the life of the community" and that the "man revealed in the work of the great Greeks is a political man" (1:xxv), reconciling those ideals with the social and political exigencies of the present leads to several problems. Much of volume 2 of Jaeger's *Paideia* is concerned with contrasting what he calls "sophistic" and "Socratic" paideia. There he confronts the sophists Protagoras, Gorgias, and Callicles and outlines a perspective on knowledge, virtue, and the state informed predominantly by Plato. Though Jaeger insists that the state depends on the virtues inculcated by *paideia*, he concurs with Plato's

---

[42] Jaeger explains that the Greeks knew the "formative" power of education "to shape the living man as the potter moulds clay and the sculptor carves stone into preconceived form" (ibid., xvii).

pessimistic conclusion in the *Republic* that a state governed by an ideal, philosophical order will never exist. What does the educator/ statesman do in the face of this unattainable ideal? According to Jaeger, he will work to create a private version of that state within himself: "For lack of a perfect state in which he can be active," he will "mould himself" (2:353). The "true state" that he carries "in his soul" will be his singular object of attention: "He will take care that nothing in it is altered; and his attitude to the good things of this earthly life—money, property, honour, and so on—will depend on the possibility of acquiring them without contravening the law of the state within him" (2:353, 354).

What relationship will the state within hold to the state without? In other words, as Jaeger asks of the educator/statesman, "Is he to take part in politics?" (2:354). Jaeger offers the following summary of Plato's answer in the *Republic:*

> All the previous argument debars him from doing so; and Socrates' young interlocutor correctly concludes that he will not. But Socrates says he will. In *his* state, he will certainly take part in politics with all his energy, but perhaps not in the country in which he happens to live, unless a divine tychē makes it possible for him to act according to his own lights. *His* state, the Republic, lies in the world of Ideas, for it does not exist anywhere on earth. But . . . it makes no difference whether it exists or not. Perhaps it exists in heaven, an eternal pattern for the man who can see it, and, by looking at it, build himself into the true state. (2:354)

The humanist subject that is the product of Jaeger's paideia is caught in a matrix of contradictions. His politics deride power. For example, Jaeger insists that the argument of Plato's *Gorgias* is that "in the new state, power is not the sole standard"; instead, "the standard is man; spiritual value; the soul" (2:355). The only state he can inhabit is one in his own mind, and he is incapable of political intervention. The result: the public realm is utterly privatized. As Jaeger puts it himself, "We started out with Plato to find a state. Instead, we have found a man" (2: 354). By whatever means Jaeger attempts to identify his paideia with some form of political virtue, his conception of civic aretē is clearly far less a matter of political and social intervention than it is a normative ideal of subjectivity.

If Plato's subject is defined by philosophical knowledge and virtue, then Isocrates' subject is defined by honor and esteem. Both honor and

esteem, however, are accrued only by the rhetor's successful intervention in the affairs of the polis. They are the product of the rhetor's
ability to seize the advantage in a given situation—to overreach and
redefine boundaries that are social, political, and economic. That act
of overreaching changes not only the polis but also the rhetor, since
for Isocrates there is little distinction between public rhetorical ēthos
and private character. Isocrates insists that his instruction encompasses knowledge directed toward both the management of one's own
household and the governance of the polis; he reproaches those who
refuse the name "students of philosophy" to those "who pursue and
practise those studies which will enable us to govern wisely both our
own households [*ton idion oikon*] and the commonwealth [*ta koina
ta tēs poliōs*]" (*Antid.* 285). If a distinct boundary holds between the
public and private, it is one marked only to be transgressed.

Plato's and Isocrates' models of knowledge begin and end at different loci. Plato's student begins with the soul and moves to the polis
only after acquiring knowledge by way of *dianoia*—that discourse
with one's own soul that should lead to judgment concerning truth
and falsity.[43] In the *Phaedo*, Socrates describes two types of goodness,
or virtue: philosophical aretē and "popular goodness"—also called political aretē. According to Plato, true virtue is equivalent to true
knowledge, and political virtue is knowledge only to the extent that
it is philosophical.[44] The philosopher consequently finds himself in a
paradoxical relationship to the polis. For example, in the discussion in
the *Phaedrus* of rhetoric's relationship to true knowledge, Socrates asserts that since attaining true knowledge requires "considerable diligence, . . . the wise man should exert not for the sake of speaking to
and dealing with his fellow men, but that he may be able to speak what
is pleasing to the gods" (273e). In other words, if the philosopher apprehends true political aretē, he will be more likely to use it to please
the gods than to deliberate in the Assembly.

Isocrates, however, begins with the polis to describe wisdom in the
individual soul: "For the same arguments which we use in persuading
others when we speak in public, we employ also when we deliberate
[*bouleuomenoi*] in our own thoughts; and, while we call eloquent
those who are able to speak before a crowd, we regard as sage those
who most skilfully debate their problems in their own minds" (*Antid.*

---

[43] See Burnet, *Early Greek Philosophy*, 289.
[44] See ibid., 174.

256–57). The very word here for deliberation, *bouleuein*, is related to the name of the democratic *Boule*, the Council which was to serve the citizen Assembly.[45] The point of reference for both knowledge and goodness in Isocrates' paradigm is deliberation in the polis, not discourse that pleases the gods: "The power to speak well is taken as the surest index of a sound understanding, and discourse which is true and lawful and just is the outward image of a good and faithful soul" (*Antid.* 255–56). The polis provides the model for the soul; indeed, it is in the polis that virtue is most important: "It behoves states much more than individuals to cultivate the virtues and to shun vices; for a man who is godless and depraved may die before paying the penalty for his sins, but states, since they are deathless, soon or late must submit to punishment at the hands both of men and of the gods" (Isocrates, *On the Peace*, 120).[46]

Isocrates' pedagogical project is centrally concerned with the construction of character; however, for Isocrates, character is measured neither by an external, ideal standard nor by a private, internal plumb line but rather by the esteem one earns from one's peers: "The stronger a man's desire to persuade his hearers, the more zealously will he strive to be honourable and to have the esteem of his fellow-citizens" (*Antid.* 278). Isocrates' sense of character contrasts with the traditional humanist "subject" at several points. Isocratean "character," or ēthos, is invariably rhetorical; it is always tied to discourse and to specific social and political exigencies. This radical temporalization of subjectivity also precludes the Isocratean pedagogical project from being determined by a normative ideal of subjectivity. The goal of Isocrates' pedagogy is successful intervention in the exigencies of the polis, and in those acts of intervention the rhetor's ēthos is both a product and a tool.

Plato and Isocrates would appear to agree on one point: for both "philosophers," neither the subjects nor the objects of knowledge are defined by inherent features; rather they are defined by their place in a set of social, political, and economic relations.[47] One of the earliest and most specific discussions of a program of studies that would eventually be identified with the humanities is found in Plato's *Protago-*

---

[45] *OCD*, 178.

[46] For one perspective on the elevation of the "public" sphere in classical Athens, see Cohen, *Law, Sexuality, and Society*, chaps. 4 and 9.

[47] See Cicero, *De Oratore* I.xvi.72.

ras. Socrates describes the early education of one of his students as instruction in language, music, and sports, taken "not in the technical way, with a view to becoming a professional [*dēmiourgos*], but for education [*epi paideiai*], as befits a private gentleman [*ton idiōtēn kai ton eleutheron*]" (312a–b).[48] This paideia is explicitly contrasted with the technical, professional knowledge of the dēmiourgos (associated with the tradition of technē). What is translated here as "gentleman" is the Greek *eleutherios*, the "freeman," who contrasts specifically with the "public man" (LSJ, 532).[49] A similar association is made by Cicero in *De Oratore* when Crassus refers to the education necessary for the accomplished orator as "those arts that befit the well-bred" (I.xvi.72).[50] In both cases, education is defined less by curricula than by the class characteristics of the "learner." Moreover, despite the fact that humanist treatises frequently assert that the humanities aim to "democratize" virtue, virtue retains its identification with a set of values far more concerned with markers of class than with the everyday needs of the polis.

Rhetoric and Humanism

Perhaps the most critical question facing traditional humanism is the extent to which it remains committed to the production of a normative subject, a subject designed to embody and reproduce specific cultural values and social relations rather than examine and transform them. Rhetoric's relationship to this cultural project could hardly be more complex. Humanism's cultural and intellectual origins are not always

---

[48] The translation cited is from the Loeb edition, trans. W. R. M. Lamb. In Hamilton and Cairns's *Collected Dialogues*, Guthrie uses the term "liberal education" to describe this curriculum (312b).

[49] The problem of translation centers largely on how one interprets Greek paideia (or enkuklios paideia) and the classical conceptions of "public" and "private." In W. R. M. Lamb's translation in the Loeb edition of Plato's *Protagoras*, Socrates describes the curriculum of a young student as "education [*paideia*] as befits a private gentleman [*ton idiōtēn kai ton eleutheron*]" (312a–b). In Hamilton and Cairns, however, Guthrie translates paideia as "liberal education" learned by a "layman and gentleman." The fifth- and fourth-century conceptions of public and private are more complex than the public/private binary suggests. See Cohen, *Law, Sexuality, and Society*, chap. 4, and Ober, *Mass and Elite in Democratic Athens*, chap. 3.

[50] A similar transformation takes place in George Norlin's translation of Isocrates' *Antidosis*, in which paideia is translated as "liberal education."

given Jaeger's philosophical cast. Traditions of humanism persist that place their origins in the rhetoric of Rome, not the philosophy of Greece, and in the paideia of Cicero and Quintilian, not Socrates.[51] These paideia traditions of rhetoric are frequently identified with pedagogies explicitly concerned with the construction of character, and they have served as both prototypes and rationales for a humanist education. Quintilian's *Institutio Oratoria* is the most obvious case of a "rhetorical" education aimed expressly at the production of character. But traditions of "broad learning," generally identified with the paideia of Cicero, have also served as humanist models of education. The recuperation of Cicero by Italian Renaissance humanists is the most obvious example. Rhetoric's historical identification with these paideia traditions raises a number of questions, but one question in particular confronts us here. When does rhetoric's concern with ēthos, or character, become a project of producing a normative subject? In other words, is Cicero's "ideal orator" equivalent to Quintilian's vir bonus?

Examining the fate of rhetoric's social and political function is further complicated by what is sometimes referred to as "statesman-orator" traditions of rhetoric. These traditions frequently overlap with paideia traditions and similarly refuse to identify virtue, or aretē, with philosophical knowledge. Virtue is civic, not speculative; rhetoric is characterized as a part of civic virtue.[52] Defining rhetoric's relationship to civic virtue is a complicated task, far beyond the boundaries of this study. Even approaching such a definition is difficult for a number of reasons. The concept of aretē alone has a long and intricate history, and the extent to which civic virtue can be identified with Protagoras's art of social and political intervention is a complicated issue that yields no simple resolutions. The problem of defining rhetoric's relationship to social and political exigencies is compounded by the fact that outside humanist educational institutions, oratory has had its own life in forensic, religious, and political discourse, flourishing and waning often with little support or even influence from the academy.[53] What is at issue, however, is whether these traditions reclaim

---

[51] Kennedy (*Classical Rhetoric,* 31) also places Isocrates at the fountainhead of this tradition.

[52] See Kennedy's discussion of philosophical rhetoric in *Classical Rhetoric* and Conley's treatment of the statesman-orator tradition in the *Renaissance in Rhetoric in the European Tradition,* 112–14.

[53] These traditions have been traced by scholars in speech and history. Cmiel's *Democratic Eloquence* is a more recent examination of public discourse.

for rhetoric the social and political intervention embodied in Protagoras's political technē, Isocrates' logōn technē, and Aristotle's conception of productive knowledge.[54]

From an Art of Social and Political Intervention to the Content of Humanist Curricula

R. S. Crane offers one of the most explicit descriptions of a humanist paideia that locates its origins in the statesman-orator tradition. Crane writes that the humanities follow Cicero and Quintilian in determining "those arts and subject matters which are best suited to the formation of the orator, who was, for them, the virtuous and wise man par excellence" ("Idea," 1:5). The humanist project of the twentieth century, according to Crane, is not as explicitly tied to practical ends as its Roman counterpart; however, it is still centrally concerned with the formation of character. The importance of the humanities resides not "with certain subjects of study merely, or with the pursuit of certain abstract *ends*," but rather with the "cultivation" of "man's" distinctive features (1:7–8).

Crane's characterization of the end of rhetoric as the production of ēthos is largely a restatement of Quintilian's conception of the vir bonus. Yet both depictions of rhetoric would appear to be the product of the superimposition on the oratorical tradition of Plato's equation of knowledge to virtue. What Crane's interpretation of classical rhetoric ignores is the possibility that Quintilian's assertion—that the objective of a rhetorical education is the production of the vir bonus—was a radical reorientation of the ends of rhetoric. No longer did the teacher of rhetoric promise to enable success in specific social and political contexts, as did Protagoras, Isocrates, Aristotle, and Cicero. Instead, the paideia of Quintilian would produce the "man" of learning, whose eloquence would proceed from "honor" (*Inst.* XII.i.30) and who would be the "good man" first and the orator second (XII.ii.1). Rather than providing strategies for acts of social and political intervention,

---

[54] The history of "civic virtue" is as mottled as that of "civic humanism." In *Virtue Transformed*, Burtt notes that despite scholarly examinations of eighteenth-century "civic virtue," the term simply doesn't appear in eighteenth-century political discourse. One can find such terms as "public virtue, private virtue, public spirit, politick virtues," but not "civic virtue" (4). Thus, like "civic humanism," the birthplace of "civic virtue" was more likely the research library or the classroom than sites of public deliberation.

rhetoric would provide the curricular content for a developmental process of education. At the end of that process, the powers of the "vir bonus" would shine with the greatest "splendor" when he was "called upon to direct the counsels of the senate and guide the people from the paths of error to better things" (XII.i.26)—this despite the fact, as Michael Winterbottom notes, that in the Flavian empire such endeavors were "absurdly out of date."[55]

Though Aristotle asserts in the *Rhetoric* that "the true and the just are by nature stronger than their opposites" (Kennedy, 34; 1355a21–22), he also offers a compendium of topics, advising the student of rhetoric to take whichever "argument is useful" (Kennedy, 114; 1376a33). Aristotle's *Rhetoric* outlines an "art" of ēthos, not an ethical subject or an ethical and political ideal. Moreover, though Aristotle maintains that rhetoric is a rational art, what it offers are strategies for the *appeal* to reason, not a static body of philosophical knowledge, apprehended by a stable, knowing subject. Static subjects and objects of knowledge are the concerns of philosophy; determining the means to the end of "the good life" is the business of ethics and politics, not rhetoric.

This transformation of rhetoric from an art of social and political intervention into the curricular content of a humanist education is acceptable only if one dismisses these alternative rhetorical traditions and overlooks the context in which Quintilian's art was formulated. The institutionalization of rhetoric had already begun in the Hellenistic period, and Cicero's rhetorical treatises were aimed in part at reviving rhetoric's social and political function. For most of Cicero's career in the waning years of the Roman republic, however, he was forced to balance persuading audiences with assuaging senatorial powers.[56] After the murder of Julius Caesar, Cicero's criticism of Mark Antony brought about his own death. In contrast, Quintilian, born a century after Cicero's death, was, as Kennedy notes, hardly a critic of the imperial powers: "He accepted honor and advancement from the Flavians; he indulged in flattery when prudent" (*Rhetoric in the Roman World*, 488). And when the emperor Vespasian assumed the

[55] For a discussion of the political contexts of Quintilian's anachronistic characterization of rhetoric's deliberative function, see Winterbottom, "Quintilian and the *Vir Bonus*" (quotation from 97).

[56] Kennedy discusses these conflicting demands in his analysis of Cicero's speeches before his consulship. See *Rhetoric in the Roman World*, chap. 3, especially 171–72.

throne in 69 C.E., Quintilian was awarded the first state professorship in rhetoric.[57]

Quintilian's career stands in sharp contrast to that of Cicero, whose life was tied to the tumultuous political affairs of the state. The consequences of this shift in rhetoric's contexts—from the assembly, courts, and senate to the classroom—are apparent throughout Quintilian's *Institutio*. The "commonplaces" that in Aristotle's *Rhetoric* provide propositions for persuasive appeals to *logos* become themes for declamations (*Inst.* II.iv.22). Though Quintilian is frequently critical of the artificial character of declamation, he still identifies certain "theses" with the "deliberative class of oratory"; these theses provide the subjects for classroom declamation on such weighty questions as "'Whether marriage is desirable' or 'Whether a public career is a proper object of ambition'" (II.iv.25). Similarly, the status category of conjecture, which played such an important role in Roman forensic rhetoric, provides the basis for "useful and attractive" exercises on such questions as "'Why in Sparta is Venus represented as wearing armour?'" or "'Why is Cupid believed to be a winged boy armed with arrows and a torch?'" (II.iv.26).

The effects of this transformation of rhetoric from an art of social and political intervention into the content of a liberal arts education is further underscored by Quintilian's descriptions of the types and purposes of rhetoric. Aristotle defines the province of rhetoric by three primary principles: its contexts, the time with which it is concerned, and its ends. The site of deliberative discourse is the Assembly; its concerns are those of the future, and its ends are exhortation toward the advantageous and dissuasion from the harmful. The site of forensic discourse is the law court; its concerns are those of the past, and its ends are the determination of justice and injustice. The contexts of epideictic discourse are ceremonial—funereal in particular; its concerns are those of the present, and its ends are to elicit honor or dishonor for its subjects (Kennedy, 47–49; 1358a36–b29). While Quintilian acknowledges these traditional divisions (*Inst.* III.iv.12–16), he insists that three new aims transcend Aristotle's divisions of discourse. Whatever the discourse type, the orator must "instruct, move and charm his hearer" (III.v.2). Quintilian's developmental curriculum

---

[57] Winterbottom maintains that in the Flavian empire, oratory could scarcely claim the "traditional political justification" by which Athenian rhetoric had been defined. He notes that the suppression of deliberation left "room only for panegyric . . . and the driest of legal advocacy" ("Quintilian and the *Vir Bonus*," 97).

is based far more on discourse genres than on rhetorical contexts. The young student begins with *narratio* and then moves on to epideictic, which has come to comprise the second most elementary form of declamation, "first attempts at passages of praise or denunciation" (II.i.8–9).

Although this appropriation of rhetoric by pedagogical traditions would appear to be a severe domestication of the art, it is precisely rhetoric's promise to produce the vir bonus that secured its centrality in certain humanist curricula. The rhetorical paideia of the vir bonus was specifically defined against the rhetorical art of social and political intervention purveyed by sophists such as Protagoras. Rhetorics that stressed success in specific rhetorical contexts (which would have to include Aristotle's *Rhetoric*) were judged seriously wanting according to the moral and intellectual standards of such paideia models as that of Quintilian. Even Bruce Kimball, in a study that otherwise carefully resists mutating rhetoric into either philosophy or ethics, still attributes what he describes as the disintegration of the "pedagogical century" (450–350 B.C.E.) to the "amoral" rhetorics of the sophists, which "attended more to devising persuasive techniques than to finding true arguments, and this amoralism exacerbated the disintegration of the ethical tradition" (*Orators and Philsophers*, 17).

Kimball's description underscores how poorly rhetoric fares under the template of Plato's models of knowledge, virtue, and subjectivity. As long as knowledge is something distinct from subjectivity, one is left with only two ways of adjudicating its value: an instrumentalist approach, whereby knowledge is a "thing" that can be used for good or ill; or an idealist approach that equates knowledge to virtue by making knowledge an end in itself.

Indeed, the logōn technē of Isocrates and the paideia of Quintilian would appear to divide precisely on the issue of the production of ēthos. Isocrates acknowledges—even "advertises"—his instruction as concerned with the construction of character; at the same time, he maintains that his logōn technē is an art of "seizing the advantage." Neither character nor rhetorical success is a single end in his instruction; knowledge and subjectivity simply are not figured in a means/end relationship. As Jaeger was well aware, Isocrates' paradigm of knowledge and subjectivity fails to conform to humanist ideals precisely on this point: it does not provide a normative subject; it does not produce the "ideal man." Jaeger notes that although Isocrates recognized that the educational value of philosophy was its "lofty moral ideal," Isocrates "believed neither that its ideal was the only one with any claim to respect, nor that the means chosen by the philosophers were likely to attain it" (*Paideia*, 3:71). According to Jaeger's own definition of rhetoric as "an instrument of practical politics" (3:71), Isocratean education would indeed pose a problem as long as "rhetoric lacked a great mission" (3:71). According to Jaeger's means/end calculus, it is impossible to confer value on rhetorical interventions that fail to justify themselves by transcendent norms of value and knowledge. Less grandiose acts of specific social and political intervention can only be opportunistic; they are, indeed, simply acts of "seizing the advantage."

The transformation of rhetoric we find in Quintilian would seem to negate any serious claim that the rhetorical humanist paideia preserved rhetoric's social and political function. One cannot raise rhetoric's relationship to the humanist paideia, however, without confronting two issues: Cicero's conception of the rhetorical paideia and Renaissance rhetorical traditions that claim to revive a kind of "civic humanism." Does Cicero's paideia conform to the humanist project of aiming primarily at the production of a specific subject? Is Cicero's "consummate orator" identical to Quintilian's vir bonus?[58] Did the invocation of Roman rhetorical traditions in Renaissance humanism reclaim a serious social and political function for rhetoric? Though the detailed responses these questions deserve are beyond the boundaries of this study, several points may suffice to argue for a provisional "no" to all three questions.

Cicero's *Paideia* and Quintilian's *Vir Bonus*

Cicero's paideia is often viewed too simply as broad learning or cultural funding that yield the exemplary orator. Such interpretations tend to idealize the orator, transforming him into a hero of culture rather than a model of rhetorical success. Though the conception of

[58] Ēthos in Ciceronian rhetoric is, of course, largely determined by its primary context: the rhetoric of advocacy. See Kennedy, "Rhetoric of Advocacy in Greece and Rome," and May, "Rhetoric of Advocacy and Patron-Client Identification." For a discussion of Cicero's conception of "personhood" in his ethical treatise De Officiis, see Gill, "Personhood and Personality." Another approach to analyzing Ciceronian rhetorical ethos may be found in Leff's discussion of attributional invention in "Topics of Argumentative Invention." For other treatments of Ciceronian ēthos, see May, Trials of Character, and Wisse, Ethos and Pathos from Aristotle to Cicero. For a brief general discussion of rhetorical ēthos, see Sattler "Conceptions of Ethos in Ancient Rhetoric."

general learning, or paideia, is central to Cicero's program of rhetorical education, one thing that is frequently ignored is that the enkuklios paideia was only part of a complex formula for the training of the orator. That training included a number of factors—natural talent, art (method and precepts), imitation, practice—as well as general knowledge. Indeed, much of *De Oratore* is a debate concerning the proper emphases among different constituents of a rhetorical education. Antonius observes, "In oratory three things are necessary to discovery of arguments, first acuteness, secondly theory, or art, as we may call it if we like, and thirdly painstaking" (II.xxxv.147).[59] Crassus often appears to devalue formal study in rhetoric, yet his description of the orator's education always includes instruction in precepts and practice—in addition to natural talents and a "liberal education":

> Only let the intending speaker or writer, thanks to the training given by a liberal education in boyhood, possess a glowing enthusiasm as well as the assistance of good natural endowments, and, having had practice in the abstract discussions of general principles, have selected the most accomplished writers and orators for study and imitation: then of a certainty such a one will not have to come to your professors to be shown how to put words together and how to invest them with brilliance of style. (III.xxxi.125)

Although eloquence may require broad learning, the primary end of that paideia is certainly *not* self-construction and self-knowledge. Knowledge, virtue, and subjectivity are simply not figured according to humanism's chain of equivalences.[60]

---

[59] Discussion of the importance of a tutor is added in *De Oratore* III.xxiii.87–88.

[60] The concept of "general knowledge" itself is the subject of debate throughout *De Oratore*. How does one determine the border between special and general knowledge? Is general knowledge enough for the orator, or should he be knowledgeable in the specialized material of law? Another question arises concerning the character of general knowledge. In *De Oratore*, Cicero appears to agree with Plato's definition of the "liberal arts" or the enkuklios paideia as "the arts that befit the well-bred" (I.vxi.72). In contrast to Plato, however, Cicero describes his enkuklios paideia as the knowledge of the "common practice, custom, and speech of mankind, so that, whereas in all other arts that is most excellent which is farthest removed from the understanding and mental capacity of the untrained, in oratory the very cardinal sin is to depart from the language of everyday life, and the usage approved by the sense of the community" (I.iii.12). Indeed, this "common knowledge" is specifically contrasted with the "private" and the hidden: "The subjects of the other arts are derived as a rule from hidden and remote sources, while the whole art of oratory lies open to the view" (I.iii.12).

Like Quintilian, Cicero offers a model of character—the "consummate orator."[61] What is at issue, however, is the extent to which this model of ēthos is an end in itself, as it is for Quintilian. In other words, is Cicero's ideal orator simply the older sibling of Quintilian's vir bonus?

Though Cicero clearly delineates the "ideal orator," Cicero's ideal is never exclusively a model of knowledge and virtue: he is also a model of rhetorical success. Cicero never claims that the "consummate orator" is the embodiment of "true" knowledge. Crassus insists that the "one and only true and perfect orator" is "able in Aristotelian fashion to speak on opposite sides about every subject and by means of knowing Aristotle's rules to reel off two speeches on opposite sides on every case" (III.xxi.80).[62] Even the most forceful identifications of rhetoric with virtue and knowledge still ground eloquence in rhetorical contexts and rhetorical success:

Eloquence is one of the supreme virtues. . . , which after compassing a knowledge of facts, gives verbal expression to the thoughts and purposes of the mind in such a manner as to have the power of driving the hearers forward in any direction in which it has applied its weight; and the stronger this faculty is, the more necessary it is for it to be combined with integrity and supreme wisdom, and if we bestow fluency of speech on persons devoid of those virtues, we shall not have made orators of them but shall have put weapons into the hands of madmen. (III.xiv.55)

Eloquence without integrity may yield dangerous madmen, but eloquence without rhetorical success is simply not eloquence.

Indeed, the kind of merit identified with the orator would appear to resemble Isocrates' conception of honor more than Quintilian's vir bonus.[63] Crassus describes the exemplary orator as one "from whom every blemish has been taken away, and one who moreover is rich in every merit" (I.xxvi.118). That merit, however, is finally determined

---

[61] My discussion is not intended to oversimplify Cicero's notion of the consummate orator but rather to contrast it to Quintilian's vir bonus. For one treatment of this concept, see Gilleland, "Development of Cicero's Ideal Orator."

[62] For a discussion that situates any conception of "truth" in Roman rhetoric in its historical and rhetorical contexts, see Dorey, "Honesty in Roman Politics."

[63] "Honor" in Ciceronian rhetoric would impinge on *dignitas*. Balsdon observes that "in politics a man's *dignitas* was his good name" ("*Auctoritas, Dignitas, Otium*," 45). See also Wirszubski, "Cicero's *Cum Dignitate Otium.*"

not by knowledge and virtue but by the esteem of the rhetor's audiences and the success of his rhetorical endeavors: "Our orator must carefully see to it, that he not only contents those whom it is necessary to satisfy, but is wonderful as well in the eyes of such as have the right to judge freely" (I.xxvi.119).

Cicero's "consummate orator" may even be the obverse of an ideal, universal type. In *De Oratore*, Scaevola insists that the consummate orator can be the achievement only of a specific personality. Contrasting the "competent" with the "consummate" orator, Scaevola describes what the teacher of rhetoric should be able to promise his students:

> What you are able to guarantee is . . . that in the courts whatever case you present should appear to be the better and more plausible, that in assemblies and in the Senate your oratory should have most weight in carrying the vote, and lastly, that to the intelligent you should seem to speak eloquently and to the ignorant truthfully as well. If you can achieve anything more than this, therein you will seem to me not an orator but a Crassus, who is making use of some talent that is peculiarly his own and not common to orators in general. (I.x.44)

In other words, the ideal orator will be a peculiar exception rather than a general model.[64]

By philosophical standards, Ciceronian rhetoric would appear to be epistemologically and ethically equivocal. It remains committed to rhetorical success, not ideal models. Quintilian's question concerning the orator's commitment to virtue as opposed to rhetorical success would most likely never have occurred to the characters in *De Oratore*. Although rhetorical success may be enhanced by a virtuous character, virtuous character without rhetorical success would be no model of virtue at all.

Renaissance Civic Humanism and Political *Technē*

The relationship of rhetoric to Renaissance civic humanism poses another complication in determining the fate of rhetoric's social and political function. The Renaissance humanism of Europe is frequently

---

[64] See also Antonius: "I am not speaking of the inspired genius of a consummate orator but of the moderate level attained by practice and habituation" (*De Oratore*, II.lxxiii.298).

characterized as the recovery of rhetoric's civic function and the expression of civic virtue's affinity with a literary education. The curriculum of the humanists was to have healed the breach between wisdom and eloquence inflicted by medieval scholasticism. Taking their literary ideals from such orators as Cicero, Renaissance humanists are frequently credited with negotiating a merger between the public domain associated with rhetoric and more private spheres of value, judgment, and taste.[65] The political character of Renaissance civic ideals, however, remains the subject of significant debate.[66] Scholars long accepted Burckhardt's contention that Renaissance humanists were largely indifferent to politics (Rabil, "Significance of 'Civic Humanism,'" 141); and Burckhardt's depiction of the possibilities of political dissent in Renaissance despotisms and republics echoes the political quietism of Quintilian's vir bonus: "Each individual protested inwardly against despotism but was disposed to make tolerable or profitable terms with it rather than to combine with others for its destruction" (Burckhardt, *Civilization of the Renaissance*, 39). Cicero was not admired for his statesmanship; rather, according to Burckhardt, he was "recognized universally" for providing "the purest model of prose" (151). It was not until the middle of the twentieth century that scholars such as Hans Baron and Eugenio Garin began to argue for the existence of a strong civic tradition of Renaissance humanism.[67]

Reexaminations of Renaissance civic humanism, however, have tended to confirm Burckhardt's earlier interpretation. The argument at large is that Renaissance humanism served in part to "depoliticize" patterns of economic distribution. For example, Albert Rabil observes that when Francesco Barbaro invokes authors of antiquity to outline "'the genuine civic spirit in humanistic literature,'" he refers to the defenses of private wealth in the state offered by both Aristotle and Xenophon ("Significance of 'Civic Humanism,'" 145). Anthony Grafton and Lisa Jardine are similarly critical of the discovery of civic virtues in Renaissance humanism, arguing that, on the whole, humanist

---

[65] See also Seigel, "'Civic Humanism' or 'Ciceronian Rhetoric.'?" For a treatment of Renaissance conceptions of rhetoric, see Gray, "Renaissance Humanism."

[66] Rabil notes that Seigel argues that civic humanism never existed ("Significance of 'Civic Humanism,'"153).

[67] See Baron, "Leonardo Bruni," and Garin, *Italian Humanism*. For summaries of this debate, see Rabil, "Significance of 'Civic Humanism,'" and Seigel, "Civic Humanism."

education gave a new elite "an indelible cultural seal of superiority," while inculcating in "lesser members" a "properly docile attitude towards authority" (*From Humanism to the Humanities*, xiv). Renaissance institutions, they argue, served the needs of a "new Europe" to "close off debate on vital political and social questions" (xiv), while the conception of taste implicit in Renaissance eloquence was "equivalent to confirmation of contemporary values" (xv).[68] Even the most elegant defenses of Renaissance rhetoric reach something of an impasse when they confront rhetoric's political functions.[69] Victoria Kahn, for example, argues that the deliberative tradition of Greek rhetoric appears in Renaissance perspectives on prudence and reading: "Literature is not only the activity in which the self-reflexive nature of the linguistic act is most in evidence, but also the place where that self-reflexivity—conceived in prudential terms, may be seen to have practical and political significances" (*Rhetoric, Prudence, and Skepticism*, 21). Kahn's work is an explicit attempt to resituate Renaissance reading and rhetoric in twentieth-century literary and reader-response theory; at the same time, the relatively private nature of this political gesture may speak worlds about the character of the Renaissance "civic."[70]

Productive Knowledge and the Democratization of Virtue

As we shall see, the disciplinary character of rhetoric in nineteenth- and twentieth-century interpretations of Aristotelian rhetoric has been largely determined by philosophy, generally precluding rhetoric's reformulation as a political technē, a logōn technē, or productive knowledge. Though traditions of rhetorical paideia have promised to produce a kind of "culture hero," that heroic model has retained its authority largely to the extent that it divorced itself from evolving social and political contexts. Consequently, rhetoric's confrontation with culture, at least within academic institutions, has often served the function of securing specific lines of cultural authority and effac-

[68] The extent to which Renaissance humanists were seriously engaged with the texts of antiquity is also the subject of debate. Grafton and Jardine cite significant scholarly evidence that Gabriel Harvey, the humanist professor of rhetoric in England, received his Cicero and Quintilian primarily through Ramus. See *From Humanism to the Humanities*, 184–96.

[69] See Struever, *Language and Thought in the Renaissance*.

[70] See also Kahn, *Machiavellian Rhetoric*.

ing both social and historical difference. Ironically, this "depoliticiza-tion" of rhetoric has frequently made the discipline a far more effec-tive instrument of social, political, and economic power. On the one hand, as long as the rhetorical paideia promised to produce a norma-tive subject, that subject would both embody and reproduce existing lines of power. On the other hand, more philosophical traditions of rhetoric would produce normative bodies of knowledge and normative descriptions of social realities, equally effective at naturalizing con-tingent social relations and universalizing specific class values.

What is at stake is far more than rhetoric's disciplinary character. At stake is the very character of the humanist paradigm and the lib-eral arts. To what extent are both constituted by the commitment to reproduce normative subjects and normative bodies of knowledge? What powers and institutions does this commitment serve? To what extent have these principles created a cultural paradigm that con-strues "difference" primarily as "deviation"?

One broad rationalization for humanism's universalization of a spe-cific set of class values has been the promise of "democratizing" virtue. Recent challenges to the traditions and canons of the liberal arts, however, have suggested that this commitment has done more to subvert than to secure democracy.

Again, Jaeger's treatment of paideia and rhetoric betrays the often problematic relationship between traditional humanism and democ-racy. Jaeger insists that the values that underwrite both culture and law are simply inapplicable for the demos at large.[71] The "nobility" is the "prime mover in forming a nation's culture": all culture, "how-ever high an intellectual level it may reach, and however greatly its content may change, still bears the imprint of its aristocratic origin. Culture is simply the aristocratic ideal of a nation, increasingly intellectualized" (*Paideia*, 1:4). What, then, is the role of paideia in a democratic society? What Jaeger outlines is largely a program of edu-cation for democracy's representatives, an education for "exceptional"

---

[71] In a treatment of his theory of class, Jaeger explains that "all higher civilization springs from the differentiation of social classes," a differentiation that is born of "nat-ural variations between man and man" (*Paideia*, 1:4). This social stratification yields a kind of cultural homeostasis, according to Jaeger, because the "hereditary principle which rules" the "highly privileged class" is "counterbalanced by the new supplies of strength which pour in from the lower classes" (1:4). Even in the face of "violent change" in which "the ruling caste is deprived of all its rights or destroyed," what re-mains constant is the formative influence of the ruling class (1:4).

citizens.[72] He explains the importance of strong leaders in a democracy in his treatment of Pericles' "archaic ideal of isonomia" (1:289–90):

> The logic of history led to the conclusion that, if the democratic state was to maintain itself, it must have the right kind of man as its leader. That was in fact the chief, the *only* problem of democracy, for the democratic principle was bound to develop *ad absurdum*, whenever the democratic state attempted to be more than a strictly regulated system of ratifying the decisions of its representatives, and really became the domination of the masses. (1:290)

Jaeger's argument concerning democracy and the aristocratic values embedded in the humanist paideia is not peculiar to his supremacist view of Greek culture. The political philosopher Leo Strauss also takes aristocratic values as the starting point for his definitions of both democracy and liberal education:

> What is modern democracy? It was once said that democracy is the regime that stands or falls by virtue: a democracy is a regime in which all or most adults are men of virtue, and since virtue seems to require wisdom, a regime in which all or most adults have developed their reason to a high degree, or *the* rational society. Democracy, in a word, is meant to be an aristocracy which has broadened into a universal aristocracy. (*Liberalism*, 4)

The type of democracy set forth by Strauss is explicitly dependent on the paradigm of liberal humanism: "Liberal education is the ladder by which we try to ascend from mass democracy to democracy as originally meant. Liberal education is the necessary endeavor to found an aristocracy within democratic mass society. Liberal education reminds those members of a mass democracy who have ears to hear, of human greatness" (5).

Clearly, the problem of such a perspective on both democracy and education concerns the status of these auditors of "human greatness." How are they determined? How are they created? What secures the standards of human greatness on which they depend? As Richard Lan-

---

[72] See Jaeger's comparison and contrast of the sophistic educational project and Platonic ideals in ibid., vol. 1, bk. 2, chap. 3, and vol. 2, specifically bk. 3, chap. 5, as well as the general discussion of Plato, legislation, and cultural ideals in vol. 3.

ham observes, this perspective on the democratization of virtue in the university has generally left "'nontraditional'" students to "learn our ways as best they can" ("Extraordinary Convergence," 36). In other words, those who have ears to hear are likely to be those who already embody dominant standards of "human greatness"; and those who do not hear are responsible for their own failure to ascend the ladder of liberal virtue. Both Jaeger and Strauss point to a troubling paradox in traditional conceptions of democracy and humanism: "subjects" of democracy are not the citizens of the state but rather the state's exceptional leaders. Such a theory of both education and politics is far less likely to disperse "virtue" than to justify its scarcity.

Productive Knowledge and the Democratization of Advantage

Jaeger found it necessary to distinguish very carefully the paideia of the sophists from that of Socrates. The objective of his Socratic paideia is aretē, translated as both "virtue" and "excellence"; and aretē is incarnate in the "ideal man." But Jaeger also explains a principle behind this notion of excellence: "Aretē or excellence in a utensil, a body, a soul, or a living being, does not come about by chance, but only by right order and deliberate art. Everything becomes good when its own peculiar type of order, its cosmos, becomes supreme and is realized in it" (*Paideia*, 2:146). According to this functionalist perspective—explicit, as we shall see, in both Plato and Aristotle—virtue is secured when both people and "things" realize the proper order within and find their place in the proper order without.

In his discussion of Plato's *Gorgias*, Jaeger insists that it is precisely this order that is threatened by the technē of such rhetoricians as Callicles. By affirming the sophistic position that rhetoric is finally a matter of making the weaker stronger, Callicles admits that his logōn technē is bound to no single standard of knowledge or value—truth or virtue. As Jaeger observes, such an art would inevitably disrupt the lines of order by which excellence is secured:

> Wise men tell us that heaven and earth and gods and men are held together by community and friendship and orderliness and moderation and justice, and that is why the universe is called the Order, the Cosmos. It is not *pleonexia*, the greed for more, that is powerful among gods and men; it is geometric proportion. But Callicles does not care about geometry! (*Paideia*, 2:146)

In Jaeger's paradigm, pleonexia challenges not only standards of value but also the very classificatory principles by which people and objects are defined.

Jaeger's characterization of pleonexia stands in sharp contrast to that of Isocrates. It is precisely the art of "overreaching" that Isocrates aims to teach; and the lines of order that Plato's aretē secures are the very boundaries that productive knowledge will transgress. At the same time, simply to equate Isocrates' art of advantage to an art of subversion may be only to recast his logōn technē in the paradigm of philosophy—to prescribe merely a different instrumental use for "knowledge" per se. As long as both knowledge and subjectivity are "things" that can be extricated from temporal social, political, and economic relations, humanism's key terms remain unchanged. Normalized subjects will continue to reproduce existing lines of power, and normalized bodies of knowledge—whether empirically objective or philosophically universal—will naturalize contingent social realities.[73] Consequently, transgressing the boundaries of the humanist paradigm may be less a categorical challenge to specific relations of power than the opening of spaces for the construction and *expression* of alternative models of subjectivity, knowledge, and value.

The question that persists is whether contemporary challenges to the humanist paradigm should lead us either to abandon the notion of excellence or to reformulate the terms in which it has been cast. Where do we begin with such a reformulation, and will we have a humanist paradigm once we have finished? In a sense, these questions can be addressed only by other questions raised in this book.

What if Protagoras and Isocrates do indeed proceed from a different paradigm—a paradigm that Aristotle acknowledges even though he does not embrace it? What if the art of Protagoras and Isocrates is concerned with not only the construction of speeches but also the construction of subjectivities? We know that Isocrates' rhetor is *not* defined by his success in either forcefully communicating ideas or absolutely predicting and controlling the business of the state. Isocrates outlines neither a subject of virtue nor a subject of knowl-

---

[73] "Every theory, as the word itself suggests, is a programme of perception." according to Bourdieu. "Even the most strictly constative scientific description is always open to the possibility of functioning in a prescriptive way, capable of contributing to its own verification by exercising a theory effect through which it helps to bring about that which it declares" (*Language and Symbolic Power*, 128, 134).

edge but rather a rhetorical ēthos constructed by the shifting fortunes of honor, which the polis can both confer and withhold. Ēthos is produced by the rhetor's intervention in the affairs of the polis; and the affairs of the polis intervene in the production of the rhetor's ēthos. What would it mean to recast our conception of the subject in terms of rhetorical ēthos—a contingent, temporal subject that exists only in a situated, discursive exchange?

Dispersing the humanist chain of equivalences will require finding alternative measures of knowledge and value, as well as alternative models of subjectivity. When Isocrates enjoins his students to "seize their advantage," he points to a renegotiation of these terms at two levels. First, in seizing the opportunity for instruction, his students change their own cultural authority; they increase their likelihood of accruing honor and esteem. But their success as rhetors also depends on their ability to seize their advantage in a particular moment of discourse—to discern a point of indeterminacy, overreach a boundary, and intervene in the systems of classification and standards of value that are secured by the social cosmology of humanists such as Jaeger and Strauss. Such acts of intervention are described by Bourdieu as "the denunciation of [a] . . . tacit contract of adherence to the established order"; it is there, "strictly speaking," he contends, that "politics begins."[74] At this moment of indeterminacy, a very profound kind of invention takes place—a renegotiation of the real, the valuable, and the human.

Is it possible to envision the humanist project as the democratization not of virtue but of "advantage," the negotiation and invention of diverse standards of value, subjectivity, and knowledge?[75] Only those who insist that value be assessed by a single historical scale would fear that such an alternative would lead to the death of excellence and

---

[74] Ibid., 127. "Politics begins, strictly speaking, with the denunciation of this tacit contract of adherence to the established order which defines the original doxa; in other words, political subversion presupposes cognitive subversion, a conversion of the vision of the world" (ibid., 127–28).

[75] This principle is embedded in theories of democracy which maintain that the critical principle of democracy is the equalization of occasions to give "voice"—or to represent—interests and concerns. See Arblaster, *Democracy;* Lefort, *Democracy and Political Theory;* and Bowles and Gintis, *Democracy and Capitalism.* This principle is also implicit in Iris Marion Young's argument in *Justice and the Politics of Difference* that justice should be defined not solely in terms of the distribution of rights but also as the alleviation of domination and oppression.

virtue. Indeed, it is more likely that it is the suppression of such alternatives that accounts for the poverty of virtue in our own time.

In the discussion of technē and productive knowledge that follows, I examine the shifting characterizations of art in myth, science, and ancient Greek society. I also trace the story of technē in various Prometheus narratives from Hesiod through Isocrates, concluding by exploring the occlusion of productive knowledge by the theory/practice opposition as it appears in the nineteenth- and twentieth-century commentaries on Aristotle's *Rhetoric*. Though this examination employs the methodologies of the very tradition that it critiques, this attempt to define productive knowledge is as heuristic as it is descriptive. Indeed, rather than resisting the paradox of critique—that the past we critique exists only in the present—I embrace that paradox as the rhetorical purpose of this account: to define a past that might be used in responding to the epistemological and ethical crises of the present.

2 *Techne* and the Transformation of Limits

> The sense of limits and of the legitimate transgression of limits . . .
> is the basis at once of the ordering of the world (known, since Par-
> menides, as *diakosmesis*) and of the ritual actions intended to au-
> thorize or facilitate the necessary or unavoidable breaches of that
> order. "The world is based on the limit [*thalasth*]," said an old
> Kabyle. "Heaven and earth are separated by the limit. The eyes have
> an enclosure [*zerb*]. The mouth has a limit. Everything has a limit."
> To bring order is to bring distinction, to divide the universe into op-
> posing entities.
> —Pierre Bourdieu, *Outline of a Theory of Practice*

One of the earliest uses of the term "techne" is found in a passage
in the *Odyssey* that poses some problems for translators. In book III, a
smith comes at Nestor's request to overlay a heifer's horns with gold
in order to make the animal a fitting sacrifice for Athena. According to
Homer, the artisan arrives "bearing in his hands his tools of bronze,
the implements of his craft [*peirata technes*], anvil and hammer and
well-made tongs" (III.433–34). The indeterminacy of the passage turns
on the noun *ta peirata*, translated here as "implements."[1] "Ta peirata"
is the Homeric plural of *to peras*, which generally means "end, limit,
boundary" (LSJ, 1365). A nineteenth-century commentary on the
passage attempts to accommodate these senses of the word as both
"implement" and "boundary" by suggesting the following translation
of 'ta peirata": "'wherein lie the issues of art,' i.e. on which art depends
for its accomplishment" (Merry and Riddell, *Homer's "Odyssey,"* 131).
In other words, one can account for both meanings if we accept that
the accomplishments of art are, paradoxically, tied to its boundaries.

---

[1] For a discussion of *peras*, see Detienne and Vernant, *Cunning Intelligence*,
279–326.

The ambiguity of the limit is the same ambiguity we find through-out characterizations of technē. Athena, the patron goddess of the arts and crafts of the smiths, also brings under her aegis spinning and weav-ing, the arts of the Moirai, or Fates.[2] In these ancient contexts, technē is never reducible to an instrument or a means to an end. Instead, art intervenes when a boundary or limitation is recognized, and it creates a path that both transgresses and redefines that boundary. Fate and ne-cessity may set temporary limits for invention, but their boundaries are perpetually redrawn by technē.

In this chapter I begin to create a context for the ancient conception of technē by outlining its mythic traditions and several of the terms by which it is defined. Some of these terms, such as *mētis* and *kairos*, are part of a lexicon that defines technē as a model of knowledge with a distinctive form of intelligence and sense of time. That lexicon also includes forces and limits *against* which technē is defined: *bia* (com-pulsion), *kratos* (force), *anankē* (necessity), and *moira* (fate). Technē challenges those forces and limits with its power to discover (*heuriskein*) and invent new paths (*poroi*). The definition of technē in Chapter 1 is only elaborated in these contexts, not changed.

(1) A technē is never a static normative body of knowledge. It may be described as a dynamis (or power), transferable guides and strategies, a cunningly conceived plan—even a trick or trap. This knowledge is sta-ble enough to be taught and transferred but flexible enough to be adapted to particular situations and purposes.

(2) A technē resists identification with a normative subject. The sub-jects identified with technē are often in a state of flux or transformation. For example, when an art is employed or exchanged, characters fre-quently change their identity. They cross the boundaries that separate animals from humans and mortals from immortals. Since a technē is al-ways transferable, no matter how brilliant the plan or strategy, it is never confined to a specific human or god. In other words, technē is never "private" knowledge, a mysterious faculty, or the product of unique genius.

(3) Technē marks a domain of intervention and invention. A technē is *never* knowledge as representation. Technē appears when one is out-numbered by foes or overpowered by force. It not only enables the trans-gression of boundaries but also attempts to *rectify* transgressions.

[2] See Merry and Riddell, *Homer's "Odyssey,"* 273, and OCD, 138–39.

Gods and Goddesses of Art

The most significant mythic tradition of techne is found in various Prometheus accounts, discussed in detail in Chapters 4 and 5. But techne is associated with other gods and goddesses who are identified with invention, craft production, and the disruption of lines of power. The one characteristic shared by these deities is an ambiguity of identity. They are either caught between dual identities, as is Prometheus, crossing and recrossing the boundary between humankind and the gods, or like Metis, they are defined by the power of transformation itself.

Prometheus

The character of Prometheus remains at the heart of mythical and political discussions of techne.[3] His name means literally "forethought" (*prometheia*), and he is known for his sympathy for humankind, which motivates his theft of fire from heaven to give to mortals. Frequently depicted as the prototypic "man," Prometheus's gift of the power of art and technology (symbolized by fire) is credited with precipitating the division of labor that brings about complex social organizations, such as the city. Some of the most detailed accounts of the Prometheus story in the Greek tradition are found in Hesiod's *Theogony* and *Works and Days*, Aeschylus's *Prometheus Bound*, and Protagoras's "Great Speech," which we have by way of Plato's dialogue *Protagoras*. Though key elements of the plot are consistent, the characterizations of Prometheus range from the trickster, as depicted by Hesiod, to the tragic hero, as depicted by Aeschylus.

Hephaestus

Whereas Prometheus is the archetypal craftsman, Hephaestus is the patron god of fire and craft. Hesiod describes him as "skilled in crafts [*techneisi*] more than all the sons of heaven" (*Theog.* 928). He is the son of Zeus and Hera, banished from heaven by his mother, according

---

[3] Though I focus primarily on Prometheus accounts of techne, Thomas Cole, in *Democritus and the Sources of Greek Anthropology*, has demonstrated in detail the extent to which these accounts are a subset of a wider group of narratives describing the theft or discovery of the technai and their distribution.

to Homer, because he was born with misshapen (curved) feet. Detienne and Vernant argue that Hephaestus's crooked feet bear witness
to his polymorphic character, associating him with such creatures as
the crab, which "half-belong to the element of the sea" (CI, 273). Hephaestus is the god of the smith, frequently referred to as the "famous
god of the two strong arms" (*Od.* VIII.349, 357). In Hesiod's version of
the Prometheus myth, he appears as the artisan who crafts the first
woman, Pandora, whereas in Homer's *Odyssey*, he is husband to
Aphrodite.

Hermes

Hermes appears in Protagoras's version of the Prometheus narrative
to deliver to humankind *dikē* (justice) and *aidōs* (respect), which
constitute Protagoras's political technē. Hermes is known as the
messenger god, hence identified with good speaking or oratory (OCD,
503). He is also associated with invention; he created the lyre, for example, on the very day of his birth (*Homeric Hymn to Hermes*, 25–61).
His characterizations frequently overlap with those of Athena and
Prometheus. His eyes are described as flashing, as are Athena's, and he
possesses the same cunning, crafty intelligence we find in Hesiod's
Prometheus. His invention of the lyre is given the following description in the hymn: "As bright glances flash from the eye, so glorious
Hermes planned both thought and deed at once" (45–46). Later in the
same hymn, he is credited with seeking the "art of fire" (108) and inventing "fire-sticks and fire" (111).

Mētis

The goddess Mētis is described as "counsel personified" (OCD, 679).
As Detienne and Vernant explain, Metis's unique character lies in her
power of metamorphosis: "She can, in succession, become a lion, a
bull, a fly, a fish, a bird, a flame or flowing water" (CI, 20). According
to Hesiod's *Theogony*, Metis is Zeus's first wife, the "wisest among
gods and mortal men" and mother of Athena (886–88). Having been
warned by Earth and Heaven of the wisdom and power of Metis's children, Zeus "craftily deceived her with cunning words and put her in
his own belly . . . that the goddess might devise for him both good and
evil (888–900).

Athena

"Flashing-eyed Athena" is the armed goddess who oversees cities and the crafts and arts. *Homeric Hymn XI* describes Athena as one who "loves deeds of war" but who "saves the people as they go out to war and come back." The indeterminacy of Athena's character turns on her sexual identity. She is an androgynous figure, dressed always in armor. In the *Odyssey*, for example, she visits Telemachus in the guise of a man, "lord over the oar-loving Taphians," to warn him of the suitors in his home and of the fate of his father, Odysseus (I.181).

Athena's role as goddess of arts and crafts is raised explicitly in a Homeric epigram that addresses her as the goddess of the kiln:

> Potters, if you will give me a reward, I will sing for you. Come, then, Athena, with hand upraised over the kiln. Let the pots and all the dishes turn out well and be well fired: let them fetch good prices and be sold in plenty in the market, and plenty in the streets. Grant that the potters may get great gain and grant me so to sing to them. (XIV.1–6)

The poet clearly makes no attempt to disguise the commercial dimension of the arts of song or pottery. While other texts will illustrate the potential of techne as a set of teachable skills to be transferred or "exchanged," the Homeric Athena underscores the economic value of techne .

Hephaestus and the Bonds of Love and Art

One brief tale in the *Odyssey* brings two of these characters together and illustrates how techne shifts a balance of power and reverses a transgression. In book VIII Hephaestus seeks revenge for Aphrodite's infidelity with Ares. According to the Homeric poet, Hephaestus was told by Helius that Ares and Aphrodite have been lovers. After hearing the news, Hephaestus went to his smith and on his anvil "fashioned the snare" (276)—a trap of forged "bonds which might not be broken or loosed, that the lovers might bide fast where they were" (274–75). Hephaestus then took the snare to his bed chamber and "everywhere round about the bed-posts he spread the bonds, and many too were hung from above, from the roof-beams, fine as spiders' webs, so that no one even of the blessed gods could see them, so exceeding craftily were they fashioned" (278–81). After setting the trap, he pretended to journey to Lemnos, leaving Aphrodite alone. As soon as Ares saw him depart, he came to Aphrodite, saying "come, love, let us to bed and take our joy, couched together. For Hephaestus is no longer here in the land, but has now gone" (292–94). As soon as they lay down, "about them clung the cunning bonds [*desmoi technēentes*] of the wise Hephaestus, nor could they in any wise stir their limbs or raise them up" (296–97).

When Hephaestus saw that the lovers could not escape, he returned to his home. Standing at the gate, he cried to the gods, "Father Zeus, and ye other blessed gods that are forever, come hither that ye may see a laughable matter and a monstrous, even how Aphrodite, daughter of Zeus, scorns me for that I am lame and loves destructive Ares because he is comely and strong of limb, whereas I was born misshapen" (306–11). Hephaestus's lameness, however, has not prevented him from taking revenge. His art has literally transformed their desire into bondage: "Yet, methinks, they will not wish to lie longer thus, no, not for a moment, how loving soever they are. Soon shall both lose their desire to sleep; but the snare and the bonds shall hold them until her father pays back to me all the gifts of wooing that I gave him for the sake of his shameless girl" (315–20).

The story concludes with a moral that succinctly summarizes the value of technē: "'Ill deeds thrive not. The slow catches the swift; even as now Hephaestus, slow though he is, has outstripped Ares for all that he is the swiftest of the gods who hold Olympus. Lame though he is, he has caught him by craft [*technēisi*]'" (329–32). Though the story remains an unhappy tale of retribution, it reinscribes two persistent themes regarding technē. Art makes up for a lack—in this case, the lack of speed due to Hephaestus's lameness and his lack of physical attractiveness. His technē also has a pitiless transformative power, for it changes the bed of love into a trap and love's embrace into imprisonment.

Power, Cunning Intelligence, and Time

Technē and Power

The earliest uses of technē found in Homer and Hesiod frequently convey the sense of trick or contrivance that is illustrated by Hephaestus's bonds (LSJ, 1784–85). Technē is often associated with *apatē*, or "deception," and the product of a techné is often a ruse—something that is not what it appears to be. *Dolos* often occurs with techné and is similarly defined as "any cunning contrivance for deceiving or catching . . . any trick or stratagem . . . craft, cunning, treachery" (443). Other senses of techné often overlap and sometimes appear contradictory. Techné may refer to a "set of rules, system or method of making or doing," but it may also denote artistic products and concrete examples that might be used to illustrate those methods (1785). For example, a techné can refer to a "treatise on Grammar . . . or on Rhetoric" (1785); this is the sense often used by scholars to refer to ancient handbooks—or *technai*—of rhetoric, which can include already composed speeches as well as figures of speech.

Techné also refers to a craft or trade that can generate economic capital (LSJ, 1785); it is generally identified with artifice as opposed to nature.[4] Though the material of techné may be taken from nature, by skill the artist produces something that nature on its own could not create. "Technology" is an obvious cognate of techné, which in present usage generally marks the splintering of techné into craft, as opposed to high art, and technical knowledge as instrumental means.[5] These distinctions, however, were largely ignored in ancient traditions of techné. Generally foregrounded in the various uses of techné are its economic value and its location in culture as opposed to nature.

One of the most important dimensions of ancient conceptions of techné is its complex relationship to subjectivity. In his discussion of technique, Cornelius Castoriadis explains that "techné" is related to the ancient verb *teuchein*, which in Homer means "'to fabricate', 'to produce', 'to construct'" (*Crossroads*, 231). At the same time, its noun form *teuchos* can mean "tool" or "instrument" (231).[6] Vernant observes

---

[4] For example, *to technēton*, the "product of a craft," contrasts with nature (LSJ, 1785).

[5] See Heidegger, "The Question concerning Technology," in *Basic Writings*, ed. Krell, and Mumford, *Technics and Civilization*. An interesting observation is made by Gayatri Chakravorty Spivak in her attempt to reframe the "humanist" project in *In Other Worlds:* "A simple test case of how politics-economics-technology (i.e., technocracy) becomes a collective determinant where 'the last instance' can only be situated provisionally, temporarily, and in a slippery way, is the revisions of Edison's technological systems as recorded in the publications of the Edison Electric Institute. A humanist analysis of technology, choosing to ignore this transformation in the definition of technology, situates techné as the dynamic and undecidable middle term of the triad *theoria-techné-praxis*" (283 n. 10).

[6] See also LSJ, 1784.

that Homer depicts the "tool," or *organon*, as both an instrument "manipulated by man" and an "extension of his own organs" (MT, 281). In other words, the organon "transmits and amplifies the force of man" (281). Both descriptions suggest that technē is inseparable from the subject it enables, and, reciprocally, the intervention enabled by technē redefines that subject.

In one sense, technē very concretely determined subjectivity because the possession of a technē was an explicit class marker. Artisans always made up a distinct social group; as early as Solon, the third census class was defined as the *moira technourgos* (LSJ, 1785). The *technitēs*, or "craftsman," contrasted with the freeman (1785), for the technitēs made his living from his professional knowledge, or his art.[7] Vernant argues that the social status of the artisan was likely at its highest point in Homer's age, when artisans formed groups similar to religious brotherhoods and worked at the behest of the nobility (MT, 292). Vernant is careful to distinguish these artisans from what we might call "engineers" because, as he maintains, artisans in the Greek tradition did not concentrate on developing forms of technology to apply to agricultural or production problems. Their products are more accurately characterized as *agalmata*, luxury items that served less as "utilitarian object(s)" than as symbols of "personal value and social superiority" (292). In this context, the artisan's products could be classified as *thaumata*—objects designed to evoke wonder and awe (290, 292–93). Moreover, as these brotherhoods of artisans were in competition, rather than sharing and developing new techniques, they jealously guarded their technai as trade—even cult—secrets.[8]

As technai grew more specialized, hierarchies developed within the artisan class itself. Thus, as Vernant notes, *cheirotechnēs* comes to refer to the manual laborer, who works with his hands (*cheires*) (MT, 293)—despite the fact that the Hippocratic writer of *Ancient Medicine* still refers to the physician as an "acknowledged handicraftsman [*cheirotechnēs*]" (VII.2).[9] Vernant maintains that democratic principles helped to hasten the decline in status of the Homeric artisan because obvious markers of material wealth were more likely

---

[7] Plato also uses *technikos* to refer to any skilled person, but particularly to grammarians and rhetoricians (LSJ, 1785).

[8] On the spirit of competition (*eris*) among brotherhoods, see Vernant, MT, 202.

[9] See also Aristotle, *Met.* 981b4.

to bring higher taxes than social prestige. Once the crafter of thaumata, the artisan came to be identified with the merchant and banausic classes. For the most part, however, democratic reforms, as
Vernant observes, left the artisan "relegated to a position that corre-
sponded to his function in the state, and confined to a subordinate
role" (MT, 293).

As this discussion suggests, techne's value and class status were
largely dependent on one's perspective. For the banausic classes,
techne was a means to some degree of economic and social power. For
Plato, techne referred to a kind of professional knowledge, directly
opposed to the paideia of the freeman (*Protag.* 312b). Despite his reform program for rhetoric, outlined in the *Phaedrus*, Plato's assessment
of sophistic instruction remains fairly constant: "The activity as a
whole, it seems to me, is not an art, but the occupation of a shrewd
and enterprising spirit" (*Gorgias* 463a). Though in the *Gorgias* and the
Phaedrus Plato outlines his criteria for a true art, by the time those
criteria are met, we are left with something that resembles philosophy far more than it does rhetoric.[10]

Techne and Metis

What passes for art in this realm of appearances is the product of a
different kind of reasoning, known as metis. In *Cunning Intelligence
in Greek Culture and Society*, Marcel Detienne and Jean-Pierre Vernant trace the Greek conception of metis, a "cunning intelligence"
more akin to the "shrewd and enterprising spirit" of the sophists than
to the dialectical reasoning of Plato. A number of terms might be used
to describe metis: "flair, wisdom, forethought, subtlety of mind, deception, resourcefulness, vigilance, opportunism, various skills, and
experience acquired over the years" (CI, 3). According to Detienne and
Vernant, Athena and Hephaestus are "the deities of *metis*" (18); metis
informs not only Hephaestus's forging of the "snare" and "bond" but
also Prometheus's efforts to deceive Zeus (125–26). For Detienne and
Vernant, it is the sophist who, "in contrast to the philosopher. . . , embodies the scheming intelligence of the man of *metis*, plunged into the
world of appearance and of Becoming" (45).

Detienne and Vernant are not alone in identifying techne with

___

[10] See also *Gorgias* 465, 501a, and *Phaedrus* 245d. Plato will be discussed in detail
in Chapter 5.

mētis. Lowell Edmunds observes that mētis is associated with technē in Homer and Empedocles (*Chance and Intelligence*, 106, 106 n. 26). For Empedocles, men are "well-learned in their crafts [*technēs*] because of cunning [*mētios*]" (Inwood, 219). Mētis is also explicitly identified with technē in Hesiod's *Works and Days* and *Theogony*. Prometheus is called "Prometheus the crafty," *Prometheus ankulomētēs* (WD 48; *Theog.* 546). The adjective *ankulomētēs* is a compound of mētis and the word for crooked or bent; thus an alternative translation to "cunning" could be "crooked of counsel" (LSJ, 10).[11]

The goddess Mētis takes her name from this kind of intelligence, which denotes "wisdom, skill, craft," as well as "counsel, plan, undertaking" (LSJ, 1130). In contrast to philosophical *nous*, which is concerned with timeless principles, mētis is "applied to situations which are transient, shifting, disconcerting, and ambiguous, situations which do not lend themselves to precise measurement, exact calculation or rigorous logic" (CI, 3–4). Mētis is associated with the indeterminacy of both subjects and objects. It is used to create deceptive identities, such as the Trojan Horse, that disguise "inner character" with deceptive artifice. Mētis even transgresses the boundaries separating the gods, humankind, and animals. Mētis frequently refers to animal intelligence, particularly the "cunning" that allows a weaker animal to subvert the stronger. Detienne and Vernant observe how Pindar uses mētis (here translated as "cunning") to describe the intelligence of the fox: "The cunning of the weaker has taken the stronger by surprise and brought about his downfall" (in CI, 36). Similarly, in Oppian's second-century c.e. *Treatise on Fishing*, mētis enables the fishing frog to transform part of its own body into bait to attract prey, and it is "by *technē*" that the octopus camouflages itself, merging "with the rock to which it clings" (CI, 28, 29). Mētis and technē undermine the rule of force in the animal world. Oppian explains: "Those which have not been allotted strength by some god and which are not equipped with some poisonous sting to defend themselves have as their weapons the resources of an intelligence fertile in cunning tricks and stratagems (*doloi*). They can kill a fish which is easily their superior in size and strength" (in CI, 28). Mētis occurs throughout the stories of technē that we shall examine; the significance of technē often lies in the power of transformation that mētis enables.

---

[11] For a discussion of *ankulomētēs*, see West's commentary on *Theogony* 18, p. 158.

Techné and Kairos

If mētis is the intelligence identified with technē, then kairos is the time "associated with technē." Kairos contrasts with *chronos*, which denotes "time in the abstract . . . a definite time, period" (LSJ, 2008). Kairos signifies, on the one hand, the "exact or critical time, season, opportunity," but it can also mean "advantage, profit" (LSJ, 859, 860).[12] Kairos would appear to embody the apothegm "time is money." Another sense of kairos refers to "due measure, proportion, fitness" (859). In Hellenistic depictions, the god Kairos often holds a pair of scales, and sometimes, as Debra Hawhee Wilhoit has pointed out, the god is portrayed surreptitiously depressing one pan of the scales in his favor.[13]

The significance of the identification of technē with a different order of time is easily underestimated. For example, Aristotle is generally careful to distinguish technē from metaphysics, mathematics, and the natural sciences; at points, however, he insists that technē involves rational intellection, comparable with that in the sciences. The point on which Aristotle decisively distinguishes the rationality of technē from philosophical reasoning is its relationship to time. For both Plato and Aristotle, the highest and most true knowledge transcends time; it is knowledge about things that "could not be otherwise" because the subjects of philosophical knowledge are immune to the contingencies of time and context. In contrast, the reasoning associated with mētis and technē is explicitly temporal.

In mythic accounts, the contingency of technē on the opportune moment may be a matter of waiting for a god to fall asleep or turn his back. The opportune moment plays a critical role in the arts of medicine, sea navigation, and rhetoric. G. E. R. Lloyd notes that according to some Hippocratic treatises "*every* disease can be cured, if you hit upon the right moment (*kairos*) to apply your remedies."[14] Detienne and Vernant describe the significance of kairos in the art of navigation: "Alcaeus devotes an entire poem to the theme that the sea voyage is won or lost on dry land. Zeus *Ourios* may blow the wind of departure but to profit from it the navigator must have foreseen it and wait for it.

---

12 See the debate recorded by Wilson, "Kairos as 'Profit.'"

13 For an important treatment of kairos, see Wilhoit, "Kairos Revisited." For the portrayal of Kairos, see 59–61.

14 See Lloyd, "Science and Morality," in *Methods and Problems*, 362. It is only fair to note that Lloyd is not necessarily praising the scientific method used here.

Kairos, associated with Zeus *Ourios* who represents the opportunity, stands for the propitious moment which the good pilot must seize, having foreseen from afar the opportunity which will arise for him to exercise his *technē*" (CI, 224).

The sophists were keenly aware of the importance of "knowing when" to gesture, exhort, and intervene. Protagoras is credited by Diogenes Laertius with being the first "to expound the importance of the right moment [*kairou*]" (Sprague, 4; DK, A. 1. 52). Isocrates insists that his instruction is distinguished by its concern with "the qualities of fitness for the occasion [*tōn kairōn*], propriety of style, and originality of treatment" (*Against the Sophists*, 13). Similarly, Aristotle calls attention to the importance of kairos in the arrangement of a speech; in this case kairos is translated as "opportunity":

> Making the audience attentive is a feature common to all parts of a speech, if there is need of it [at all]; for these remedies are sought everywhere, not just when beginning. Thus, it is ridiculous to amass them at the beginning, where all listeners are most paying attention. As a result, whenever there is an opportunity, one should say [things like] "And give me your attention, for nothing [that I say] pertains more to me than [it does] to you" and "I shall tell you something strange, the like of which you have never heard." (Kennedy, 264; 1415b12–14)

Deploying an art at the "right moment" in a particular situation is the sign of the true rhetor, yet it is something that cannot be taught by explicit precepts or rules. Isocrates is especially sensitive to the notion that acquiring a "sense" of the right way and right moment requires careful inculcation and the imitation of masters, which he describes as "habituation." In the *Antidosis*, Isocrates describes the development of the man who will "speak or write discourses which are worthy of praise and honor" (276): "He will select from all the actions of men which bear upon his subject those examples which are the most illustrious and the most edifying; and, habituating [*sunethizomenos*] himself to contemplate and appraise such examples, he will feel their influence not only in the preparation of a given discourse but in all the actions of his life" (277). "Habituating" is an apt translation for "*sunethizomenos*," which could also be rendered "becoming accustomed to." The student does not simply imitate a discrete subjectivity but rather submits to the influence of a context that includes "men," texts, and actions.[15]

---

[15] For a treatment of the complex and indeterminate relationship between rhetor and exemplars, see Leff, "Genre and Paradigm in the Second Book of *De Oratore*."

Isocrates' descriptions of his logōn technē affirm the notion that the transmission of a technē has as much to do with constructing a subject as with transferring rhetorical strategies. Knowing the right moment bears witness to a very complex kind of mimesis—what Bourdieu would call the "embodiment" of an art. What is "learned by body," according to Bourdieu, "is not something that one has, like knowledge that can be brandished, but something that one is" (LP, 73). Only this kind of embodiment creates the mastery that "makes it possible to appreciate the meaning of the situation instantly, at a glance, in the heat of the action, and to produce at once the opportune response" (LP, 104). "Knowing how" and "knowing when" are at the heart of kairos, distinguishing technē from rule-governed activities that are less constrained by temporal conditions. Bourdieu succinctly defines the "pedagogical" problem raised by kairos: "The pedagogy of the Sophists, forced, in order to realize its aim, to produce systems of rules, such as grammars or rhetorics, came up against the problem of the rules defining the right way and right moment—*kairos*—to apply the rules, or, as the phrase so aptly goes, to *put into practice* a repertoire of devices or techniques" (OTP, 20).

What is at stake for the rhetor's performance is twofold. On the one hand, the successful performance of the rhetor who has appropriated both rules and proper timing is often a testimony not to his mastery of an art but, paradoxically, to his "natural" ability—and even "natural" virtue. It is when art "appears to disappear" that it has been most successfully appropriated—or transformed into "nature." On the other hand, the unsuccessful performance of the rhetor who appropriates rules without this practical sense of the "right time" will only expose the "inadequate" and "unnatural" character of his art—and consequently his "virtue." Put more pointedly, decontextualized principles and rules are usually markers of the successful mastery of the art of "going to school"; they point to success in a pedagogical context that only underscores the initial "lack" in the rhetor.

In the mastery of the moment lies the rhetor's best chance to intervene in and transform a situation. Like the enabling peirata of Homer's artisan, a technē works together with the limits of "what is." This sense of limits is invoked by Aristotle in one of his most precise definitions of rhetoric: "Rhetoric may be defined as the faculty of observing in any given case the available means of persuasion" (*Rhet.* 1355b25–26).[16] The successful rhetor understands and responds to the

---

16 W. Rhys Roberts's translation, in *Complete Works*, ed. Barnes.

limits of the "given case." An art deployed at the "right time," however, may do more than redefine the limits of specific situations; it may also create alternative situations.

Arts of Resistance and Transformation

Mitigating Force and Power

Bia and kratos are personified in Hesiod's and Aeschylus's versions of the Prometheus myth, and because I discuss them in my treatments of these narratives, their examination here will be brief. What is important to observe is the extent to which technē mitigates bia and kratos. Though both bia and kratos can refer to bodily strength, kratos is more explicitly identified with the sense of "*power over*" either subjects or another force (LSJ, 992). Kratos often refers to a kind of master/slave relationship and to "mastery" itself, as well as to victory (992). Bia may denote force and even a specific act of violence; it is, for example, the term for rape in Attic law (314). Bia is frequently associated with compulsion. As part of Zeus's retinue in the Prometheus stories, Bia and Kratos are agents of the old theocratic cosmos, challenged by Prometheus's technē. More literally, they are the tools of a predemocratic society in which violence is used to maintain social order, and invasion and plunder are legitimate means of acquiring economic capital.

Bia and kratos are explicitly set against technē in a number of contexts. In the pseudo-Hippocratic text *The Art*, dated in the fifth century B.C.E., the terms are used to describe both the character of medical art and the challenge presented to it by "obscure" or internal diseases, the causes of which are difficult to determine:

> For it is only when art sees its way that it thinks it right to give treatment, considering how it may give it, not by daring but by judgment, not by violence [*biēi*] but by gentleness. As to our human constitution, if it admits of being seen, it will also admit of being healed. But if, while the sight is being won, the body is mastered [*kratēthēi*] by slowness in calling in the attendant or the rapidity of the disease, the patient will pass away. (XI. 28–35)

The description, as a whole, is arcane to modern ears. But, in its own context, the agonistic struggle between disease and therapeutic treat-

ment that is expressed by the bia/kratos pair would have been very familiar.[17]

In a more general treatment of medicine in *The Art*, kratos is used
to define the limits of techné itself:

> For in cases where we may have the mastery [*epikratein*] through the
> means afforded by a natural constitution or by an art [techné], there we
> may be craftsmen, but nowhere else. Whenever therefore a man suffers
> from an ill which is too strong for the means at the disposal of medicine,
> he surely must not even expect that it can be overcome [*kratēthēnai*] by
> medicine. (VIII. 13–19)

The writer is quite explicit that the discovery of art shifts the balance
of power between humankind and nature:

> When . . . nature herself will yield nothing of her own accord, medicine
> has found means of compulsion [*biastheisa*], whereby nature is con-
> strained, without being harmed, to give up her secrets; when these are
> given up she makes clear, to those who know about the art [*technēs*]
> what course ought to be pursued. (XIII, 12–15)

Though Hesiod concludes that techné will never overcome the forces
of nature and the gods, the writer of the Hippocratic treatise maintains
that techné transposes that relation of power so that nature is now
compelled by art.

For Aristotle, bia and kratos generally refer to an external agency,
force, or source of motion.[18] Bia specifically refers to political force.
In two passages in the *Politics*, bia is paired with deception (apatē),
here translated "fraud": "Revolutions are effected in two ways, by
force [*dia bias*] and by fraud [*di'apatēs*]. Force may be applied either at

[17] Such rhetoric is no doubt also responsible for scholarly interpretations that credit
a sophist rather than a physician with authorship of *The Art*. See also Pedro Laín Entralgo, *The Therapy of the Word in Classical Antiquity*, especially chap. 4, "The Word
in Hippocratic Medicine."

[18] In the *Rhetoric*, bia appears in judicial topics on "wrongdoing" as Aristotle
describes different causes for human action. He suggests that people generally act
"either not on their own initiative or on their own initiative" (Kennedy, 89;
1368b32–33); and in this context, actions may be taken by means of seven causes:
"through chance [*tychē*], through nature [*physis*], through compulsion [*bia*], through
habit [*ēthos*], through reason [*logismos*], through anger, through longing" (Kennedy,
89; 1369a5–7).

the time of making the revolution or afterwards. Fraud, again, is of two kinds; for sometimes the citizens are deceived into acquiescing in a change of government, and afterwards they are held in subjection against their will" (1304b7–12). A similar relationship between force and fraud is raised in a discussion of tyranny: "Any one who obtains power by force [*bias*] or fraud [*apatēs*] is at once thought to be a tyrant" (1313a9–10).

In other contexts, bia and kratos are set against the alternative power of persuasive speech. Though Plato questions the epistemological validity of the technē of persuasive speech, he does not underestimate its power. In the *Republic*, the misologist, who is called a "stranger to the Muses," is depicted in the following manner: "He no longer makes any use of persuasion [*peithoi*] by speech but achieves all his ends like a beast by violence [*biai*] and savagery, and in his brute ignorance and ineptitude lives a life of disharmony and gracelessness" (411d–e). As we shall see in the Prometheus narratives, the art of effecting change through words—or persuasion—is what distinguishes humankind not only from animals but also from the brutal and capricious gods.

Challenging the Boundaries of Necessity and Fate

Although technē can mitigate lines of force and power, its most challenging boundaries may be *anankē* and *moira*. Generally translated as "necessity," anankē can also refer to "force, constraint" (LSJ, 101). Anankē appears in myth and philosophy as a "binding" force frequently identified with bia and kratos. Aristotle also uses anankē in a technical sense in logic, philosophy, and the natural sciences to describe operations or processes that "cannot be otherwise." Both terms appear throughout the Prometheus narratives, where they frequently refer to a "limit" or boundary that technē has challenged—sometimes successfully and sometimes not.

The conflict depicted in the Prometheus narratives largely turns on Prometheus's disruption of the *harmonia*, or "order," of Zeus. The punishment Zeus orders, depicted by both Hesiod and Aeschylus, is to leave Prometheus "bound" with bands or chains "of necessity." The poet concludes at the end of the *Theogony* narrative: "It is not possible to deceive or go beyond the will of Zeus: for not even the son of Iapetus, kindly Prometheus, escaped his heavy anger, but of necessity [*hup'anankēs*] strong bands confined him, although he knew many a wile" (613–16). Aeschylus concludes the same. Prometheus's crime was "to benefit mortals beyond due measure [*kairou pera*]" (*Pr.* 507). Chained by Hephaestus as the tragedy opens, Prometheus laments, "My allotted doom I needs must bear as lightly as I may, knowing that the might of Necessity [*tēs anankēs*] brooketh no resistance" (103–5). After a description of the range of arts he bestowed on humankind—from metalworking to medicine, from the art of combining letters to augury (458–506)—Prometheus still concludes that "art [*technē*] is feebler than Necessity [*anankēs*]" (514).

Moira is a complex and ambiguous term with regard to technē and the demarcation of limits. Though moira is generally associated with "fate," its meanings vary and, at times, appear almost contradictory. On the one hand, moira refers to "one's portion of life" in the sense of destiny or fate (LSJ, 1141). At the same time, moira can denote a lot or portion that may be divided and redistributed (1140). For example, moira can signify the "lot, portion or share which falls to one," particularly in "the distribution of booty" (1141).[19] Thus, in the second sense, moira can signify a reapportionment that would seem to change one's "fate" in the first sense. Moira's intricate relation to technē is illustrated by a more obscure sense of moira as a way of "making one's living," particularly by means of a technē (Vlastos, "Solonian Justice," 80 n. 101).[20]

Moira also appears as a goddess. In Homer she is the goddess of fate and death, whereas in Hesiod the Moirai refer to three goddesses: Clotho (the Spinner), "she who spins the thread of man's life"; Lachesis, the Disposer of Lots, who "assigns to each man his destiny"; and Atropos, literally, "she who cannot be turned" (*Theog.* 217–18; translator's note, p. 95 n.1). On the one hand, the fates give "men at their birth both evil and good to have," but they also "pursue the transgressions of men and of gods" (219–20).[21] Ananke and Moira are brought together in the *Republic*'s Myth of Er, discussed in chapter 5, where Ananke appears as the mother of the three Fates, or Moirai (X.617c). When moira is not personified in mythic accounts, it frequently refers

[19] For this sense of *moira*, see the *Iliad* 9.318.

[20] For more on moira, see George Thomson, *The Prehistoric Aegean*, pt. 3, chaps. 8 and 9.

[21] At one point in the *Theogony*, the Moirai are described as the daughters of Night (211–17), and at another point, as the daughters of Themis and Zeus (901–5). See also *Iliad* IV.517 and XVIII.119.

to a portion distributed by a mighty god.[22] F. M. Cornford observes that in Homer, for example, moira refers to a system of provinces, whereby the three sons of Cronos and Rhea are assigned their portions to rule: Poseidon, the sea; Zeus, the earth; and Hades, the underworld (*From Religion to Philosophy*, 15–16). According to Hesiod, the powerful goddess Hecate, capable of bestowing great honor and wealth, receives from Zeus "a share [moiran] of the earth and the unfruitful sea" (*Theog.* 413).

References to moira appear throughout the Prometheus narratives. Gregory Vlastos places technē and moira at the heart of Hesiod's versions. According to Vlastos, Hesiod's tales embody an ancient doctrine of technē, whereby the "arts of fire . . . symbolize the whole of man's endeavor to change his *moira* for the better by the skilful adjustment of means to ends" ("Solonian Justice," 77). Hesiod's pessimistic conclusion that "art is feebler than necessity" amounts to a conservative orthodoxy articulated by Solon. Though Solon acknowledges that the accumulation of wealth can be "unjust," riches are for the most part "given of the Gods": "Aye, surely Fate [Moira] it is that bringeth mankind both good and ill" (*Elegy* 13). By this doctrine, as Vlastos notes, wealth "belongs to this realm of *moira*," and "*technē* cannot undo what is fated to be" ("Solonian Justice," 77). This conception of fate underlies an aristocratic sense of justice that goes back to Homer: "Man or god, everyone has his place in the order of 'honor' established by *moira*; and the essence of justice is to deal with others in accordance with their place in this order, not to covet their 'honor' or encroach upon it" ("Solonian Justice," 80).

As Solon's concerns with wealth and fate suggest, references to moira as a redistributed portion are not confined to myth. Vlastos argues elsewhere that the democratic notion of *isonomia*, "equality before the law," displaced an older sense of equality, *isomoiria*, "equality of distribution or portion":

Long before the term *Isonomia* had been coined there had been a perfectly good word for "equal distribution": *Isomoiria*; the adjective *isomoros* already occurs in Homer (Il., XV, 209). When the embattled peasantry of Attica rebelled against eupatrid oppression they did ask for *Isomoiria*, and their demands included redivision of the land as well as

[22] See also Thomson's discussion in *Aeschylus and Athens*, 38–54.

redistribution of political rights and privileges. We know what happened to their demands. They got under Solon a share, though nothing like an equal share, of political power. On the score of economic equality they got nothing at all, beyond cancellation of debts secured on the debtor's person and the emancipation of those who had fallen into slavery through debt. ("*Isonomia,*" 352–53)

The demand for "equal portion" made to Solon was not a historical anomaly. Vlastos acknowledges that the claim of equal allotment "must have been an old, deep-rooted tradition" ("Solonian Justice," 79). In this context, the ascent of democratic law was an ambiguous victory, for it formalized—indeed, legalized—the separation of justice before the law from the just distribution of resources.[23] The justice of isonomia was constitutional and legal, not social and economic. According to equality before the law, citizens could expect the law to apply equally to all; at certain times in Athenian democracy, each citizen could equally expect to participate in lawmaking and the administration of justice. However, these claims to "political" equality were expected to efface claims to other forms of equality. From this perspective, Vlastos argues, the triumph of isonomia was actually "the record of a defeat for the poorest section of the *demos*"; it revealed "the paradox of Greek democratic society: the astonishing fact that the man who, as citizen, shares the kingly dignity, the sovereign power of the *demos*, may yet as a private individual labor under the indignity of utter destitution" ("*Isonomia,*" 355).

As we shall see, Plato and the sophist Protagoras divide largely on the issues that surround moira, techné, and the distribution of art and power. Questions concerning allotment are at the heart of Protagoras's version of the Prometheus myth: What share should humankind have in the powers of the gods? What principles should determine the distribution of political techné?[24] Though Protagoras will insist that all must have a share in the art of politics, his "democratic" disposition is grounded on isonomia, which is a long way from the traditions of isomoiria.[25]

---

[23] See Vlastos's discussion of this "bifurcation of justice" in "Solonian Justice," 75–78.

[24] See Chapter 5 for a full discussion.

[25] For another discussion of ancient conceptions of justice, see Michael Gagarin, "*Diké* in Archaic Greek Thought" and "*Diké* in Works and Days."

Technē, Philosophical Inquiry, and the Invention of New Paths

In the simplest form of Socratic dialectic, the questioner and respondent begin with a proposition or a "stock question," such as, What is courage? Then, through the process of dialectical interrogation, the questioner attempts to lead the respondent into contradiction.[26] The Greek term for the contradiction that generally signals the end of a round of dialectic is *aporia*. Formed from the word *poros*, meaning "path," aporia means literally "no path," as John Burnet puts it, "no thoroughfare"—or in more contemporary usage, "no exit."[27]

The distinctions between *aporia* as "no exit" and *poros* as a "way out" may mark the differences between philosophical and rhetorical traditions of inquiry and invention.[28] *Aporiai*, the plural form of aporia, also refers to the set problems of the ancient philosophical schools.[29] These aporiai are similar to Thomas Kuhn's "exemplars" in that they define the boundaries of a professional community. They contrast with the exemplars of modern science in that their function was not always—or even necessarily—to be solved.[30] Often the objective of dialectic was to sharpen intellectual skills; always its objective was to reauthorize and reproduce the community's values, conventions, and methodologies. Solutions to specific political exigencies were not the objective of dialectic, in spite of the fact that those who were trained in dialectic likely possessed the cultural authority to wield significant political power.

The images that depict artistic invention are frequently topographical. They refer to paths, places, and roads. Some of those paths lead to familiar "places"; other paths are themselves new trajectories. The term "poros' also denotes a means or passageway; it may refer as well to a contrivance or device—particularly one that provides a "way out" of danger (LSJ, 1450–51). Poros is closely identified with technē, but it

[26] I use G. E. L. Owen's description of Socratic dialectic in *Logic, Science, and Dialectic*, 214.

[27] I refer here to Burnet's treatment of dialectic in the introduction to his commentary in *The "Ethics" of Aristotle*, xl–xli.

[28] Owen observes that the focus on aporia in Plato's early dialogues gives way to the examination of more serious paradoxes in the later dialogues (*Logic*, 214).

[29] See Burnet, *"Ethics,"* xl–xli. "Aporiai" is something of a synonym for *problemata*, which I discuss in chapter 3 in the context of ancient conceptions of science.

[30] See the postscript to the second edition of Kuhn, *Structure of Scientific Revolutions*.

is also associated with *hodos* and *heuriskein*.[31] Like *poros*, "hodos" may denote a "way, road," as well as a "method, system" (1199), whereas "heuriskein" means to "find out, discover" or "devise, invent" (729).

Topos/topoi, which define rhetorical invention, literally refer to "place"/"places."[32] These topographical depictions persist into the Renaissance and beyond in various senses of "commonplace." Thomas Wilson's treatment of logic reinscribes the Greek sense of *topos* and the Roman notion of *loci* in the metaphors of the English hunt:

> A place is, the restyng corner of an argumente, or els a marke whiche geveth warning to our memorie what wee maie speake probably, either in the one parte, or the other, upon al causes that fal in question. Those that bee good harefinders will soone finde the hare by her fourme. For when thei see the ground beaten flatte round about, and faire to the sighte: thei have a narrowe gesse by al likelihode that the hare was there a litle before. Likewise the Huntesman in huntyng the foxe, wil soone espie when he seeth a hole, whether it be a foxe borough, or not. So he that will take profeicte in this parte of Logique, must bee like a hunter, and learne by labour to knowe the boroughes. (Quoted in Ong, *Ramus, Method,* 120)

The indeterminacy between "place," on the one hand, as a spatial "corner" and, on the other, as the "marke" of a "thing" betrays the extent to which the contest between rhetoric and philosophy remained alive. Generally, the more invention is concerned with the distinctive mark of a "thing" rather than a "path" to an end, the more it reflects philosophy's concerns with substance, identity, and attributes. Another definition of "place" in a sixteenth-century dialectical treatise (which according to Ong is virtually plagiarized from Agricola) reveals the further "displacement" of "place" by a "thing" or substance: "A place is some common distinctive mark of a thing by the help of which it is possible to discover readily what can be proven [or what is probable] with regard to any particular thing; or, as Cicero describes it, it is the seat of an argument" (in Ong, *Ramus, Method,* 117). Such form/content oppositions are difficult to find in the earliest depictions of techne. The detemporalized and frequently decontextualized senses

---

[31] See Lauer and Enos on *heuriskein* in "The Meaning of *Heuristic.*"
[32] See Isocrates, *Panegyricus* 40

of form and content that increase in postclassical rhetoric simply have little relevance in a domain that is characterized by discovery paths, places, and signs.

These topological images are neither naïve nor accidental. Descriptions of the mapping of a domain of technē are a case in point. Detienne and Vernant use poros to describe the distinctive character of metis: "Its suppleness and malleability give it the victory in domains where . . . each new trial demands the invention of new ploys, the discovery of a way out (*poros*) that is hidden" (CI, 21). They also observe that poros is frequently identified with *tekmōr*, which refers to a "distinctive mark, an indication, or sign" (150).[33] In the *Iliad*, Menelaus is trapped on his island, unable to take to the sea, because the gods "have bound his path by chaining up the winds" (CI, 151). He searches for a tekmōr to "escape from this *aporia*" because the sea is an "undifferentiated expanse of waters" (151). His technē consists of determining "points of reference"—the signs identified with tekmōr (151). In this way, Menelaus both *finds* and *makes* a path that will provide him with a way out. Detienne and Vernant compare Menelaus's sea to Hesiod's Tartarus—a region that cannot be traversed "because it contains no fixed or established directions" (153). It is an "opaque mass in which there is neither top nor bottom, neither right nor left, a space lacking all orientation" (153). The signs that the technē of seafaring attempt to determine are regularities of the stars, the atmosphere, and the sea—points of reference for what would otherwise be chaos. Topological images recur in Aeschylus's *Prometheus Bound*, where humankind is given both "arts" and "paths" (CI, 150). In contrast to philosophical inquiry, a technē aims to create paths in uncharted territories—to help one find one's way in the dark.

Similarly, the Hippocratic treatise *The Art* attempts to define the province of technē in the previously uncharted expanse between two extremes or limits—those of correctness and incorrectness:

> Mistakes, no less than benefits, witness to the existence of the art; for what benefited did so because correctly administered, and what harmed did so because incorrectly administered. Now where correctness and incorrectness each have a defined limit, surely there must be an art. For the absence of art I take to be absence of correctness and of incorrectness; but where both are present art cannot be absent. (V.26–35)[34]

---

[33] "Tekmōr" appears in Homer; elsewhere the word is spelled *tekmar* (LSJ, 1767).
[34] See also Hippocrates, *The Art* I.4–8.

What is important to observe is that the boundaries of art are *not* fixed; they are strategic and subject to revision. Moreover, the signs associated with healing are not referential; instead, they are signs that constitute the path toward the end of "producing" health.[35]

In sum, the aim of artistic inquiry and invention is neither to formalize a rigorous method nor to secure and define an object of study but rather to reach an end by way of a path that can be retraced, modified, adapted, and "shared." The purpose of such a path, at least in ancient depictions of invention, is not to find a "thing." A techné deforms limits into new paths in order to reach—or better yet, to produce—an alternative destination.

[35] This contrasts with Grimaldi's interpretation of *sēmeia* as representational rather than heuristic. See his *Studies in the Philosophy of Aristotle's "Rhetoric,"* 104–11.

3 Arts of Invention and Intervention

> It is not only in itself that technique is creation; it is an essential dimension of the overall creation represented by every form of social life. This is so above all because technique just as much as language, is an element of the constitution of the world as a human world, and in particular of the creation by each society of what is, for it, the real-rational. . . . Every society is immersed in a milieu which is resistant, and a similar milieu runs through it internally. This milieu is not, however, resistant in any way, and it is not simply resistant full stop. . . . What makes possible not just technique, but making/doing of any kind is the fact that brute reality is not fixed, but bears within it immense interstices which allow of movement, assembling, alteration, division. . . . Technique thus brings about a division of the world into these two regions fundamental to human making/doing: the region which resists in every way, and the region which (at a given historical stage) resists only in a certain way. It constitutes, within brute reality, that in relation to which nothing can be done, and that in relation to which some kind of making/doing is possible. Technique is creation in that it makes arbitrary use simultaneously of the rational make-up of the world *and* of its indeterminate interstices.
>
> —Cornelius Castoriadis, *Crossroads in the Labyrinth*

The complex relationship of technē to limits is at the heart of its inventive power. Only because technē intervenes in an already existing procedure, method, or calculus of value can it transform "what is" into "what is possible." Because technē defines itself in terms of intervention and invention, it is concerned solely with situations that yield indeterminacies that would allow one to discern the opportune moment and to "seize the advantage." For this reason, technē is frequently defined against *physis* (nature), *automaton* (spontaneity), and *tychē* (chance), each of which both enables and constrains invention. In this chapter I further situate technē in the context of ancient conceptions of knowledge, exploring the points of indeterminacy into which technē intervenes.

Technē/ology, Science, and Ancient Medicine

Ancient Greek Science and Art

Ancient technē requires us to put aside much of our common wisdom about science and technology, for both bear little resemblance to anything now called by those names. Until the fourth or third century B.C.E., the Greeks most likely did not have a conception of technology per se. While more recognizable forms of science and engineering developed in Egypt and the East, intellectual speculation in Greece was qualitatively different. What was understood to be pure science, or *epistēmē*, in Greece was highly deductive and, by definition, not the kind of knowledge to be applied to everyday life. In this context, the careful observations of Aristotle in the fourth century B.C.E. are significant turning points in intellectual inquiry. At the same time, Aristotle still proceeds from this deductive tradition. Lloyd makes the following observation concerning Aristotelian science:

> If we turn to the treatise called the *Physics* of Aristotle in the expectation of finding anything *we* would recognise as physics, or even anything we would immediately recognise as the ancestor of our physics, we shall be disappointed. Instead of dealing with fundamental particles, or even with matter and energy, Aristotle devotes much of his time to problems to do with causation, time, infinity, continuity. *They* seem to *us* to belong not to physics but to metaphysics and philosophy of science. (*Methods and Problems*, 418).

A brief look at the Aristotelian *Problems* also helps to contextualize Greek science. These texts address such questions as "Why do men generally themselves yawn when they see others yawn?" (886a25); "Why is it that in summer men are less capable of sexual intercourse and women more so?" (879a26); and in E. S. Forster's eloquent translation, "Why is it that it is not those who are very drunk that are most troublesome in their cups, but those who are only half blotto?" (871a7). These questions most likely remain unanswered and, no

doubt, retain perennial interest. Despite their questionable authorship, however, they remain a part of the "scientific" milieu of fourth-
century B.C.E. Greece.

With regard to applied science—or what we generally think of as
technology—those differences may be even more pronounced. The inventions of Greek science, according to Nicholas Lobkowicz, were
"little more than toys; one only has to think of the various gadgets invented by Hero of Alexandria, which include curiosities such as an al-
tar, at the side of which figures offer libations when a fire is raised on
it" (*Theory and Practice*, 41). As another example, Lobkowicz cites a
defense of catoptrics, the science of mirrors, as a science "worthy of
study" because it "produces spectacles which excite wonder in the observer, for example, the view of one's own back" (41). Though Aristotle's *Mechanics* includes important understandings of force and
weight, it is hardly an engineering treatise. Vernant describes the extent to which Aristotle's *Mechanics* is determined by dialectical traditions and sophistic thought:

> In Aristotle's work, mechanical problems are considered not so much as
> such and for their own sakes, but rather in connection with the diffi-
> culties of a logical order to which they give rise. Aristotle is interested
> in mechanical constructions because he sees them as "paradoxical" phe-
> nomena that the philosopher must explain. ... *Mēchanē* still has a
> meaning close to that of a trick or expedient; it is defined as an ingenious
> invention which enables a man to extricate himself from an embarrass-
> ing situation or *aporia* and assume the advantage over some natural
> force that is contrary and superior to him.[1]

Vernant goes on to point out that the sophists' technē of the *dissoi logoi*, or the art of arguing both sides of an issue, is a kind of "dynamic
view of argument" (MT 286). Just as the mechanics of weights and
forces (for example, the pulley) enabled the "smaller" to dominate the
"larger," the sophistic arts of discourse could make the weaker argument appear to be the stronger (287–88). Such a view of technology, as

---

[1] Vernant adds: "Even if certain passages of his demonstrations resort to mathematical reasoning, and—in order to state certain problems—take material facts as their
starting point, his thought remains essentially logical and dialectical in its inspiration.
The form, the terminology, and the conceptual framework of the theory in which it is
expressed remain strangely close to those of the sophistic method" (MT 286).

Vernant points out, blurs the boundaries between humans and machines and between mechanical arts and arts of discourse.

Vernant is hardly alone in observing the shifting boundaries between Greek science, dialectic, and rhetoric. François De Gandt, in "Force et Science des Machines," points out the dependence of Aristotelian science on the topical tradition (a tradition of inherited maxims, set problems, and topoi), locating the sources of many arguments developed in Aristotle's *Mechanics* and *Physics* in the dialectical treatise the *Topics*. G. E. L. Owen has also written extensively on similar issues in Greek science. In *"Tithenai ta phainomena,"* for example, he examines the contradictions between the scientific method outlined in the *Analytics* and the discussions in such "scientific" treatises as the *Physics* and *Meteorology*. Owen points out that the aporiai examined in these treatises are not restricted to the "unexplained or recalcitrant data of observation"; instead, they are frequently "logical or philosophical puzzles generated, as such puzzles have been at all times, by exploiting some of the things commonly said" (241). Owen draws the following conclusion concerning Aristotle's *Physics*: "By such arguments the *Physics* ranks itself not with physics, in our sense of the word, but with philosophy. Its data are for the most part the materials not of natural history but of dialectic, and its problems are accordingly not questions of empirical fact but conceptual puzzles" (242).

The seemingly arcane concerns of ancient Greek science do not mean that epistemological boundaries were unimportant to these thinkers; they simply used different taxonomic principles for drawing them. Some of the best evidence for the relative autonomy of technē as a model of knowledge comes from ancient medical texts in the Hippocratic corpus.[2] As we shall see, these texts frequently outline specific characteristics of art as a model of knowledge in order to distinguish medicine from philosophy; they also depict a complex relationship between medicine and the art of discourse. W. H. S. Jones, translator of *The Art*, maintains that the text was authored by a sophist, rather than a physician. According to Jones, the style, logic, and general "rhetorical character" of the text are virtually conclusive

---

[2] For discussions of art as a model of knowledge, see Charlton, "Greek Philosophy." For technē and ancient medicine, see Miller, *"On Ancient Medicine* and the Origin of Medicine" and *"Technē* and Discovery in *On Ancient Medicine."*

evidence that the author was a sophist— perhaps even Protagoras or Hippias.[3]

The arts of the physician and the rhetor overlapped at a number of points. In the fifth century B.C.E., both medicine and rhetoric were known as technai, and as such they were accorded ambiguous class status. In "Medicine as a 'Liberal Art' and the Question of the Physician's Income," Fridolf Kudlein makes the following observation regarding the early art of medicine: "Its practitioners were subject to a social stigma which, in spite of the increasing respect the *technai* won in ancient society, never disappeared completely; all *technitai* practised their profession for money in order to earn a living" (448). He rightly notes that "the roots of this class-bound stigma" are found in the aristocratic social structure of Homeric society in which "the lot of the propertyless person who was forced to earn his living was an unhappy one" (448). R. G. A. Buxton makes the following comparisons between doctors and sophists: "Like sophists, doctors were marginal figures in relation to the social structure of the polis. Like sophists they travelled from city to city in the performance of their professional duties. Like sophists, they had to drum up a responsive group of clients by 'presenting' themselves as credibly and as persuasively as they could" (*Persuasion in Greek Tragedy*, 20). He goes on to cite an anecdote from Plutarch concerning Antiphon's attitudes toward medicine and rhetoric: "He advertised that he had the power of curing those that were in trouble by means of speech; and discovering the causes of their sickness by enquiry he consoled the sick; but thinking that the profession was beneath his dignity he turned to rhetoric" (20).[4]

Both *The Art* and its contemporary *Ancient Medicine* illustrate the shifting status of medicine in relation to philosophy, not rhetoric. In *Ancient Medicine*, the writer confronts those who say that physicians must be philosophers: "Certain physicians and philosophers assert that nobody can know medicine who is ignorant of what man is" (XX.1–3). The question of "what man is" belongs to philosophy; it is essentially a question of definition, which in the fourth century B.C.E. might have been addressed by either Plato's dialectics or Aristotle's analytics. Despite the fact that philosophy would have been accorded

---

[3] See the basis for Jones's dating in the introduction to *The Art* by Hippocrates, 188. Jones notes that Gomperz attributes the text to Protagoras and suggests an equally strong case could be made for attributing the text to Hippias (187).

[4] For a detailed study of rhetoric and medicine, see Laín Entralgo, *Therapy of the Word in Classical Antiquity*.

a much higher social status than medicine, the Hippocratic writer insists that his art is distinct from philosophy: "But the question they raise is one for philosophy: it is the province of those who, like Empedocles, have written on natural science, what man is from the beginning, how he came into being at the first, and from what elements he was originally constructed" (XX.4–8).[5] He goes on to assert that what these philosophers and "physicians" have "said or written on natural science no more pertains to medicine than to painting" (XX.8–11). The examples given of Empedocles' questions should provide us a clear picture of the character of his "natural science"; science refers to what we would likely call philosophy, whereas medical research remains in the domain of technē.[6]

Technē, Theōria, and Representational Knowledge

Although Aristotle likely offers the most extensive treatment of technē, one of the most important (and least recognized) dimensions of his discussion is its consistency with earlier treatments of technē found in such texts as *The Art* and *Ancient Medicine*. Traces of Aristotle's four causes (material, formal, final, and efficient) appear in *The Art*, written as much as a century before Aristotle wrote his treatises. The passage below extends the discussion of "obscure" diseases raised in Chapter 2. The problem with obscure diseases is that unlike lesions they may not be "seen." The writer maintains that only a true master of the art of medicine can understand such diseases: "Men with an adequate knowledge of this art [technē] realize that some, but only a few, diseases have their seat where they can be seen: others, and they are many, have a seat where they cannot be perceived" (IX.4–9). In response to criticism that the art pronounces some patients incurable,

[5] The Greek here is simply *physis*. Even the translator notes the problem of rendering physis as "natural science." Jones defines physis here as "how the universe was born and grew out of primal elements" (Hippocrates, *Ancient Medicine*, 53 n. 2).

[6] One Hippocratic treatise, entitled *Decorum*, inconclusively dated sometime after 300 B.C.E., makes precisely the opposite argument. This treatise invokes the lofty status accorded the philosopher during the classical period, attempting to associate medicine with the "highest" knowledge: "For the physician who is a lover of wisdom is the equal of a god" (V.3–4). For discussion of dating, see Jones's introduction on 269–72. The text must be read more as a cultural artifact than a medical guide; the translator notes that the text is written in poor Greek and shows influence of Pythagorean secret societies (269–76).

the writer points out that the true power of the art should be evident in its success in treating obscure diseases:

> Now the power of the art [*technēs*], when it raises a patient suffering from an obscure disease, is more surprising than its failure when it attempts to treat incurables. . . . So in the case of no other craft that has been discovered are such extravagant demands made; those that depend on fire are inoperative when fire is not present, but operative when one has been lighted. And the arts that are worked in materials easy to shape aright, using in some cases wood, in others leather, in others— these form the great majority—paint, bronze, iron and similar substances—the articles wrought, I say, through these arts and with these substances are easily shaped aright, and yet are wrought not so much with a view to speed as to correctness. (xii.1–15, ellipses in Loeb edition text)

The passage invokes what will become Aristotle's material and efficient causes. The complicated "materials" of the art of medicine are contrasted with leather, paint, bronze, and iron, the material causes of other arts. Like fire, the doctor functions as an efficient cause, making the art of medicine "operative." The writer notes that the peculiar excellence of the art of medicine resides in its ability to intervene in a condition in which the "matter" is so indeterminate and the stakes are so great.

Ironically, Aristotle preserved these ancient traditions of technē only by refusing to "elevate" art to the status of philosophy, science, or ethics. Moreover, though the critical difference between Plato and Aristotle could be said to turn on their differing conceptions of technē, the primacy of philosophy was a point on which both firmly agreed. They maintained that the "highest" knowledge transcended the specificities of time and place, and it remained true knowledge only as long as it was pursued for no earthly purpose. In the *Metaphysics*, Aristotle describes the highest and most exact sciences as the study of first principles; these principles are the hardest to know because they are "furthest from the senses" (982a25). At the same time, this knowledge is the most certain because it rises above such indeterminacies as individual sense perception and temporal change. Aristotle explains: "Understanding and knowledge pursued for their own sake are found most in the knowledge of that which is most knowable" (982a30–32). Aristotle elaborates his definition of theoretical, or philosophical, knowledge in a passage that begins by distinguishing it from the science of production (*poiētikē*):

> That it is not a science of production is clear even from the history of the earliest philosophers. For it is owing to their wonder that men both now begin and at first began to philosophize. . . . And a man who is puzzled and wonders thinks himself ignorant (whence even the lover of myth is in a sense a lover of wisdom, for myth is composed of wonders); therefore since they philosophized in order to escape from ignorance, evidently they were pursuing science in order to know, and not for any utilitarian end. And this is confirmed by the facts; for it was when almost all the necessities of life and the things that make for comfort and recreation were present, that such knowledge began to be sought. Evidently then we do not seek it for the sake of any other advantage; but as the man is free, we say, who exists for himself and not for another, so we pursue this as the only free science, for it alone exists for itself. (982b11–28)

Aristotle's epistemological taxonomy will be discussed in more detail in Chapter 6, but the passage above points to two important issues surrounding technē: the extent to which epistemological boundaries are equivalent to social boundaries, and the sense of theoretical knowledge as spectacle (*theōria*) rather than representation.

Aristotle's identification of philosophy with the leisure class was a commonplace in the fourth century B.C.E.. His description of "free science" resembles Plato's description of paideia as knowledge befitting the freeman in his private life (*Protagoras* 312b). The defining characteristics of Plato's paideia were social and economic. Both Aristotle's "free science" and paideia were defined against the education of the dēmiourgos. In the *Metaphysics*, Aristotle outlines the distinctive characteristics of theoretical knowledge:

> We suppose first, then, that the wise man knows all things, as far as possible, although he has not knowledge of each of them individually; secondly, that he who can learn things that are difficult, and not easy for man to know, is wise. . . ; and of the sciences also, that which is desirable on its own account and for the sake of knowing it is more of the nature of wisdom than that which is desirable on account of its results, and the superior science is more of the nature of wisdom than the ancillary; for the wise man must not be ordered but must order, and he must not obey another, but the less wise must obey *him*. (982a8–19)

Aristotle's summary description invokes a familiar tautology: knowledge is defined by the class subject who seeks it; free science is that knowledge sought by the free man.

This equation of epistemological and social boundaries is particularly important in understanding the ancient conception of theoretical knowledge. Our own word for theory is from the Greek *theōrein*, meaning "to look at, behold, observe, perceive, speculate" (LSJ, 796–97).[7] *To theōrēma* may refer to a sight or spectacle, as well as to an object of speculation (LSJ, 796). Various forms of the Greek word for "wonders" (*ta thaumata*) and the verb "to wonder" also appear in discussions of theoretical knowledge, such as *Metaphysics* 982b11–28 quoted above. A Pythagorean doctrine, discussed in more detail in Chapter 6, identifies theōria with the "best" group of men who attend the Olympics, "those who simply come to look on (*theōrein*)" (Burnet, *Greek Philosophy*, 42). Theoretical knowledge is more than nonutilitarian knowledge; it is knowledge as spectacle.

The significance of theōria as spectacle is described by John Burnet. In the following passage, he suggests that the love of spectacle is one with the Greek spirit of inquiry:

> The visit of Solon to Croesus which Herodotos describes, however unhistorical it may be, gives us a good idea of this spirit. Croesus tells Solon that he has heard much of "his wisdom and his wanderings," and how, from love of knowledge (*philosopheon*), he has travelled over much land for the purpose of seeing what was to be seen (*theories heineken*). The words *theorie*, *philosophie*, and *historie* are, in fact, the catchwords of the time, though they had, no doubt, a somewhat different meaning from that they were afterwards made to bear at Athens. The idea that underlies them all may, perhaps, be rendered in English by the word *Curiosity*; and it was just this great gift of curiousity, and the desire to see all the wonderful things—pyramids, inundations, and so forth—that were to be seen, which enabled the Ionians to pick up and turn to their own use such scraps of knowledge as they could come by among the barbarians. (*Early Greek Philosophy*, 24–25)

Clearly, this quote is full of ironies. What according to Burnet is to evince the seeds of scientific inquiry is more likely to associate that

---

[7] When describing mental activity, theōrein frequently refers to contemplation and consideration (LSJ, 796); Aristotle consistently identifies theōria with the science that studies first principles or causes (*Met.* 982a29). Aristotle's conception of theoretical knowledge will be discussed in detail in Chapter 6.

spirit with the tradition of thaumata. Later Burnet notes that one of the few issues on which both early and late accounts of Pythagoras agree is that he was known as a "wonder-worker" (*Early Greek Philosophy*, 87). Perhaps what Burnet's characterization best illustrates, however, is the transformation of an ancient local prejudice against the non-Greek-speaking world into a normative human value.

It is these traditions we must remember if at any point we are tempted to identify ancient Greek conceptions of theory with Enlightenment notions of representational knowledge. There are no visual metaphors that even remotely suggest theōria "re-presents" knowledge by "reproducing" a conceptual framework that corresponds to a formal object or discrete practice. Theōria may be concerned with "sight," but it is sight as a perspectival "gaze"—not an "accurate" vision. Even classical depictions of mimēsis offer little support for an interpretation of theōria as a mirror of practice or phenomena. Ancient mimēsis was associated with imitation and copy (LSJ, 1134)—more like the "imitation" identified with "mimes."[8] The "representation" related to theōria is more appropriately identified with a situated, temporal performance than with the reproduction of a concept or "idea."

Empeiria and the Boundaries of Art

Outside of Plato's discussions of art, *empeiria* most clearly distinguishes technē from ancient speculative traditions. "Empeiria" is generally translated "experience," but it also refers to "practice"—even "craft" (LSJ, 544). Empeiria differentiates technē not only from philosophy but also from magic, chance, and the irrational. For Plato, empeiria has only negative connotations; it is mere knack as opposed to true knowledge. Other traditions, however, ground technē in empeiria, for it is empeiria that separates the knowledge of such arts as medicine, rhetoric, and seafaring from the deductive inquiry of philosophy.[9]

According to the writer of *Ancient Medicine*, empeiria is at the heart of the technē of medicine. *Ancient Medicine* itself is a very specific response to the challenges of a "new school" of medicine based

[8] See Else, "'Imitation' in the Fifth Century." For more on mimēsis, see Gebauer and Wulf, *Mimesis*.

[9] See Edmunds on Pericles' conception of the relationship between experience and technē in *Chance and Intelligence*, 24.

on deductive inquiry. Empeiria is the one element that most clearly distinguishes the writer's art from that of the rival school; the text impugns the new school's reliance on "hypotheses."[10] As Jones explains in the introduction to his translation of *Ancient Medicine*, these "hypotheses" differ radically from modern scientific conceptions of "hypothesis." While modern senses of hypothesis are tied directly to empirical verification, in ancient thought, as Jones explains, "hypothesis" is "not a summary of phenomena; it is a postulate, intended to be accepted, not as an explanation, but as a foundation (*hypo-tithēmi*) upon which to build a superstructure" (introduction to *Ancient Medicine* 7). *Ancient Medicine* opens with a direct attack on the "new" science. In the following passage, Jones translates "hypotheses" as "postulates":

All who, on attempting to speak or to write on medicine, have assumed for themselves a postulate as a basis for their discussion—heat, cold, moisture, dryness, or anything else that they may fancy—who narrow down the causal principle of diseases and of death among men, and make it the same in all cases, postulating one thing or two, all these obviously blunder in many points even of their statements, but they are most open to censure because they blunder in what is an art [technēs]. . . . Some practitioners are poor, others very excellent; this would not be the case if an art of medicine did not exist at all, and had not been the subject of any research and discovery, but all would be equally inexperienced and unlearned therein, and the treatment of the sick would be in all respects haphazard. But it is not so; just as in other arts the workers vary much in skill and in knowledge, so also is it in the case of medicine. Wherefore I have deemed that it has no need of an empty postulate as do insoluble mysteries, about which any exponent must use a postulate, for example, things in the sky or below the earth. If a man were to learn and declare the state of these, neither to the speaker himself nor to his au-

[10] In "Who Is Attacked in *On Ancient Medicine?*" Lloyd surveys a number of inconclusive arguments concerning date and audience, noting that some scholars maintain that Plato is the audience, particularly because the use of hypothesis in the treatise is so consistent with Plato's use of the term (50–51, 54). M. R. Wright, on the other hand, maintains that Empedocles is the writer's target (*Empedocles*, 13). Lloyd argues that the audience is the Pythagorean Philolaus; as Lloyd observes, it is generally agreed that the text at least refers to the deductive methodology associated with the Pythagorean school (50, 54–68); and by these scholars' accounts the text was probably written sometime between the second half of the fifth century and the first half of the fourth century B.C.E.

dience would it be clear whether his statements were true or not. For there is no test the application of which would give certainty. (I.1–27)

The treatise as a whole offers a number of important insights into technē because the writer's argument commits him both to defining art and to persuading his audience that this is the kind of knowledge that is appropriate for medicine.

The Hippocratic writer admits that his art and the knowledge of the "new school" both require research, discovery, and learning. For example, if members of the Pythagorean school are the text's audience, they could claim that geometry is the product of research and discovery because it required learning and could be done "naturally." Moreover, it is the nature of geometry to be guided by methodological proof, which can be taught and learned. What the geometrician could not claim to possess, however, would be the kind of experience with individual cases that medicine requires. In other words, in geometry one gains experience by repeating proofs of certain theorems. Like an algorithm, however, the proof always yields the same answer. In contrast, medicine requires the "adaptation" of principles to specific cases and situations in which a number of contingencies are in play. A single treatment will not have the same effect on all patients. For this reason, the physician's accumulated lore concerning the many possible responses to a treatment is a critical dimension of the art of medicine.

The passage's most significant criticism is that the "new school" of medicine has tried to "narrow down" the causes of illness to "one thing or two" and to "make it the same in all cases." In contrast, the "ancient" art of medicine proceeds on the basis of *archai* (II.1), which, in this case, are flexible principles based on accumulated experience. It is for this reason that memory is an important component of art. The physician remembers, compares, and reevaluates methods tried in the past, adjusting principles on the basis of what seemed to succeed or fail.

Aristotle insists that this capacity to recall, combine, and evaluate is the source of art and the critical difference between humankind and animals:

> The animals other than man live by appearances and memories, and have but little of connected experience [*empeirias*]; but the human race lives also by art [*technēi*] and reasonings. And from memory experience

is produced in men; for many memories of the same thing produce finally the capacity for a single experience. Experience seems to be very similar to science [*epistēmēi*] and art, but really science and art come to men *through* experience. . . . And art arises, when from many notions gained by experience one universal judgement about similar objects is produced. For to have a judgement that when Callias was ill of this disease this did him good . . . is a matter of experience; but to judge that it has done good to all persons of a certain constitution, marked off in one class, when they were ill of this disease . . . this is a matter of art. (*Met.* 980b25–81a12)

The Hippocratic writer says much the same thing when he explains:

Now to learn by themselves how their own sufferings come about and cease, and the reasons why they get worse or better, is not an easy task for ordinary folk; but when these things have been discovered and are set forth by another it is simple. For merely an effort of memory is required of each man when he listens to a statement of his experiences. (*Ancient Medicine* II.17–23)

For both Aristotle and the Hippocratic writer, the experience of the practitioner is critical in an art; and it is memory, rather than postulates, that ties the principles of art to particular situations.

Ancient Medicine provides another important insight into the role of empeiria in a technē. Both excerpts from *Ancient Medicine* point to the significance of audience. As the writer observes in the first excerpt I.1–27, a medical principle based on experience should be both intelligible and defensible to the patient. This perspective is reinforced in the second excerpt where the writer asserts that learning about symptoms and healing is difficult for "ordinary folk," but it is not impossible. This claim dissociates medicine from cult mysteries identified with many circles of learning, particularly the Pythagoreans.

These treatments of empeiria underscore the extent to which technē was a well-defined model of knowledge, distinct from philosophy, as early as the fifth century B.C.E. For the Hippocratic writers, as well as Aristotle, empeiria bore witness to the complexity of the principles that guide an art. Rational and repeatable without being rule governed, these principles lay somewhere between algorithms, or strictly deductive procedures, and natural genius—even magic.[11]

----

[11] See Jacqueline de Romilly, *Magic and Rhetoric in Ancient Greece*; John O. Ward, "Magic and Rhetoric from Antiquity to the Renaissance"; and William Covino, *Rhetoric, Magic, and Literacy*.

The Interstices of Nature, Spontaneity, and Chance

Marking the Boundaries of Nature

In Western traditions, the most persistent limit imposed on technē has been that of *physis,* or "nature." Various senses of "nature" and "the natural" have been used to authorize specific models of virtue, power, and distribution; and technē has frequently served as the dividing line, separating these models of "nature" from human culture. Nature has defined the character of technē at a number of points. For example, the extent to which technē as "trick" is identical to technē as pure deception depends on one's definition of the absence of deception—or "the true"—and "nature" has long been invoked to provide that standard. Lloyd observes that physis performed a powerful rhetorical function for the Greeks. As Lloyd explains it, they "invoked the natural to contrast it with the deviant, to justify their own particular attitudes, beliefs and behaviour, including, not least, their prejudices on gender difference and on sexual practices, where what passes for natural to insiders appears to outsiders as all too obviously culturally determined" (*Methods and Problems,* 417). As Lloyd observes elsewhere, a look at the ways *physis* was used to authorize the male body as the single human model against which woman be could only an inferior aberration should also remind us just how "conventional" views of "nature" can be.[12]

Cultural constructions of "nature" continue to play an important role in authorizing specific models of the state and of education. One could cite here Jaeger, Crane, and many others. Leo Strauss's discussion of the role of a liberal education in the democratic state invokes nature in a subtle but powerful way. The question addressed by Strauss is, In a society in which free choice is possible, why do so many choose not to ascend the ladder of liberal accomplishment? Strauss argues that education makes that ascent possible. At the same time, he acknowledges that we are hardly a virtuous society, considering that a "basic" education is supposedly available to all. His response to this paradox is a careful qualification regarding the subjects who will respond to such an education. Having already asserted that this education is based on aristocratic values, Strauss, as we noted, concludes that a liberal education only "remind(s) those members of a mass democracy who have ears to hear, of human greatness" (*Liberalism,* 5).

Obviously, Strauss's reference to the physical body is metaphorical;

---

[12] See Lloyd, *Science, Folklore, and Ideology,* especially pt. 1, chap. 3, and pt. 2.

however, when we try to extricate his argument from the metaphor of the body, we are confronted with both its intractability and rhetorical force. Why is it that some do not "hear"? Are they deaf—or disabled— "by nature"? If these standards of human greatness are so obvious (hence, implicitly "self-evident") to some, why must they be taught? In other words, if these are "natural" human values, why are so many elaborate cultural mechanisms required for their inculcation? In a now familiar tautology, those who ascend the ladder of a liberal education have heard the call of human greatness; the call of human greatness beckons only those who already speak with its voice.

In contrast to "modern" treatments of nature, the pre-Socratics and Aristotle often foregrounded the contingent character of physis. In part, because physis was so central to intellectual inquiry in these traditions, it was also the subject of persistent debate. In many depictions, the boundary between nature and culture is the product of negotiation; thus nature's borders are simply a provisional stopping point in the negotiation.

The briefest survey of pre-Socratic definitions of "physis" underscores the futility of attaching a single meaning to the term. "Physis" is often referred to as "underlying substance," and Ionian science is filled with debates concerning whether that substance is composed of a single element or more. For example, according to Burnet, Empedocles argued that physis is composed of four elements, "each with a *physis* of its own," whereas the Atomists believed the underlying substance to be "an infinite number"—yet they still called it "physis" (*Early Greek Philosophy*, 11). William Heidel questions Burnet's assumption that the many treatises from the sixth and fifth centuries B.C.E. entitled *Peri Physeōs* necessarily refer to "primary substances." Heidel maintains that the primary meaning of "physis" is "growth"— as either process per se or as the beginning or end of process; moreover, that process could be either concrete or abstract ("*Peri Physeōs*," 97).

Many of Aristotle's descriptions of physis are attempts to resolve questions raised by these earlier debates. Aristotle's theory of four causes responds to the pre-Socratic tendency to reduce all questions to the problem of determining a single definition for physis. Referring to these earlier debates, Aristotle maintains, "That nature exists, it would be absurd to try to prove; for it is obvious that there are many things of this kind" (*Phys.* 193a3–4). He goes on to point to the narrow character of earlier investigations: "If we look at the ancients, natural science would seem to be concerned with the matter. (It was only very slightly that Empedocles and Democritus touched on form and essence.)" (194a18–21). Though Aristotle retains the ancient sense of physis as growth, he insists that an adequate definition of physis requires the different perspectives of the four causes (*aitia*): material, efficient, formal, and final. In the simplest terms, what distinguishes nature for Aristotle is that it contains within itself its own source of motion (efficient cause), matter (material cause), form, and end (telos, or final cause, sometimes referred to as that "for the sake of") (LSJ, 563).

Aristotle depicts an especially complex relationship between art and nature. His definition of physis is completely dependent on technē.[13] The mutually constitutive relationship between art and nature is part of the very structure of Aristotelian thought. Two principles undergird Aristotle's philosophy: first, inquiry must be guided by more than one "cause," or perspective, and second, these different perspectives are woven together in the notion of purpose, end, or telos. For Aristotle, art is the paradigm for nature, because art exemplifies change for a purpose: "Action for an end is present in things which come to be and are by nature" (199a7–8). The critical distinction between art and nature concerns their different efficient causes: nature is its own source of motion, whereas technē always requires a source of motion outside itself. Aristotle's definition of nature is relatively simple: "Nature is a principle or cause of being moved and of being at rest" (*Phys.* 192b21–22). Conversely, artificial products are distinct in that "none of them has in itself the principles of its own production" (192b28–29). In other words, an art does not contain within itself its form (formal cause) or source of motion (efficient cause).

Aristotle also uses technē to distinguish form and matter—or formal and material causes. This distinction impinges on a number of important issues. What concerns us here, however, is the way it informs

---

[13] The Hippocratic author of *The Art* writes, "Some too there are who blame medicine because of those who refuse to undertake desperate cases, and say that while physicians undertake cases which would cure themselves, they do not touch those where great help is necessary; whereas, if the art existed, it ought to cure all alike" (VIII.1–6). The writer responds that such accusations are based on a misunderstanding of art: "For if a man demand from an art a power over what does not belong to the art, or from nature a power over what does not belong to nature, his ignorance is more allied to madness than to lack of knowledge. For in cases where we may have the mastery through the means afforded by a natural constitution or by an art, there we may be craftsmen, but nowhere else" (VIII.10–16).

Aristotelian mimesis.[14] Aristotle begins with a simple explanation of matter, form, and artistic intervention: "Some identify the nature or substance of a natural object with that immediate constituent of it which taken by itself is without arrangement, e.g. the wood is the nature of the bed, and the bronze the nature of the statue. As an indication of this Antiphon points out that if you planted a bed and the rotting wood acquired the power of sending up a shoot it would not be a bed that would come up, but wood"(*Phys.* 193a9–14). In a later passage in the *Physics*, Aristotle offers the following discussion of technē, physis, and mimēsis:

> Where there is an end [telos], all the preceding steps are for the sake of that. Now surely as in action, so in nature; and as in nature, so it is in each action, if nothing interferes. Now action is for the sake of an end; therefore the nature of things also is so. Thus if a house, e.g., had been a thing made by nature, it would have been made in the same way as it is now by art; and if things made by nature were made not only by nature but also by art, they would come to be in the same way as by nature. The one, then, is for the sake of the other; and generally art in some cases completes what nature cannot bring to a finish, and in others imitates nature. If, therefore, artificial products are for the sake of an end, so clearly also are natural products. (199a8–18)

"Form," per se, is not what art imitates in this passage. Art imitates the *action* of nature; like nature, art is "making for a purpose." Aristotle offers an example: "It is both by nature and for an end that the swallow makes its nest and the spider its web" (199a26–27).

Form is directly related to the action of making. Indeed, form precipitates motion toward an end. However, Aristotle will always ascribe movement to an efficient cause. Matter is set in motion toward a telos by efficient causes, and form directs that motion. Aristotle describes a number of efficient causes: "The seed and the doctor and the deliberator, and generally the maker, are all sources whence the change or stationariness originates" (195a21–23). In the examples of wood, tree, and bed, the artist is the efficient cause of wood being made

---

[14] Clearly, the character of Aristotelian mimesis can be debated. I am aware that my interpretation, which I have attempted to support with other ancient sources, is particularly at odds with neo-Aristotelian interpretations, especially those of the Chicago school. See McKeon, "Literary Criticism and the Concept of Imitation in Antiquity."

into a bed; and the formal principle of the bed, or its definition, is possessed by the artist. In artistic production—whether it be the production of health or belief—the artist is the efficient cause. Nature is unique in that it possesses within itself its own efficient cause; in the case above, the seed possesses its own material, formal, efficient, and final causes. Thus, in Aristotle's teleological system, what distinguishes physis is that within it all four causes converge.

If we take seriously Aristotle's comparison of artistic production to the action of nature, some common assumptions about Aristotelian mimesis must be put into question (see *Phys.* 194b27). Outside the domain of metaphysics, form is seldom something static. For the most part, form refers to the dynamism by which a functional—or teleological—process unfolds. As Aristotle explains, "It is both by nature and for an end that . . . plants grow leaves for the sake of the fruit and send their roots down (not up) for the sake of nourishment" (199a26–29). It is the form or definition of a plant to grow leaves, to develop, and to bear fruit. In this case, as in art, form is not a static idea; rather, it describes a purposeful, directed movement. Perhaps even more important is that the telos of the purposeful actions of art *is not* the artistic product. Though this notion will be discussed in more detail later, in no place does the Aristotelian corpus assert that the telos of art is the product itself. The end of an art is invariably outside the artistic process. As we shall see, the telos of the art of rhetoric is belief (*pistis*) in the audience. In the same discussion in book II of the *Physics*, Aristotle could hardly be more unequivocal regarding the telos of medicine: "Doctoring . . . leads not to the art of doctoring but to health. Doctoring must start from the art, not lead to it" (193b13–14). Even Aristotle's art of tragedy does not have its telos in the drama itself but catharsis in the audience.

The complexities of form, imitation, and telos play an important role in marking the boundaries of ancient "professions." In *Ancient Medicine*, the Hippocratic writer maintains that the question concerning "what man is" belongs to philosophy, not medicine. Aristotle invokes a similar dispute in the *Physics* when he argues that natural science should be concerned with the form as well as matter:

> If . . . art imitates nature, and it is part of the same discipline to know the form and the matter up to a point (e.g. the doctor has a knowledge of health and also of bile and phlegm, in which health is realized and the builder both of the form of the house and of the matter, namely that it

is bricks and beams, and so forth): if this is so, it would be the part of natural science also to know nature in both its senses. (194a21–27)

In this case, "both its senses" refers to formal and material causes.

As with many places in the corpus, once Aristotle probes his own assertions, new and often confusing distinctions proliferate. Aristotle acknowledges that arts must be of at least two different kinds, since clearly the art that determines the structure and dimensions of the house must differ from the art used in making bricks and beams. Aristotle's own example refers to the arts involved in shipbuilding and navigation:

> The arts, therefore, which govern the matter and have knowledge are two, namely the art which uses the product and the art which directs the production of it. That is why the using art also is in a sense directive; but it differs in that it knows the form, whereas the art which is directive as being concerned with production knows the matter. For the helmsman knows and prescribes what sort of form a helm should have, the other from what wood it should be made and by means of what operations. In the products of art, however, we make the material with a view to the function, whereas in the products of nature the matter is there all along. (194b1–8)

In other words, the helmsman evaluates the construction of the helm by the standards of his own art of seafaring. The artist or artisan who builds the helm masters the art of shipbuilding, not navigation. This distinction does nothing to undermine Aristotle's insistence that the telos of an art resides in the "user" of the artistic product.

Aristotle goes on to make a more important distinction between the natural scientist and the philosopher. The question is asked again:

> How far then must the student of nature know the form or essence? Up to a point, perhaps, as the doctor must know sinew or the smith bronze. . . ; and the student of nature is concerned only with things whose forms are separable indeed, but do not exist apart from matter. Man is begotten by man and by the sun as well. The mode of existence and essence of the separable it is the business of first philosophy to define. (194b9–15)

The student of nature may be concerned with the form of plants, trees, and animal. These forms are inseparable from matter because they direct growth from "within"; nature, we remember, contains its own source of motion, or efficient cause. In contrast, the work of first philosophy is to define the terms used to study nature—in other words, to define per se the terms "form," "matter," "motion," and "end."

Despite his taxonomies and definitions, Aristotle's concept of physis remains difficult to define once and for all. As the "nature" of something, physis can mean a variety of things. Nature is most clearly distinguished from other elements in that it has "in itself the principle of its own production" (192b28–29). But nature can also denote a kind of persistent "character," what he refers to as *kata physin*, or "according to nature." Nature consists of those "things" that can act only kata physin. He explains: "The term 'according to nature' is applied to all these things and also to the attributes which belong to them in virtue of what they are, for instance the property of fire to be carried upwards—which is not a nature nor has a nature but is by nature or according to nature [kata physin]" (192b35–93a).

This sense of "persistent character" brings physis into contexts that illustrate the often flexible boundary between Greek conceptions of nature and culture. Liddell and Scott note that physis may refer to the "natural form or constitution of a person or thing," which may include a mental disposition and character (LSJ, 1964). In this sense, physis overlaps in a number of ways with ēthos—the word from which we derive both the ethical appeals of the rhetor and the study we call "ethics." West notes, for example, that ēthos "is not immutable 'character' but a pattern of behaviour which is subject to influence from others" (Commentary on *Works and Days*, 169).[15] This is *not* a biological or "natural" sense of character, even though, as West notes, by the fifth century B.C.E. ēthos could refer to "the innate disposition which will have its way" (160). For the most part, the "nature," or physis, of a person is the result of a consistent "pattern of behaviour," which, in turn, is the product of cultural forces.[16]

As this sense of physis suggests, the Greeks were aware that nature often requires complicated and well-orchestrated mechanisms for its production and maintenance. A fragment from Empedocles offers a

[15] This reference is to ēthos in Hesiod. West provides other citations, but his argument applies to ēthos in general (Commentary on *Works and Days*, 169).

[16] This issue is at the heart of Peter Rose's examination of the cultural and economic significance of the identification of physis with "inherited character" and "inherited excellence" in the fifth and fourth centuries B.C.E. See *Sons of the Gods, Children of Earth*, especially 201, 205–15, 270–73.

brief example. Empedocles is generally believed to have been a pupil of Pythagoras, and by tradition he is famous for "combining the roles of philosopher, scientist, poet, orator, and statesman with those of mystagogue, miracle-worker, healer, and claimant to divine honours" (OCD, 382).[17] The following passage refers to Empedocles' four elements—Earth, Air, Fire, and Water—and two other important agents, Love and Strife. According to M. R. Wright, Empedocles is urging the audience, Pausanias, to take the words he has spoken on these topics and, using the "language of initiation rites, to contemplate them with the correct disposition, and with assiduous and uncontaminated attention" (*Empedocles*, 259). Empedocles is as explicit as possible: "If you push them firmly under your crowded thoughts, and contemplate them favorably with unsullied and constant attention, assuredly all these will be with you through life, and you will gain much else from them, for of themselves they will cause each thing to grow into the character [ēthos], according to the nature [physis] of each."[18] These "words" are to grow "according to nature," but that growth requires attention and the severe discipline of contemplation. The result of that development is the transformation of physis into ēthos. Thus, while physis generally marks a boundary of technē, the intervention of instruction is an explicit means of renegotiating that boundary.

Negotiating the Limits of Spontaneity

To automaton is generally translated as "the self-acting, spontaneous" (LSJ, 281). The spontaneous frequently marks a limit of technē because it often refers to a phenomenon or a domain that does not yet admit human understanding or intervention. What appears to act on its own may not be viewed as such for all time. As research extends the domain of technē, it encroaches on that of spontaneity.

The role of spontaneity in the discovery of new knowledge and methods is central to the art of medicine. One of the most critical determinations the physician must make is to decide when the art of medicine has intervened to enable healing and when that healing is the result of the body's own processes or the simple, intuitive actions

---

[17] For a detailed treatment of sources of Empedocles' biography, see Wright, *Empedocles*, 1–17.

[18] The Greek text is on page 132 and the translation is on page 258 of Wright, *Empedocles*.

of patients. Whereas *Ancient Medicine* defends its methods against the "new" deductive science, *The Art* is largely a refutation of arguments that medical art is incapable of intervening in the natural processes of healing. According to the writer's accusers, healing occurs either spontaneously, on its own, or by virtue of *tychē*, "luck" or "chance." The defender of the art is put in the complicated position of acknowledging the legitimacy of self-treatment, while still defending a professional art of medicine: "Now my opponent will object that in the past many, even without calling in a physician, have been cured of their sickness, and I agree that he is right" (Hippocrates, *The Art* V.1–3). The Hippocratic writer concedes that it is possible "to employ in self-treatment the same means as would have been employed had a physician actually been called in" (V.5–8). He insists, however, that this should confirm rather than question the existence of an art of medicine.[19] According to the writer, even those who treat themselves know "that their recovery was due to doing something or to not doing something; it was caused in fact by fasting or by abundant diet, by excess of drink or by abstinence therefrom" (V.13–16). In other words, some people "have learnt, by having been benefited, what it was that benefited them" and similarly what caused them harm (V.18–21).

Having made his case that it is a common belief that intervention in illnesses is possible, the author goes on to build an argument for the professional status of the physician. He insists first that "it is not everybody who is capable of discerning things distinguished by benefit and things distinguished by harm" (V.21–23). In other words, intuition is fallible. Some forms of intervention may be harmful; and some laypeople are better than others in intervening in their own illnesses and facilitating their own recovery. The writer takes the argument a step further. In contrast to the layperson, the physician both studies and masters, as far as possible, types of intervention (or methods of treament), as well as how and when to apply them. Thus, the writer insists that "what benefited" them did so "because it was correctly administered" (V.28–29). It is the true physician who not only discerns what benefits and what harms the patient but also knows how to administer treatment at the right time and in the right way. Just because

---

[19] "And it is surely strong proof of the existence of the art, that it both exists and is powerful, if it is obvious that even those who do not believe in it recover through it" (Hippocrates, *The Art* V.8–10).

the layperson has access to treatment the doctor might have prescribed does not mean there is no art of medicine.

> Seeing then that there is nothing that cannot be put to use by good physi-
> cians and by the art of medicine itself, but in most things that grow or
> are made are present the essential substances of cures and of drugs, no
> patient who recovers without a physician can logically attribute the re-
> covery to spontaneity [to automaton]. Indeed, under a close examination
> spontaneity disappears; for everything that occurs will be found to do so
> through something, and this "through something" shows that spon-
> taneity is a mere name, and has no reality. Medicine, however, because
> it acts "through something," and because its results may be forecasted,
> has reality, as is manifest now and will be manifest for ever. (VI.8–20)

According to the writer, everything that occurs does so by some means
and not by accident. This sense of means is *not* reducible to "instrument" or instrumentality; rather it refers to an interpretable, pre-
dictable process. For example, a person suffering jaundice may either
by chance or for a reason that has nothing to do with her physical condition spend a day in the sun. By "means" of a number of physical
processes related to the sun, her jaundice may improve; and she might
attribute that improvement to spontaneity. From her perspective, she
simply "got better." What the physician would insist, however, is that
those physical processes activated by the sun were critical "means"
in alleviating the illness. It is the work of technē to discover or invent
those means. Thus, the job of the physician/researcher is twofold: to
determine those means and to "exploit" them—or to administer them
more effectively by art.

Spontaneity also plays a role in Aristotle's concepts of technē and
the four causes. To automaton is very closely related to tychē, which
I discuss below, but it is also tied to the theory of causes. Aristotle
maintains that both spontaneity and chance are causes (*Phys.* 195b31).
He explains: "First then we observe that some things always come to
pass in the same way, and others for the most part. It is clearly of neither of these that chance, or the result of chance, is said to be the
cause—neither of that which is by necessity and always, nor of that
which is for the most part. But . . . there is a third class of events be-
sides these two" (196b10–14). Chance and spontaneity comprise the
third class. They are distinguished from each other with regard to the
ability of agents affected by them to reason and deliberate. Aristotle

continues: "Chance and what results from chance are appropriate to agents that are capable of good fortune and of action generally. Therefore necessarily chance is in the sphere of actions. . . . Hence what is not capable of action cannot do anything by chance" (197b1–6). For Aristotle, action requires choice (*proairesis*): "Thus an inanimate thing or a beast or a child cannot do anything by chance because it is incapable of choice" (197b6–8). He adds that "the spontaneous on the other hand is found both in beasts and in many inanimate objects" (197b13–15).

Aristotle's examples of chance and spontaneity are not particularly helpful: "We say, for example, that the horse came spontaneously, because, though his coming saved him, he did not come for the sake of safety. Again, the tripod fell spontaneously, because, though it stood on its feet so as to serve for a seat, it did not fall so as to serve for a seat" (197b15–18). What is rather obliquely at stake in these examples is the issue of action directed toward ends.[20] To use an earlier example, if a child (who is incapable of "choice," according to Aristotle) with jaundice played in the sun long enough to be cured, her healing would have been "spontaneous." On the other hand, should the disease return a decade later when the child had become an adult, the evaluation would be different. The adult might still know nothing about jaundice and sunlight. Still, if she were to spend the day in the agora and return home cured of jaundice, that healing would be attributed to chance. Aristotle's distinctions between chance and spontaneity may seem naïve and capricious. Yet they underscore one persistent feature of Aristotelian thought: the situational, perspectival, and temporal character of his epistemology.

Exploiting the Indeterminacies of Chance

Like to automaton, tychē marks a limit of art, but it marks that limit in an intricate way. Though "tychē" is generally translated as "chance," it has a constellation of meanings and connotations. Tychē can refer, on the one hand, to the "act of a god," but also to the "act of a human being." Tychē can be characterized as "an agent or cause beyond human control"; as such, it may be identified with providence and good fortune. In other contexts, however, tychē may refer to

---

[20] "Where there is an end, all the preceding steps are for the sake of that" (Aristotle, *Phys.* 199a9).

necessity and fate (LSJ, 1839), thus invoking moira's sense of portion or allotment. For example, in Aeschylus's *Prometheus Bound*, H. W. Smyth translates tychē as "lot" in Prometheus's response to Oceanus: "Save thyself, as thou best knowest; while I will drain to the dregs my present lot until such time as the mind of Zeus shall abate its wrath" (377–78).

Lowell Edmunds observes that in some ancient Greek perspectives tychē was viewed as the operative cause in human life (*Chance and Intelligence*, 61); while good birth might be attributed to physis, tychē explained the "lot" of the peasant farmer. If tychē is identified with fate, then technē would be one of fate's most threatening adversaries— or humankind's most beneficial ally. This is the sense of techne's relationship to tychē in Plato's *Laws*. The Athenian asserts that "human history is all an affair of chance"—that "chance [tychē] and circumstance [kairos], under God, set the whole course of life for us" (*Laws* IV:709b). At the same time, he maintains that "we must allow for the presence of a third and more amenable partner, skill [technē]" (709b–c).

Tychē frequently refers to a point of indeterminacy that can be exploited by technē. We remember that the Hippocratic author of *The Art* had to refute arguments that the acts of healing for which he claimed credit were actually due to either spontaneity or chance. The accusation is raised in the context of the question of why not all patients are healed by way of medical treatment. If not all are healed, one could just as easily argue that the patient was healed "through luck [tychēi] and not through the art [dia technēn] (IV.7–8). The writer does not deny the power of tychē. He asserts that he is unwilling to "rob luck of any of its prerogatives" (8–9).[21] At the same time, however, he argues that he has observed "that when diseases are badly treated ill-luck generally follows, and good luck when they are treated well" (10–11). Those who submit to medical treatment, he goes on to say, simply show their "unwillingness to behold nothing but the reality of luck, so that while freed from dependence upon luck they are not freed from dependence upon the art" (14–19). He concludes that both luck and spontaneity simply mark the temporary limits of human investigation—and those limits are set only "by the capacity of the sick to be examined and of researchers to conduct research" (XI.5–7).

---

[21] As the translator notes, what is here translated "prerogatives" is *ergon*, meaning "work" or "effect" (Hippocrates, *The Art*, p. 194 n. 1).

In the art of navigation, tychē marks more explicitly both a limit of knowledge and an indeterminacy that may be exploited. Edmunds describes Thucydides' view of the technē of navigation as the mastery of tychē—in this case, the threatening indeterminacies of the sea. As Edmunds puts it, the technē of sailing takes these contingencies and "converts the sea to usefulness" (*Chance and Intelligence*, 42). Edmunds explains this perspective on the technical mastery of the contingent as follows: "The technical skill of the naval commander, Phormio, who, because he knew from experience that a breeze would come up at a certain time, was able to make this breeze a part of his tactics, whereas the same breeze appeared to the Spartans a matter of chance" (170–71).

Detienne and Vernant similarly observe the significance of tychē to the art of navigation. They note that Tychē also appears as a "goddess of the sea" (CI, 223). According to Hesiod, she is a sister of Metis (*Theog.* 358, 360), and "like the sea, she symbolises change and mobility" (CI, 223). The double nature of tychē is embodied in the goddess. She represents "one entire aspect of the human condition" in which the individual is "buffetted by the waves, whirling with the winds, rolling helpless hither and thither without respite"; but she is also the one who "takes charge of the tiller and guides the ship unerringly to harbour" (223). According to Alcman, Tychē is the daughter of Prometheia, the offspring of "foresight" (CI, 223). Detienne and Vernant explain: "Just as the human art of foresight develops against the background of a future that is opaque and unpredictable, the art of the helmsman can only be exercised within the framework of the uncertainty and instability of the sea. The play of the tiller cannot be dissociated from the movement of the waves. Tychē brings the indiscernible future within the bounds of possibility" (223). Because tychē refers to the indeterminacies that art may exploit, it is closely associated with temporal calculation and kairos: "Tychē and Kairos both emphasize one essential feature of the art of navigation: the necessary complicity between the pilot and the element of the sea" (224–25).[22]

---

[22] Detienne and Vernant summarize Aristotle's perspective on the art of navigation and calculation: "Aristotle says that in the art of navigation there can be no general knowledge applicable to every particular case, no certain knowledge of all the winds that furrow the waters of the sea. . . . The excellence of a navigator cannot be measured by the scope of his knowledge but rather by his ability to foresee and uncover the traps the sea sets for him which are at the same time the opportunities it offers to his intelligence as a pilot" (CI, 224).

This is one critical point that distinguishes techne from epistēmē: an art is temporal and strategic—characteristics that define the kind of "conniving with reality" that makes both intervention and invention possible.[23]

The meanings of tychē in Aristotle shift slightly depending on their context. In the *Rhetoric*, tychē is described as a cause of "good luck" and a cause of human behavior. Tychē is raised in ethical topics for deliberative rhetoric: "Chance is the cause of some things that can also be created by the arts and of many things unrelated to art. . . . In general, the kinds of good things that come by chance are those which incur envy" (Kennedy, 61–62; 1362a2–6). In forensic topics about "wrongdoing," chance appears as one of seven causes of human action: "People do everything they do for seven causes: through chance, through nature, through compulsion, through habit, through reason, through anger, through longing" (Kennedy, 89; 1369a5–9).[24] According to Edmunds, Aristotle uses tychē in "scientific" treatises the same way as does Thucydides. For Thucydides, techne is concerned only with those domains "liable to rational prediction and control, at least to some degree" (*Chance and Intelligence*, 145). Chance lies outside that domain because it is "contrary to calculation"; and it is the "aim of techne [*sic*] to defeat chance" (81, 161).[25] Similarly, Aristotle frequently uses tychē as a boundary to separate the domain of rational inquiry from the expanse that outruns prediction and calculation. This sense of tychē appears briefly in the *Rhetoric*, where it is used to outline the sphere of deliberation: "Nor is there deliberation about all contingent matters; for some benefits among those that can come to pass or not are the work of nature or happen by chance" (Kennedy, 52; 1359a34–37).[26] Tychē receives serious treatment in the *Physics*, where Aristotle asserts that tychē (like to automaton) is a cause, but an unpredictable and incalculable cause. He does not attribute divin-

[23] "The many-coloured, shimmering nature of *mētis* is a mark of its kinship with the divided, shifting world of multiplicity in the midst of which it operates. It is this way of conniving with reality which ensures its efficacity. Its suppleness and malleability give it the victory in domains where there are no ready-made rules for success, no established methods, but where each new trial demands the invention of new ploys, the discovery of a way out (*poros*) that is hidden" (CI, 21).

[24] See also Aristotle, *Rhet.* 1368b34.

[25] See also Edmunds, *Chance and Intelligence*, 187.

[26] In the Barnes collection, Roberts translates "tychē" as "accident," a translation that can be misleading because "accident" as *symbebēkos* has a technical meaning in the *Posterior Analytics* (71b10, 73b10–16).

ity or mystery to tychē; rather, he maintains that "chance is a cause, but that it is inscrutable to human intelligence" (196b5–7). Tychē belongs with to automaton in the "third class of events"—those that happen neither always, nor for the most part (196b10–11). Because there is no predictability to chance, Aristotle places it in the domain of the *paralogos*, "the unaccountable" or "the incalculable."[27] He explains: "Thus to say that chance is unaccountable [paralogon] is correct. For an account [logos] is of what holds always or for the most part, whereas chance belongs to the third type of event" (197a18–20).[28] Aristotle gives the following, rather confusing example:

> A man is engaged in collecting subscriptions for a feast. He would have gone to such and such a place for the purpose of getting the money, if he had known. He actually went there for another purpose, and it was only accidentally that he got his money by going there; and this was not due to the fact that he went there as a rule or necessarily [ex anankēs], nor is the end effected (getting the money) a cause present in himself—it belongs to the class of things that are objects of choice and the result of thought. It is when these conditions are satisfied that the man is said to have gone by chance [apo tychēs]. (196b33–97a3)

This definition is consistent with that of spontaneity; because the man is not a child or beast but a being capable of deliberation and choice, his meeting someone who owed him money was the result of chance.

Spontaneity and chance are important in defining technē largely because of art's unique relationship to time. Spontaneity is a matter of determining if and when an art has intervened in a process, and chance

[27] Liddell, Scott, and Jones define the adjective *paralogos* as "beyond calculation, unexpected, unlooked for"; the substantive *ho paralogos* means "incalculable element" (1317).

[28] Commentaries shed little light on *to paralogon*. They generally treat the issue of account or calculation in purely quantitative terms, without seriously exploring logos in the dialectical sense of a reasoned account or a theory. Ross simply avoids the term in his commentary on the *Physics*, translating it as "incalculable" in the analysis (354). Hippocrates Apostle gives the passage more attention. He translates *paralogon* as "contrary to reason" (Commentary on *Physics* 34), explaining in his commentary that "a reason is a universal statement of things existing necessarily or for the most part" (Commentary 214). No doubt commentators are sensitive to the paradox that Aristotle does indeed provide examples of chance, examples that, to some extent, deconstruct chance's definition (*Phys.* 196b33–97a8).

is largely a matter of temporal predictability. For Aristotle, at least, ty-chē marks that which cannot be predicted; tychē remains in the do-main of the paralogos (that for which one cannot give a reasoned ac-count) because its occurrences cannot be linked to any set of signs or causes.

Again, "time" distinguishes philosophy from art. The Greek sense of "logos" as a "reasoned account" applies to both epistēmē (philosophy/science) and technē. What is different about these two logoi, however, is their purpose, largely in relation to time. Greek philosophical tradi-tions aimed at defining postulates that would "hold" regardless of time and place. These "accounts" remained in the domain of theōria as "ob-jects" of speculation. The accounts of *technē*, in contrast, served to en-able an intervention—or "practice"—not to interpret it for its own sake.

The distinction between enabling practice and interpreting it will be examined in more detail later. At this point, however, several dif-ferences are worth noting. Neither the rhetorician nor the physician aimed to construct an account that simply "explained" a phenome-non in either discourse or healing. The accounts of technē were pro-visional explanations of signs or precedents for the purpose of effec-tive intervention. Ancient rhetoricians and physicians did not look at discourse or the human body as a problem to be solved or an object to be explicated; the body was seen as an integration or matrix of processes. The technē of medicine aimed to affect those processes in a way that could be explained. Similarly, the technē of rhetoric was concerned with the affairs of the polis, which included laws and pub-lic opinions, matters of war and matters of reason and emotion, con-stitutions of different states and common sayings of the young as well as the old. Though rhetoric was concerned with social behavior, emo-tions, and political formations, it was not the study "of" them. Be-cause a *technē* does not aim at interpretation *per se*, it does not have to transform the subjects with which it deals into static objects of study. Temporality is not something to be excluded but rather is con-stitutive of the "work" of technē.

Technē and the Fuzzy Art of Invention

In *Fuzzy Thinking*, Bart Kosko examines fuzzy logic in lay terms, and its distinguishing features closely resemble those of technē. One of the most important characteristics of fuzzy logic is its resistance to the either/or logic principles of strict Aristotelian logic. This principle can be simply stated: that something cannot both be and not be (or, in logic's shorthand, *A* or not *A*).[29] Though Aristotle may be a source of this logic, he carefully and consistently maintains that technē lies outside the jurisdiction of its laws. In contrast to either/or logic, fuzzy logic posits that everything is a matter of degree. In other words, in varying degrees, something *may* both be and not be. Unlike the bivalent, black/white logic that drives computer science and linear mathematics, fuzzy logic is multivalent.[30] Rather than defining black as opposed to white, fuzzy logic measures the relative shades of gray. As Kosko explains, the calculus of logical logic requires a "rounding up" or "rounding down" to turn responses into "bits" of information coded as one of two alternatives, yes or no.[31] This kind of binary logic, Kosko points out, cannot account for gradations between yes and no—the gray world of relative differences that seldom present themselves as binary alternatives.

Like ancient technē, fuzzy logic is defined against coherence and correspondence theories of truth (*Fuzzy Thinking*, 83–91). Fuzzy logic does not obey rules of internal consistency (83–84); its rationality is simply not dependent on its coherence as a formal system. Fuzzy logic similarly fails to represent or correspond to a phenomenon or a state of affairs. As Kosko points out, correspondence between theory and objective phenomenon is a rather poor criterion for a rational logic because it leads to a number of commonsense dilemmas with regard to time, change, and possibility (84–85). What happens to the truth of the statement "Grass is green" in mid-December in the northern hemisphere? As Kosko maintains, temporality and, especially, experience distinguish fuzzy logic from "logical" logic. Fuzzy logic responds to the exigencies of specific situations rather than forcing situations into a predetermined calculus. For example, in televisions equipped with fuzzy logic, each image is measured for "relative brightness, contrast,

[29] See Kosko, *Fuzzy Thinking*, 23–34.

[30] Kosko uses the simple example of posing this question to a roomful of people: "How many of you are satisfied with your jobs?" Kosko observes that some people raise their hands high, others raise them not at all, and many raise them in various heights in between. Those with arms raised, say, three-fourths of their possible length would be rounded up to yes (ibid., 13–14).

[31] For the distinction between "bit" and "fit," see ibid., 24. See also Bourdieu's critique of the theory/practice binary, especially his distinction between "fitting" and "guiding" (OTP, 29) and the "'fuzzy' logic of approximation (OTP, 123)."

and color"; fuzzy logic serves as an expert "tuner," adjusting the controls in response to each changing condition (39). Thus, like technē, the value of fuzzy logic resides precisely in its capacity to work *in* time and *with* time to respond to shifting circumstances.[32]

Perhaps the most important similarity between technē and fuzzy logic is their relationship to probability. Kosko takes great pains to demonstrate that fuzzy logic is *not* a form of probability. He maintains that probability still assumes binary logic, because, for the most part, probability attempts to "approximate" certainty.[33] What is at stake in this point of comparison with technē is greater than one may at first imagine. Few things are likely more responsible for the eclipse of rhetoric's relationship to ancient technē than Aristotle's declaration that rhetoric is the "antistrophos" to dialectic. This assertion has been widely interpreted to mean that rhetoric is modeled on philosophical logic. Like a poor, unkempt relative who is not expected to obey all the rules of fine etiquette, rhetoric is generally allowed to sit at philosophy's table—as long as it stays at the far end. This identification of rhetorical reasoning with philosophy has obscured the extent to which technē was a distinct model of knowledge, with its own boundaries, methods, and assumptions. The author of *Ancient Medicine*, for example, did not say that he wanted to "bend" the postulates of the new deductive science; rather, he insisted that the discovery procedures associated with art were of an entirely different character. Like fuzzy logic, technē is an alternative paradigm, not the adaptation of a paradigm already given.

Finally, Kosko notes that fuzzy logic "did not come of age at universities"; it "came of age in the commercial market and leapfrogged the philosophical objections of Western science" (20). Much like the art of rhetoric, which was taught by Aristotle only in the afternoon when the truly important affairs of learning had been concluded, fuzzy logic was neither welcomed nor invited into the most hallowed halls of learning. Both technē and fuzzy logic are found in the streets of interested calculation, where what is at issue is not representation but intervention and invention.

[32] The relationship between time and experience in fuzzy logic only brings it closer to ancient conceptions of technē. See Kosko, *Fuzzy Thinking*, 39.
[33] See ibid., 45–46.

4 Prometheus and the Boundaries of Art

> But art is never an end in itself; it is only a tool for blazing life lines, in other words, all of those real becomings that are not produced only *in* art, and all of those active escapes that do not consist in fleeing into art, taking refuge in art, and all of those positive deterritorializations that never reterritorialize on art, but instead sweep it away with them toward the realms of the asignifying, asubjective, and faceless.
> —Gilles Deleuze and Félix Guattari, *Thousand Plateaus*

> This *birth of society* is . . . not a passage, it is a point, a pure, fictive and unstable, ungraspable limit. One crosses in attaining it.
> Jacques Derrida, *Of Grammatology*

In *Homeric Hymn XX*, both Hephaestus and Athena are credited with distributing the power of the arts:

> Sing, clear-voiced Muse, of Hephaestus famed for inventions [*klutometin*]. With bright-eyed Athene he taught men glorious crafts throughout the world,—men who before used to dwell in caves in the mountains like wild beasts. But now that they have learned crafts through Hephaestus the famed worker [*klutotechnen*], easily they live a peaceful life in their own houses the whole year round.

Narratives like this one, which describe humankind's appropriation of techné, are known by several names: they are frequently called "prehistory" accounts and sometimes "anthropological," "genetic," or "humanistic" accounts of culture and art. Whether or not Prometheus is invoked in such narratives, the many accounts of the distribution of the arts show themselves to be parables of social, economic, and political organization. In the text above, for example, the technai both separate humankind from cave-dwelling beasts and provide the constitutive tools of civilization. The significance of the technai is depicted in a number of ways. Lowell Edmunds, for example, maintains that narratives which view the arts not as gifts from the gods but as products of human discovery signal what he calls a "humanistic theory of technē" (*Chance and Intelligence*, 28). In his analysis of the prehistory of Diodorus, Gregory Vlastos argues that the account marks a shift toward a "conventional" theory of language, which contrasts with earlier traditions that maintain that language is "'compelled' by nature."[1] Thomas Cole, in *Democritus and the Sources of Greek Anthropology*, surely one of the most detailed treatments of the prehistory accounts, compares a number of narratives from Hesiod through Polybius; and his examination iterates the uses of these accounts in setting the limits of *physis* and in authorizing specific conceptions of community, distribution, and "human nature."[2]

Interpretations of the narratives are often endowed with more explicit didactic or ideological content than are the accounts themselves. Victor Ehrenberg, for example, suggests that because Prometheus is a "suffering god," whose grief is the consequence of his "all-too-great love of man," he also serves as "a symbol for Christianity, a Christ before Christ" (*Man, State, and Deity*, 40–41). Eric Havelock describes Prometheus as the exemplary "man"—"the great prototype of the species which he endows" (*Prometheus*, 48).

The didactic purposes of these myths become even more tangled, for in some versions, what is at issue is specifically the distribution of *dikē* (justice) and the art of politics. An early precedent for Protagoras's discussion of the distribution of dikē appears in Hesiod's *Works and Days*, where the poet gives the following admonition to Perses:

> Lay up these things within your heart and listen now to right, ceasing altogether to think of violence. For the son of Cronos has ordained this law for men, that fishes and beasts and winged fowls should devour one another, for right [dikē] is not in them; but to mankind he gave right [dikēn] which proves far the best. (274–80)

---

[1] Vlastos, "On the Pre-History in Diodorus," 52 n. 6. This is part of Vlastos's larger argument that Diodorus's account is of the Democritean tradition.

[2] For treatments of nature, see Cole, *Democritus*, 61–62 and 140–43. For treatments of social organization, see especially chap. 9, "Democritean Sociology and History in the Development of Greek Thought."

The value of these accounts of technē resides in their potential to serve as cultural parables that describe something like the "birth" of a set of distinctions—a point at which differences of "kind" and portion are marked. While these technē narratives are frequently used to authorize specific conceptions of human identity, community, and order, implicitly—and sometimes explicitly—they also include definitions of dissensus, enmity, and encroachment.

In this chapter I explore the role of technē in authorizing specific models of social, political, and economic order. As valuable "know-how" that could be transformed into economic capital, such arts as metallurgy, medicine, navigation, and rhetoric were powerful catalysts in the redistribution of wealth and political power and in the construction of new modes of social identification and economic exchange.

Hesiod's Prometheus Narratives

In his commentary on *Works and Days*, M. L. West places Hesiod's birth sometime between 750 and 720 B.C.E. (44); in his earlier commentary on *Theogony*, however, that range is extended from 750 to 650 (40). Regarding the dates of composition of the poems, there is only general agreement that *Works and Days* was composed after the *Theogony* (Commentary on *Theog.*, 44). Hesiod's *Theogony* is in the tradition of cosmogonic myth, stories that explain "the origin of the world and the gods, and the events which led to the establishment of the present order" (1). *Works and Days*, on the other hand, is situated in the tradition of wisdom literature, works of instruction and exhortation that make up some of the oldest extant Western poems (Commentary on WD, 3).

Hesiod's Prometheus accounts appear in both *Theogony* and *Works and Days*, and they offer the earliest versions of the myth of the Promethean Fire Stealer.[3] Both versions describe Prometheus's attempts to shift the balance of power between humankind and the gods, and both attest to the role of technē in marking the boundaries of human identity.[4] The very name "Prometheus" means "forethinker," signifying the wit that allows Prometheus to seize the advantage over

[3] See M. L. West on myths of the Fire Stealer (Commentary on *Theog.*, 306). Though such stories were at one time most likely part of ritual ceremonies, Hesiod's poem was intended for instruction and entertainment (Commentary on *Theog.*, 15).

[4] Not all scholars agree on integrating the myths of Prometheus and the Five Ages, as I do here.

Zeus and the measure of prediction and control that art allows over nature, force, and experience.

In both versions of the myth, art and Prometheus are double-edged. Arts are always "cunning arts," very much akin to tricks; yet they are what humankind has in place of the force and domination of gods and nature. Similarly, Prometheus is referred to as "Prometheus the crafty";[5] however, he is also an ally of humankind—even a savior— since without the fire he secures for humankind culture would be impossible.[6] As future versions of the myth attest, fire signifies more than the potential for craft and invention. Technē marks the transition from a nomadic gathering culture to one of cultivation and specialized labor, a transition that created the new forms of social identity that constituted the bonds of the city.[7] Fire enables human invention that emulates the gods' creative powers and brings about a social order no longer dependent on the gods. Technē remains inextricably tied to power, and every exchange of technē disrupts a relationship of power and creates a new one.

The myth begins with Prometheus's first attempt to deceive Zeus— a ruse designed to lure the god into taking the poorer of two offerings. Prometheus's act is more than a simple trick, according to Hesiod; it is also an attempt to "match himself in wit" and rival almighty Zeus (*Theog.* 534). Prometheus begins by slaughtering an ox and setting out two offerings: meaty flesh, which he has covered with the "ox paunch," and "white bones dressed up with cunning art [*doliēi . . . technēi*]" (538–40). The cunning art is animal fat, which Prometheus intends to use to deceive Zeus into thinking the second offering is the better one. Prometheus, "thinking trickery," then bids Zeus to "take which ever of these portions your heart within you bids" (548–50). The god, however, recognizes Prometheus's trick and responds violently: "Son of Iapetus, clever above all! So, sir, you have not forgotten your cunning arts!" (559–60). In anger, Zeus refuses to give mortal men "the power of unwearying fire" (561–64). Without that power, humankind has no defense against the forces of nature and necessity.

---

[5] For a discussion of *ankylomētēs,* see West's commentary on *Theog.,* 158.

[6] As West notes, the myth in *Theogony* is an etiological account of the origin of fire, but it is also a story of the genesis of human culture. Prometheus was part of the craftsmen cult of Hephaestus, worshiped by Athenian potters (Commentary on *Theog.,* 306).

[7] According to Vernant, Hesiod's Prometheus narratives are an attempt to explain the transition in agricultural technique from gathering to cultivation (MT, 249–50).

Prometheus's second transgression, the theft of fire, permanently shifts the balance of power between humankind and the gods. Prometheus sneaks into heaven, crossing the boundary between the human and the divine; and when Zeus is not looking, he steals the fire: "The noble son of Iapetus stole again for men from Zeus the counsellor in a hollow fennel-stalk, so that Zeus who delights in thunder did not see it" (WD, 50–53). Prometheus's theft signals a conclusive break with that "golden race of mortal men" who "lived like gods without sorrow of heart, remote and free from toil and grief" (110–13). The most immediate effect of that break involves the means of human sustenance. Before Prometheus's theft, humankind was free from labor because "the fruitful earth unforced bare them fruit abundantly" (117–18). Human sustenance is now dependent on "hard toil" and subject to "heavy sicknesses" (90–93).

Prometheus's theft, however, elicits another response from Zeus. When the god sees the glow of Prometheus's fire, he declares his punishment: "Son of Iapetus, surpassing all in cunning, you are glad that you have outwitted me and stolen fire—a great plague to you yourself and to men that shall be. But I will give men as the price for fire an evil thing in which they may all be glad of heart while they embrace their own destruction" (54–58). That "plague" is woman, Pandora, the "beautiful evil" (*Theog.* 585).

If Hesiod's description of Zeus's second punishment for Prometheus illustrates the misogyny of antiquity, it also illustrates the power of art to disrupt nature's boundaries.[8] Like Prometheus's offering to Zeus, Pandora is cunning art—a trick or deception. Fashioned without by Hephaestus in "a sweet, lovely maiden-shape" (WD 62–63), she is "girded and clothed" by Athena, adorned with "necklaces of gold" by the "divine Graces" and "queenly Persuasion," and "bedecked" with "all manner of finery" by Pallas Athena (71–76). Within, however, Zeus orders his artificers to place "lies and crafty words and a deceitful nature" (88). When she is sent to earth, she is accepted as a gift by Epimetheus, who has forgotten Prometheus's warning never to accept a gift from Zeus (93–98). She carries with her a jar filled with plagues from the gods who live on Olympus (80–82), and when she removes the lid, she unleashes scourges, sorrow, and toil (90–101). The

---

[8] For a discussion of the gender relationships in Hesiod's Prometheus narratives, see Vernant, "The Myth of Prometheus in Hesiod," in *Myth and Society in Ancient Greece.*

jar is never completely emptied. What remains "under the rim of the great jar"—described as an "unbreakable home"—is Hope (96–99).

In both of Hesiod's versions, much attention is focused on Pandora as artifice. She is Hephaestus's handiwork, made from Zeus's blueprint. Pandora is not a lovely maiden herself but made in the "likeness of a lovely maiden" (71; see also *Theog.* 572). She is adorned with a panoply of arts—sewing, goldsmithing, and even rhetoric.[9] When Zeus brings the finished product out to be viewed by "the deathless gods and mortal men," they see, according to the poet, "sheer guile, not to be withstood by men" (58–59). The artifice without is supposed to conceal what Hermes has placed within her heart, "a deceitful nature," together with "lies and wheedling words" (78).[10]

To a large extent, the myth turns on two indeterminate oppositions: "true" nature set against art, and internality set against externality. Cunning art produces what is on the "outside," Athena's "embroidered veil" and golden crown. But the evil that is her "true," internal character is also the product of artifice. Though speech has been put within her by Hermes, she is decorated on the outside with a crown from which creatures speak. Like the jar, Pandora is both filled with evil and the product of art.[11] Like mētis, Pandora is "multiple" in her appearance and significance. Though she is the product of Hephaes-

---

[9] It would be difficult, at this point, to associate Peitho, the goddess of persuasion, with figures of speech, though that is what she will come to represent. Though Peitho is not mentioned in the *Theogony* account, Pandora's crown is described as having "living beings with voices" (584). It is difficult to find information on Peitho as the goddess of "queenly Persuasion." M. L. West notes that Sappho refers to Peitho as Aphrodite's daughter (Commentary on WD, 162). The OCD indicates that Peitho sometimes appears as Aphrodite's cult title and that elsewhere in the *Theogony* Hesiod refers to her as the daughter of the Ocean (794). See also Buxton, *Persuasion in Greek Tragedy.*

[10] What is translated here as "nature" is ēthos, not physis; its use here is curious because ēthos does not refer to an intrinsic, or "natural," quality. As M. L. West points out, ēthos is not "immutable 'character' but a pattern of behaviour which is subject to influence from others" (Commentary on WD, 160). West contends that it is not until the fifth century that ēthos is used to describe an "innate disposition which will have its way" (160).

[11] "Hesiod clearly thinks of the ills as what came out of the jar: formerly men were free from them, now they are everywhere; and they are contrasted with Hope which stayed inside. How is it that they are among men because they came out, while Hope is among men because it was kept in? What was Hope doing in the jar anyway, if it was a jar of ills?" (West, Commentary on WD, 169). For another interpretation of the conclusion of Hesiod's narrative, see the commentary on *Works and Days* by Tandy and Neale.

tus's art, she will be the mother of humankind—the source of nature's own "art" of reproduction; and though she is held responsible for setting loose incalculable ills upon the earth, she also guards Hope in an "unbreakable home." Prometheus is characterized by a similar indeterminacy. When Prometheus steals fire he must use a fennel stalk to transport it. In this case, nature conceals the power that enables art.

Although Prometheus emerges as the hero of the myth, Hesiod is quite explicit concerning the tale's moral: the punishment brought to earth by Pandora is proof that human intelligence will never overcome the will of the gods. He ends the story in *Works and Days* by asserting that "there is no way to escape the will of Zeus" (105). In the *Theogony*, he concludes, "It is not possible to deceive or go beyond the will of Zeus; for not even the son of Iapetus, kindly Prometheus, escaped his heavy anger, but of necessity [*hup'anankēs*] strong bands confined him, although he knew many a wile" (613–16). According to Hesiod, human guile will never conquer the force of the gods; art will never overcome fate.[12] Prometheus's theft of art has provoked the adversarial relationship to nature that now defines human labor and production; his gift of fire, however, will also be humankind's most important means of mitigating that labor.

Technē and the Standardization of Value

To read Hesiod's narratives, we must imagine a world that certainly included interested calculation, but without the objectified scales of value on which we depend. The eighth century B.C.E. out of which Hesiod emerged has been described as a midpoint between the tribe and the polis, an emergence of sorts from the Dark Age.[13] It witnessed the development of the polis community and the marketplace; but it was also a time when social order was largely determined by class and when Greek society was dominated by closed, aristocratic clans bound by shared interests and codes of conduct.[14] Social identification was

[12] For another interpretation of Hesiod's Prometheus narratives, see Havelock, *Prometheus*.

[13] See Ehrenberg, *From Solon to Socrates*, 8, 19; Wood and Wood, *Ancient Political Theory*, 17; and Burn, *World of Hesiod*, 19. The eighth century marked the end of the transformation of the Mycenaean monarchy into a Homeric aristocracy and the beginning of the movement from aristocracy to oligarchy.

[14] See Ehrenberg's discussion in *From Solon to Socrates*, 8–9, 11.

rooted in the *oikos*, or "household," which protected kinship as the primary means of social identification.[15] The oikos was not, however, a simple familial network: it was a web of religious, social, and economic affiliations. M. I. Finley, for example, points out that there are no words in ancient Greek corresponding to our conception of the family beyond the term "oikos," which also refers to "household wealth" (*Ancient Economy*, 18). Even the term Aristotle uses to describe philosophical substance, *ousia*, also meant "patrimony" or "wealth" (MT, 362). The oikos played such an important role in social and economic relations in ancient Athens that, according to Vidal-Naquet, in many cases the lot of the slave was superior to that of the agricultural laborer because the slave was connected to and thus protected by an oikos; in contrast, the wage laborer (*thete*) who was unattached to any household was without any economic, political, or social protection (*Black Hunter*, 161). In a culture in which kinship provided the primary means of social identification, the familial, religious, and economic were indistinguishable domains.[16]

From this perspective, the potential of technē to disrupt lines of power challenged existing orders at many levels. Vernant maintains that agriculture was distinguished from technē. Cultivation was not viewed as a set of techniques applied to nature; rather, Vernant suggests, it was an active "collaboration" with a divine order (MT, 253–54). Vernant points out that just before Hesiod gives instruction concerning how to hold the "end of the plough-tail" and drive oxen once plowing begins, he also admonishes, "Pray to Zeus of the earth and pure Demeter to make Demeter's holy grain sound and heavy" (WD 465–69). For Hesiod, both human identity and peace with the gods are contingent on labor, and technē threatens the redemptive function of work. Put another way, the technē of fire building may sustain human life, but one's rectification with the gods will come from work: "Through work men grow rich in flocks and substance, and working they are much better loved by the immortals" (308–9). Because work performs an important redemptive function, it becomes the standard by which both the subject and moral value are defined. Work is to be valued above wealth: "Whatever be your lot,

---

[15] For more on social identification and the oikos, see Wood and Wood, *Ancient Political Theory*, 17–19. For more on social and economic development in early Greece, see Tandy, *Warriors into Traders*.

[16] For more discussion of kinship, see Fisher's introduction to *Social Values in Classical Athens*, 5–22, and Burn, *World of Hesiod*, 111–21.

work is best for you, if you turn your misguided mind away from other men's property to your work and attend to your livelihood" (314–16). The peasant farmer is identified less by his skill than by his relationship with his land and the gods, a relationship that is secured by his labor.

Work, however, is a rather conservative standard of value; it will produce wealth but not facilitate its redistribution.[17] Despite the significance of the exchange of technē in the Prometheus myths, the transfer of wealth, for Hesiod, is generally identified with force or deception:

> Wealth should not be seized: god-given wealth is much better; for if a man take great wealth violently and perforce, or if he steal it through his tongue, as often happens when gain deceives men's sense and dishonour tramples down honour, the gods soon blot him out and make that man's house low, and wealth attends him only for a little time. (WD 320–26)

In this case, the power of language is *not* set against force; deceptive words are only an alternative to violence.[18]

On the whole, *Works and Days* underscores the extent to which human identity was couched in work, family, and agrarian cult practices.[19] The political and economic developments of the next century challenged these forms of social identification at a number of points.

---

[17] For more on the difference between work and technē, see Vernant's discussions in chapters 10 and 11 of *Myth and Thought*.

[18] See especially Vernant's discussion of Xenophon (MT, 252–53). With the progression of democratic reforms, language, particularly that of the rhetors, is increasingly identified with the seizure of property. Compare the excerpt from *Works and Days* with the following excerpt from Isocrates' *Areopagiticus*. Isocrates maintains that in the older order of the Areopagus, citizens could have "confidence" in the decisions of judges: "And so because of this confidence no one tried to conceal his wealth nor hesitated to lend it out, but, on the contrary, the wealthy were better pleased to see men borrowing money than paying it back; for they thus experienced the double satisfaction—which should appeal to all right-minded men—of helping their fellow-citizens and at the same time making their own property productive for themselves. In fine, the result of their dealing honourably with each other was that the ownership of property was secured to those to whom it rightfully belonged, while the enjoyment of property was shared by all the citizens who needed it" (35). In the *Antidosis*, Isocrates feels the need to defend himself against that accusation that "cleverness in speech results in plotting against other people's property" (230).

[19] For a discussion of the role of agrarian cults in Hesiod's time, see Burn, *World of Hesiod*, 44–48.

Standardized currency, for example, allowed for both products and skills to be viewed as commensurable and replaceable in a way that was previously inconceivable.[20] Before the seventh century, according to Vernant, premonetary symbols of exchange appear to have been restricted to the nobility, and they took the form of precious objects (*agalmata*), such as vases, jewels, and garments, which carried religious as well as economic significance (MT, 362). These agalmata would hold little value for the peasant farmer who lived outside the community that defined their aesthetic, religious, and, finally, economic value. Thus, rather than encouraging the development of systems of exchange, which was crucial to the redistribution of wealth, these gift-giving practices only reinforced existing relations of distribution and power.[21] In contrast, standardized currency allowed wealth to cross social boundaries without bringing with it class ties and responsibilities.

Transferable arts that could create capital required a radical rethinking of class, value, and power. These new technai played a powerful role in displacing the aristocratic social order, which distributed privileges according to birth.[22] The specialization of labor created new ties of interdependence, which necessarily crossed class lines, since they were based on differences of competence as opposed to sameness of clan and class. The rise of specialization required systems of exchange that would accommodate different classes. In this context, the mastery of a technē could serve as "symbolic capital" that could be transformed into economic capital; and like monetary capital, a technē could cross class lines. The arts of rhetoric, household management, and politics were, of course, express examples of technai that both redistributed social power and produced capital for those sophists, say, who charged for their instruction. However, a wide variety of arts were involved in this redistribution between the seventh and fourth centuries, including mathematics, writing (the alphabet), divination, animal husbandry, seafaring, mining, and medicine (Edmunds, *Chance and Intelligence,* 50–52). For example, naval technē functioned quite literally in concert with democratic law in the distribution of social power because it required a new class of war-

[20] See Bury, *History of Greece,* 118, and MT, 360.

[21] "The *agalma* was the medium of expression of sacred powers, social prestige, and ties of dependence among men, all belonging to the same system of symbols for wealth. When the *agalma* circulated in the form of gifts and exchanges, individuals acquired commitments and religious forces were mobilized, as well as ownership changing hands" (MT, 360).

[22] See Vernant's discussion in MT, 358.

riors, which was to be found in the artisan class (29). This elevation of the banausic class to the warrior class even required constitutional changes to allow the "practitioners of the new technē" to have their "share of the wealth and power they had helped to create" (32).

The development of both technai and currency was a powerful catalyst for class mobility; by the fifth century, however, those developments also enabled a localization of the sphere of the economic that would have been impossible in Hesiod's time. By the fifth century, a distinction was made between visible assets (*ousia phanera*) and invisible assets (*ousia aphanēs*); visible assets continued to be identified with the inalienable patrimony of land, whereas invisible assets were identified with money, credits, and securities, which could be exchanged (MT 362). This distinction encouraged a bifurcation of value into the alienable and commercial, on the one hand, and the inalienable and priceless, on the other. George Thomson goes so far as to contend that the distinction between economic and noneconomic value is responsible, in part, for the birth of philosophy.[23]

Though the specialization of the art of rhetoric as political expertise should have underscored the extent to which political power remained dependent on social and economic privilege, by the fourth century, technē was sometimes characterized as either an individual ability or a gift of nature. Both characterizations made the technai "priceless" by placing them outside the purview of economic calculation. Thus, Plato argued that the technē of politics was a rare and specialized art, the property only of those with a philosophical disposition. When technē was made this valuable, it became as inalienable as the family oikos had once been. As technē came to be seen less as a body of socially valuable knowledge and more as an individual ability, it no longer underscored the arbitrary nature of relations of power; instead of disrupting social boundaries, the concept of technē was often used to secure them.

Aeschylus's *Prometheus Bound*

Prometheus Bound was composed sometime in the first half of the fifth century, in the midst of perhaps the most successful period of

---

[23] See Thomson's discussion in the chapter titled "The First Philosophers," in *Studies in Ancient Greek Society*, vol. 2.

democratic reform.[24] Commentators have pointed out that it is an atypical example of Attic tragedy, devoid of conventions such as reversal and resolution.[25] The play presents another set of problems as well. *Prometheus Bound* is the only (complete) play that survives from the original trilogy, and scholars speculate that this is the reason for its ambiguous tone. The depictions of Zeus and Prometheus are such that it is difficult to determine whose side the audience should take. We know that Prometheus has played the hero for both Zeus and humankind, but we find him in the play defeated, angry, and bitter.

This ambiguity has enfranchised a wide range of interpretations of both the tragedy and Prometheus's character. Prometheus is invoked in the service of a number of normative conceptions of "man," and his relationship with Zeus has been used to illustrate everything from dialectical materialism to Judeo-Christian theology. Friedrich Solmsen's *Hesiod and Aeschylus* is a classic attempt to find in the tragedy a consistent, edifying moral concerning *hybris* (pride) and *sōphrosynē* (self-control).[26] The tragedy performs a number of functions for Havelock. He maintains that the story is a parable about the fate of "intellectual man," set in the context of the "tragic humanism of the Greeks."[27] He also compares Aeschylus's Zeus to Jehovah, "god of battles and a jealous god, smiter of his enemies, visiting the sins of the fathers on the children" (*Prometheus*, 58). This comparison is particularly significant because Havelock, like Jaeger, uses it to affirm the virtues of Greek culture at the expense of other Mediterranean cultures. As Havelock puts it, "Prometheus represents the intellectual humanism of the Greek mind in competition with all the inherited terrors of traditional Mediterranean cult" (58). At base, as Havelock writes, Prometheus's critical function is that of representing "the alienation of the intellectual in any society" (vi). D. J. Conacher more graciously acknowledges a number of conflicting interpretations of the myth. In his discussion of the omission of the fine arts and the art of politics in Aeschylus's version of Prometheus's great speech, Conacher observes that Thomson "comments on this feature with the enthusiasm of the dialectical materialist," whereas Solmsen "seems to find the exclu-

---

[24] See Podlecki, *The Political Background of Aeschylean Tragedy.*
[25] See Griffith, ed., *Prometheus Bound*, by Aeschylus, 13.
[26] See also North, *Sophrosyne.*
[27] See Havelock, *Prometheus*, chap. 4. Havelock also notes in the foreword to the 1968 edition that he had chosen as his first title "The Crucifixion of Intellectual Man."

sively materialistic features of these passages an embarrassment, 'almost un-Aeschylean'" (*Aeschylus' "Prometheus Bound,"* 51 n. 29).

To say that the genre of tragedy shapes the character of Aeschylus's Prometheus is to state the uncontestably obvious. Still, few scholars resist comparing Aeschylus's version to Hesiod's, despite their generic and historical differences. For our purposes, however, determining Prometheus's character is only part of the equation. As we shall see, though there is an obvious shift in the depiction of Prometheus from a cunning trickster to a tragic hero, one of the most important contrasts is between Hesiodic and Aeschylean foresight, a contrast that marks the difference between foresight that enables intervention and foreknowledge that knows the future.

Aeschylus's tragedy opens at the point where Hesiod's *Theogony* version ends. Prometheus has been brought to a cliff by two agents of Zeus—Power (Kratos) and Force (Bia). They are accompanied by Hephaestus, grieving at being forced to use his art to harm Prometheus, who is both his kin and companion (*Pr.* 139). Hephaestus obeys Zeus's order, but he cries "Oh, handicraft that I have learned so much to loathe" (45). Power responds harshly that "thy craft is in no wise to blame for these present troubles" (46–47). Before they abandon Prometheus, Power insists that Hephaestus use his hammer again to secure the manacles; he orders, "Strike harder, clamp him tight, leave nothing loose; for he is wondrous clever at finding a way out [*poron*]" (58–59). Before departing, Prometheus's name is ridiculed by Power, who taunts that the gods falsely "call thee Prometheus, for thou hast thyself need of one to take forethought [*prometheōs*] how thou shalt extricate thyself from this handiwork" (85–87). Thus, the tragedy begins with the ambiguous characterization of technē found throughout the play. Power and Force have outrun the power of art; and art (that of Hephaestus, at least) has been used to bind art "beyond all loosening" (60). Put another way, Prometheus has been restrained in such a way as to annul the power of "inventing a way out."

After the exit of his persecutors, Prometheus asks what amounts to a rhetorical question that only he can answer: "For misery present and misery to come I groan, not knowing where it is fated deliverance from these woes shall rise" (97–100). His answer reveals the contrast, which continues throughout the tragedy, between Hesiodic and Aeschylean "forethought": "And yet, what do I say? All that is to be I know full well and in advance, nor shall any affliction come upon me unforeseen" (101–3). The word used in this context for "knowing in advance" is formed from the verb *epistamai*. While this term for knowledge generally denotes a kind of certainty (it is related to Aristotle's term for science, "epistēmē"), the word is used interchangeably with Prometheus's name *promētheia*, which is based on the noun mētis. But the foreknowledge described here and throughout the tragedy is clearly more of the character of knowledge per se than the anticipation of an immediate future that allows for a specific act of intervention by way of art. Prometheus's foreknowledge concerns a future that exists "by Necessity" or it would be meaningless. This sense of foresight is in sharp contrast to that identified with mētis. Vigilance is one of the qualities of the "man of *mētis*" (CI, 31–32); he is alert to what *is* happening in order to affect what *might* happen. The foresight of Hesiod's Prometheus is not knowledge of the future; instead, it is a cunning vigilance that enabled Prometheus to seize the moment when Zeus was sufficiently distracted that Prometheus could slip into heaven and steal fire. For Aeschylus's Prometheus, on the other hand, foresight is knowledge of a "necessary" future: "My allotted doom I needs must bear as lightly as I may, knowing that the might of Necessity [*anankēs*] brooketh no resistance" (103–4). In contrast to traditions associated with moira, Prometheus's sense of fate and necessity is more concerned with the future than the past. His "allotted" portion is not what he begins with; it is his fate in the future. Prometheus's ambiguous gift of foresight only gives him knowledge of his "portion," not the power to change it.

Prometheus recounts the reasons for his punishment and for his bitterness toward Zeus: "I hunted out and stored in fennel stalk the stolen source of fire that hath proved to mortals a teacher in every art [*technēs pasēs*] and a means to mighty ends [*megas poros*] (108–10). At that point in time, Prometheus knows there is no poros for him. When the Chorus enters, however, we learn how Prometheus has the "upper hand" in his contest with Zeus. Prometheus knows what will bring about Zeus's downfall (his mother Themis has already told him); and for Prometheus, this knowledge itself is clearly a kind of power— even the power of extortion: "Not by persuasion's honied enchantments shall he charm me; and never will I, cowering before his dire threats, divulge this secret, until he shall release me from my cruel bonds and desire to proffer satisfaction for this outrage" (173–79). We learn that Prometheus's bitterness is due in part to his having come to Zeus's aid in his battle with the Titans. We also learn that fire was not Prometheus's only gift to humankind. He also "caused mortals no longer to foresee their doom [death]" (250) by causing "blind hopes to dwell within their breasts" (252).

Prometheus's account of the distribution of the arts takes place in the second episode (436–525). Commentators point out that in Aeschylus's version the dispensation of the arts is a response to a series of "needs" or practical exigencies.[28] The significance of this fact is interpreted in a number of ways. The focus on material needs prompts Thomson's interpretation of Prometheus as the archetypal proletariat. For others, Aeschylus's emphasis bears witness to an emerging anthropological perspective. Though this emphasis is at odds with Prometheus's battle with Zeus, which forms the structure of the tragedy, this interpretation asserts that the play marks a significant step in an evolving rationalist perspective that replaces the powers of the gods with human agency.

The first art mentioned by Prometheus is the art of medicine and the second, significantly, is the art whereby humankind might "read the future." This is the art of divination, which is raised in most of the prehistory accounts. It includes, as Prometheus tells us, the interpretation of dreams, voices, and "the flight of crook-taloned birds" (488–89), together with all forms of augury, including the interpretation of gall and entrails (493–98). It is worth noting that Aeschylus makes no attempt to reconcile the tragic foreknowledge that is Prometheus's gift and curse with the interpretation of signs identified with divination. Such arts as augury qualify as rational arts because they are based in experience and constructed on the observation of regularities, or "signs."

Prometheus next raises the arts of the smiths, those dealing with "bronze, iron, silver, and gold." Thomson is not strictly correct when he suggests that Prometheus's *technē* refers only to advancements in "material technique" (*Aeschylus and Athens*, 317). Prometheus refers to the fine arts before the list that begins with line 476. He takes credit for inventing the art of numbers and the art of "the combining of letters," which he describes as "the creative mother of the Muses' arts" (461). What we do *not* find in Aeschylus's list (which we do find in that of Protagoras, who is removed from Aeschylus by less than two generations) is the art of politics. An examination of the extent to which the exclusion of politics is driven by the conventions of tragedy is beyond the scope of this project. But the struggle depicted between Zeus

---

[28] See Conacher, *Aeschylus' "Prometheus Bound,"* 48–51.

and Prometheus is so personalized that it is difficult to imagine how the play could account for the bonds of *philia* and obligation that are requisite for the social order of polis. The bonds in Aeschylus's version are vertical rather than horizontal. Though Zeus and Prometheus clearly represent different orders, the tragedy remains, at some level, a tale of almost personal retribution.

As the episode comes to a close, the Chorus raises what might be interpreted as Prometheus's tragic flaw, his desire to "benefit mortals beyond due measure [*kairou pera*]" (507). At this point, Aeschylus's version recalls the crossing of boundaries found in Hesiod's narratives. Prometheus has transgressed the boundary between humankind and the gods; and whether or not the tragedy stresses this theme, the theft has changed the "lot" of humankind. Still, questions concerning Aeschylus's interpretation of the Prometheus narrative persist. Is Prometheus's crime that of trying to change the portion, or moira, assigned to humankind? Is art the means by which humankind's share is renegotiated? Aeschylus's version focuses far more on the character and foreknowledge of Zeus than on the potential agency of art. The Chorus affirms: "I am of good hope that thou shalt yet be loosed from these bonds and have power no wise inferior to Zeus" (508–10). Even Prometheus agrees because he knows the future. He will not be saved *by* art. Indeed, he concludes that "art is feebler far than Necessity" (514).

The play's next episode includes Prometheus's encounter with Io, who may be interpreted as an analogue for Pandora. As Conacher points out, Io, as the only human in the play, creates a complex bond between Prometheus and Zeus; and that bond—beyond the border of this play—will bring about resolution of their conflict (*Aeschylus' "Prometheus Bound,"* 56). Io is the object of Zeus's passion and the victim of Hera's. In an effort to protect her, Zeus begins to transform her into a heifer to hide her from Hera, consequently horns grow on Io's head. But Hera is not deceived by Zeus's actions, and she sends a gadfly to torment Io, driving her to the same hinterland in which Prometheus was abandoned. The most significant turn in the play is Prometheus's disclosure to Io of the "foreknowledge" of his own freedom and Zeus's doom. According to Prometheus, Io will join with Zeus, but from her lineage a son will be born who will release Prometheus from his bondage.

One important element of Prometheus's encounter with Io is the "map" he tries to create for her tortured wandering. By the standards of art discussed thus far, this "map" may be the tragedy's best illustration of technē. Io is characterized by confusion and disorientation. Her first speech is a series of questions: "What land is this? What people? By what name am I to call him I behold exposed to the tempest in bonds of rock?" (561–63). Chased by a gadfly, Io has wandered aimlessly, without pattern. She concludes her speech with the question, "Wither am I borne in my far-roaming wandering course?" (567–68) Prometheus uses his foreknowledge, first, to tell Io where she will go from this point. He gives her landmarks, names of countries, and descriptions of different peoples. These signs create a "way out" of, at least, Io's frenzied and disordered state of mind. To some extent, this "map" transforms her wandering into a guided journey. Prometheus provides Io a broader map by telling her that her journey has an end; and through her son she will be responsible for Prometheus's deliverance. Though commentators seldom explore the connection, Io resembles Pandora in a number of ways. Like Pandora, Io is the only source of hope in the narrative. Io is also a curiously indeterminate figure. Whereas Pandora confuses the boundary between nature and art, Io confuses the boundaries between animal life, human life, demigods, and gods.

The crossing of boundaries that ties this version to Hesiod's reappears as Io departs and the Chorus speaks: "Ah sage, sage in sooth, was he who first pondered this truth in his mind and with his tongue gave it utterance—that to marry in one's own degree is far the best" (887–89). The tragedy concludes with Hermes' attempt to extract from Prometheus his knowledge of the future. The conflict between Hermes and Prometheus again raises questions concerning the power of will and persuasion set against the force of necessity. Hermes appeals to Prometheus's self-interest and even his sanity, but Prometheus maintains:

> There is no torment or device by which Zeus shall induce me to utter this until these injurious fetters be loosed. So then, let his blazing levin be hurled, and with the white wings of the snow and thunders of earthquake let him confound the reeling world. For naught of this shall bend my will even to tell at whose hands he is fated to be hurled from his sovereignty. (989–96)

Because Prometheus will not disclose his knowledge to Hermes, the cliff begins to shake, and Prometheus is hurled into the dark chaos of

Tartarus. There he can only wait for his fate to unfold. The final in-
teractions between Hermes and Prometheus raise a number of age-old
and sometimes tedious questions. Could Prometheus have told Hermes the secret if he had so willed? If Prometheus's fate is set, what role
can exist for persuasion and will?

The character of both Prometheus and foresight are at issue here primarily for the ways they constrain and reshape technē. Clearly, in
Aeschylus's tragedy, the character of Prometheus overrides any concern with art. The only act that could affect the plot involves
Prometheus's disclosure of his special knowledge—and either by his
willfulness or his fate (we can't tell which), he does not do that. Concerns about individual will—be it of Prometheus or Zeus—are para-
mount in the tragedy. Art has created breaches between orders of
power rather than bonds *within* them.

Although it is impossible to determine the extent to which the conventions of tragedy drive Aeschylus's depiction of foresight and art,
several features of Hesiodic foresight are worth contrasting with that
of Aeschylus. In Hesiod's versions, Epimetheus (afterthought) is not
so named because he *cannot* see the future but because he does not *remember*, at a critical moment in the present, what he has been told in
the past. It is his propensity not to "think ahead" that brings about
Pandora's entrance into human affairs: "Epimetheus did not think on
what Prometheus had said to him, bidding him never take a gift of
Olympian Zeus, but to send it back for fear it might prove to be something harmful to men. But he took the gift, and afterwards, when the
evil thing was already his, he understood" (WD 85–89). The suggestion throughout the narrative is that Epimetheus's failure to remember Prometheus's warning has brought about a new dimension in human suffering. At this point, however, Epimetheus's failed memory
comes up against fate and necessity. In other words, if memory *can*
make a difference, the *necessary* character of fate is put into question.
In the *Theogony*, even Zeus is both bound and freed by the power of
memory. Throughout Hesiod's texts, Zeus is called "far-seeing Zeus"
(WD 281), the one whose eye is capable of "seeing all and understanding all" (WD 267). After Zeus perceives that Prometheus is
putting before him a trick offering, the god castigates Prometheus:
"Son of Iapetus, clever above all! So, sir, you have not yet forgotten
your cunning arts!" (*Theog.* 559–60). In the next lines, the poet writes,
"So spake Zeus in anger, whose wisdom is everlasting; and from that
time he was always mindful of the trick, and would not give the power

of unwearying fire to the Melian race of mortal men" (*Theog.* 561–63). Zeus's memory, however, also appears to be fallible. Immediately after his resolve to remember the trick, Prometheus still slips into heaven, steals Zeus's fire, and hides it in the fennel stalk. Neither Zeus's memory nor power is keen enough for the "cunning" foresight of Prometheus.

This sense of foresight in Hesiod's narratives is a critical dimension of technē. Here, foresight is *not* knowledge of a future that cannot be changed; neither is it a static representation of "fate" that holds by necessity. Instead, Hesiodic foresight is that complex, temporal dimension of art, identified with kairos, that allows for an intervention that disturbs the present and creates the future.

5 Plato and the Boundaries of Art

If, as Mill, Bentham and others constantly insist, society *is* nothing but a collection of individuals, how can 'the individual disappear' into collectivities which are simply names for such collections? And how can 'the individual' be counterposed to society or 'the people' in the ways that it so often is? What this contradiction points to is the central ambiguity in the very concept of 'the individual', between its simple meaning of 'the single human person', and its concealed, subsidiary meaning, whereby 'the individual' really means 'the exceptional individual' or 'the isolated individual.'
—Anthony Arblaster, *Rise and Decline of Western Liberalism*

A fragment in the *Dissoi Logoi* contains the following simple, ineloquent argument:

I think it belongs to <the same man> and to the same art to be able to discourse in the brief style and to understand <the> truth of things and to know how to give a right judgment in the lawcourts and to be able to make public speeches and to understand the art of rhetoric [*logōn technas*] and to teach concerning the nature of all things, their state, and how they came to be. And, first of all, how will it not be possible for a man who knows about the nature of all things to act rightly in every case and <teach the city> to do so too? (Sprague, 291–92; DK, 90 8)

The passage quickly deteriorates into a list of "if, then" clauses that detail the abilities of such a man in endeavors ranging from lawmaking to flute playing. Still, in only a few lines, the anonymous sophist cites most of the major topoi used in the fourth century B.C.E. to debate the provinces of philosophy, politics, and the arts of discourse. To "discourse in the brief style" is to engage in dialectic; and in the philosophical tradition of Plato, dialectic provides understanding of the "nature" of things. The rhetor, on the other hand, gives judgments in the "lawcourts" and "make[s] public speeches." The writer maintains that "understanding" is perfectly congruent with engaging in the affairs of the polis; knowledge and public intervention are not incompatible. With the topos of what belongs to a man and an art, the writer attempts to fuse the two lives that Socrates, in the *Gorgias*, so contemptuously divides: "the life spent in philosophy" and the life spent "speaking in the Assembly and practicing rhetoric and playing the politician" (500c).

The sophist's persuasive task is daunting, for he argues against such unequivocal pronouncements as that found in Plato's *Apology*: "The true champion of justice, if he intends to survive even for a short time, must necessarily confine himself to private life [*idiōteuein*] and leave politics [*dēmosieuein*] alone" (*Apology* 32a).[1] For Plato, the private life and the life of politics could hardly be less compatible. In contrast to the "philosopher who has applied himself to his own business and not played the busybody in his life" (*Gorgias* 526c), those who occupy themselves with affairs of the courts and the Assembly are a "riotous crew who have burst in where they do not belong, wrangling with one another, filled with spite and always talking about persons, a thing least befitting philosophy" (*Rep.* 500b). The true philosopher would never engage in such activities: "The man whose mind is truly fixed on eternal realities has no leisure to turn his eyes downward upon the petty affairs of men, and so engaging in strife with them to be filled with envy and hate, but he fixes his gaze upon the things of the eternal and unchanging order" (500b–c). Plato's state would be governed by a guardian class, who would rule by crafting and maintaining a social order based on their philosophical principles. Only in this way could the philosophical life coexist with the life of the statesman.

The sophistic fragment above provides a starting point for further exploring the logōn technē tradition of Protagoras and Isocrates and the philosophical tradition of Plato because it attempts to bridge two largely incommensurable paradigms. The sophist accepts Platonic distinctions but argues for a conclusion consistent with the logōn technē tradition. The division between the two lives is largely Platonic; however, the sophist's conclusion that both lives may merge

[1] The relationship between the public and private is not as simple in the fourth century B.C.E. as one might wish. See Ober's discussion in *Democratic Athens*, 108–12.

could hardly be less so. In contrast, both Protagoras and Isocrates assume that the lives of the philosopher and the public citizen can—even should—belong to the same man; indeed, it is unlikely that Protagoras would have made the sophist's distinction between knowledge and civic action in the first place. Thus, conflicts over philosophy, rhetoric's province, and social and political order are often conflicts between vastly different conceptions of knowledge and human identity. This chapter focuses on two specific areas of incommensurability between these two traditions: their conflicting definitions of *rhētorikē, logōn technē, paideia, philosophia, doxa,* and *epistēmē;* and their models of social, political, and economic order. My argument is that these conflicts have left us with not only an attenuated conception of the art of discourse but also a model of subjectivity, defined by internal order rather than civic action.

Philosophers versus Rhetors

Philosophers and the Polis

Plato's attitude toward the public life was likely a response in part to the activities he witnessed in the Athenian polis.[2] Two defining characteristics of Athenian democracy from the mid–fifth century B.C.E. through most of the fourth century were at odds with the very foundation of Plato's political thought: the principle of *isēgoria* and the filling of public offices by lot.[3] Isēgoria referred to the tenet that was to have held sway in the Assembly: the "right of all citizens to speak on matters of state importance" (Ober, *Democratic Athens,* 78). Josiah

---

[2] Democracy's achievements must be evaluated in context. The successes of democratic deliberation were at least facilitated by the relative homogeneity of Athen's citizens, the result, in part, of the formal exclusion of metics, slaves, and, of course, women. Athenian democracy was also situated in a culture dependent on slavery. Though there is controversy over the extent to which a slave "mode of production" freed citizens to spend their time with the affairs of the polis, that controversy hardly "humanizes" Athenian slavery. Athens' democracy also developed in the context of imperialist expansion. Foreign policies opened political and economic opportunities in the form of cleruchies and naval military service. See Edmunds, *Chance and Intelligence,* 29, and ibid., 23. For various assessments of the extent of citizen rule, see Josiah Ober, R. K. Sinclair, Mogens Herman Hansen, "The Political Powers of the People's Court in Fourth-Century Athens," in Murray and Price, *The Greek City.*

[3] See also Edmunds, *Chance and Intelligence,* 50–51.

Ober interprets Plato's criticism of democracy in the *Protagoras* as a direct response to this political environment in which any "citizen who could gain and hold the attention of his fellows in the Assembly had the right to advise them on national policy" (8). In addition, by the middle of the fifth century the most important governing bodies and offices (with the exception of certain military roles) were either open to all citizens, like the Assembly, or filled by the lottery system, as was the Council (or Boule); the selection of public officials by lot distinguished Athens as a participatory rather than a representative democracy.[4]

It is difficult to imagine a system more antithetical to Plato's principles of government than selection by lot. The lottery system was based on the assumption that all citizens were equally worthy and able to determine the affairs of the polis. By definition, the lot mitigated efforts to make politics a specialized art. As Aristotle put it, in a democracy "all persons alike share in the government to the utmost" (*Pol.* 1291b36–37); and the lot embodied the principle that all are "to rule and be ruled in turn" (*Pol.* 1317b2–3). While Aristotle is not a champion of Athenian democracy, he is not the intractable critic that Plato proved to be. Aristotle goes so far as to admit that there might be some "truth" in the "principle that the multitude ought to be in power rather than the few best" (*Pol.* 1281a40–41). For the most part, however, Aristotle's assessment of democracy proceeds from his conviction that the ideal state would be ruled by "the best," which is to say an aristocratic leisure class.[5] From this perspective, the democratic state is also antithetical to Aristotle's ideal, because, according to Aristotle, "democratic justice is the application of numerical not proportionate equality" (*Pol.* 1317b3–4).[6]

---

[4] Both the council of five hundred and the people's courts were selected by lot. See Ober, *Democratic Athens,* 141. For debates concerning numbers and attendance, see Sinclair, *Democracy and Participation in Athens,* 19, and Ober, *Democratic Athens,* 76–82. As early as 487, even the highest office of archon was filled by lot, albeit from a restricted pool. See Ober, *Democratic Athens,* 76, and Sinclair, *Democracy and Participation in Athens,* 47. The Aristotelian *Constitution of Athens* provides a catalog of other offices subject to the lot and details the sophisticated lottery system used for selecting juries. For a discussion of the authorship of *Constitution of Athens,* see P. J. Rhodes, introduction to *A Commentary on the Aristotelian "Athenaion Politeia."*

[5] See Chapter 6. See also Ober, *Democratic Athens,* 33, 164 n. 21.

[6] Noting the tendency for democracies to fall prey to demagogues, Aristotle states his preference for democracies which are "subject to the law" and in which "the best citizens hold the first place" (*Pol.* 1292a9).

For Plato and Aristotle, affecting the business of the state took the form of advising its leaders, rather than directly intervening in its affairs. Plato maintained a close association with Dion of Syracuse, who was both brother- and son-in-law to Dionysius I, tyrant of Syracuse. Dion brought Plato to Syracuse after the death of Dionysius I in the hope that Dionysius II might fulfill Plato's ideal of the philosophical ruler. Though the most tangible result of Dion's efforts was probably his own banishment from Syracuse, Plato retained a relationship with Dionysius II. Thus, while the extent of Plato's philosophical influence in Syracuse is open to question, his ambition to see his political ideals realized is not. Similarly, Aristotle sustained a relationship throughout his life with the court of Philip of Macedon, eventually serving as tutor to his son Alexander. The practical influence of both philosophers was, no doubt, limited at best; however, their political philosophies cannot be dubbed abstract theorizing. Their "ideal" states were conceived to be constructed in reality. At the same time, neither Plato nor Aristotle saw himself changing the state by engaging its conflicts and submitting to its procedures. Instead, they designed, from the outside, the principles of order that would govern the state within.[7]

Unlike many of democracy's advocates, Aristotle was keenly aware of the problem of democracy's promise of equality in the face of disparate interests and the unequal distribution of resources. After a discussion of democracy in the *Politics*, Aristotle asks these questions: "How is this equality to be obtained? Are we to assign to a thousand poor men the property qualifications of five hundred rich men?" (1318a11–14). For Aristotle, the severing of material resources from political power, which democratic law instituted, was naïve, at best. Democratic law emerged in a context in which "material progress," as Vlastos puts it, "had normally been coeval with the concentration of both political and economic power in the hands of kings and nobles" ("*Isonomia*," 355). It was democratic law that made "formally complete" the separation of economic and political justice—or the "redivision of the land" and the "redistribution of political rights and privileges" (352–53). Aristotle points to the contradiction at the heart of democratic law in his persistent reminders of the contingency of political influence on material resources. His discussion of members of

----

[7] The guardian class are described as "expert craftsmen of civic liberty [*dēmiourgous eleutherias tēs poleōs*]" (*Rep.* 395c).

the "best" kind of democracy recalls, inversely, his description in the
Metaphysics of the lover of wisdom:

> The best material of democracy is an agricultural population; there is no
> difficulty in forming a democracy where the mass of the people live by
> agriculture or tending of cattle. Being poor, they have no leisure, and
> therefore do not often attend the assembly, and having the necessaries
> of life they are always at work, and do not covet the property of others.
> Indeed, they find their employment pleasanter than the cares of gov-
> ernment or office where no great gains can be made out of them, for the
> many are more desirous of gain than of honour. A proof is that even the
> ancient tyrannies were patiently endured by them, as they still endure
> oligarchies, if they are allowed to work and are not deprived of their
> property; for some of them grow quickly rich and the others are well
> enough off. (*Pol.* 1318b10–18)

The agricultural worker contrasts with the philosopher, who is free to
seek wisdom only once "almost all the necessities of life and the
things that make for comfort and recreation were present" (*Met.*
982b19–23). Securing the "necessaries of life" requires all the farmer's
time. Consequently, this democracy functions best because it resembles aristocracy in that the common people, the dēmos, leave the most
important offices to those with "greater qualification," "special ability," and the valuable capital of *free* time (*Pol.* 1318b30–33).

Aristotle is not advocating oligarchy. His careful distinctions between aristocracy and oligarchy in the *Nicomachean Ethics* make that
clear: "All men agree that what is just in distribution must be according to merit in some sense, though they do not all specify the same
sort of merit, but democrats identify it with the status of freeman, supporters of oligarchy with wealth (or with noble birth), and supporters
of aristocracy with excellence [*aretēn*]" (1131a24–29). Still, Aristotle
knew that this kind of excellence seldom flourished where material
resources were scarce.

The democracy grudgingly affirmed by Aristotle in the *Politics* is
that instituted by Solon in the sixth century B.C.E., which divided
Athenian citizens into four census classes: *pentakosiomedimnoi*,
hippeis, zeugitai, and *thētes*. The most "democratic" dimension of
these reforms was their replacement of standards of birth with those
of wealth in determining political participation. Each class won "a
share" of political power, but a share proportionate to its resources.

Though Solon's reforms set the stage for more expansive conceptions of equality before the law that would follow, they also instituted a conception of justice whereby equality before the law could coexist with the unequal distribution of resources. Subsequent democratic reforms would legalize, if not naturalize, economic inequality. Solon's own description of his accomplishments illustrates the way such a conception of political equality protected economic inequality: "For I gave the common folk such privilege as is sufficient for them, neither adding nor taking away; and such as had power and were admired for their riches, I provided that they too should not suffer under wrong. Nay, I stood with a strong shield thrown before the both sorts, and would have neither to prevail unrighteously over the other" (Elegy 5, 6). Solon's laws permitted neither violation of the poor, on one hand, nor redistribution of resources, on the other.

Solon's displacement of standards of birth for those of wealth also helped to create a revised conception of virtue—again with ambiguous consequences. Once public law securely protects "private" property, the following sentiments are much easier to express (Plutarch attributes these statements to Solon: "Many bad men are rich, many good men poor; but we, we will not exchange virtue for wealth, for the one endureth whereas the other belongeth now to this man and now to that" (Elegy 15). "Surely equal is the wealth of him that hath much silver and gold and fields of wheatland and horses and mules, to that of him that hath but this—comfort in belly and sides and feet. This is abundance unto men, seeing that no man taketh with him the many things he hath above this when he goeth below, nor shall he for a price escape death nor yet sore disease nor the evil approach of Age" (Elegy 24). Despite their pious tone, such sentiments are most likely to be expressed by the well-fed and the well-born.[8]

Plato's *Rhētorikē*

In one sense, the relationship between the logōn technē tradition and social and political orders is quite simple. Plato effectively separates logos from technē, redefining knowledge in terms of subject mat-

---

[8] The perspectival character of Solon's conceptions of equality and virtue is difficult to ignore. Similarly, Aristotle, with characteristic frankness, maintains that it is only the weak who are concerned about "equality and frankness," "For the weaker are always asking for equality and justice, but the stronger care for none of these things" (*Pol.* 1318b4–5).

ter and making technē equivalent to social function. For Protagoras and Isocrates, logōn technē provides the means to secure, disrupt, and create social and political order. The complexity of art's relationship to social and economic various order frequently resides in conflicting definitions of rhetoric, philosophia, technē logōn, and paideia. For example, philosophia is given very different definitions by Plato and Isocrates; while they hold broadly similar definitions of paideia, their curricula differ significantly. The importance of these terms in understanding the ancient art of discourse is illustrated in the arguments made by Thomas Cole and Edward Schiappa that rhetoric did not exist as a discipline until Plato coined the term "rhētorikē."[9]

Both Cole and Schiappa assert that logōn technē referred to a recognized tradition that preceded Plato's coining of rhētorikē; both agree that this logōn technē was a more inclusive study than Plato's rhētorikē; and both conclude that rhētorikē was a philosophical invention imposed by Plato on existing arts of discourse.[10] Although their arguments are particularly valuable in confirming the logōn technē tradition, neither seriously explores the extent to which the concerns, methods, and functions of that tradition might have been largely incommensurable with those of Plato. Both Cole and Schiappa define logōn technē and rhētorikē primarily in relation to philosophy, disregarding other models of knowledge, such as technē and paideia.

In effect, Cole and Schiappa use distinctions authored primarily by Plato to interpret the significance of his demarcation of rhētorikē. For example, Schiappa suggests that the appearance of rhētorikē signaled a stage in the transition from the older logōn technē to the definition of rhetoric as a specific discipline.[11] For Schiappa, rhētorikē is Plato's means of delimiting Isocrates' philosophia, thus dividing "the goals of seeking success and seeking truth" in a way that the previous "teaching and training associated with *logos*" did not ("*Rhētorikē*," 3).[12] For

[9] See Thomas Cole, *Origins of Rhetoric*, and Schiappa, *Protagoras and Logos*.

[10] Schiappa explains that "prior to the coining of *rhētorikē*, the verbal arts were understood as less differentiated and more holistic in scope than they were in the fourth century; the teaching and training associated with *logos* do not draw a sharp line between the goals of seeking success and seeking truth as is the case once Rhetoric and Philosophy were defined as distinct disciplines"; see "*Rhētorikē*," 3. See also Cole, *Origins of Rhetoric*, 98–99.

[11] Cole maintains that rhetoric did not evolve from the sophists but was a fourth-century invention (ibid., x).

[12] Schiappa argues: "If Plato was the first person to popularize the word *rhētorikē*, he probably did so to depict the teachings of his rival Isocrates. . . . The new word

Cole, rhētorikē is a philosophical invention that is closely tied to two developments: first, the ability of audiences and composers to abstract "essential messages from verbal contexts: the informative core of any piece of communication from its non- or extra-informative—that is, rhetorical—residue" (*Origins of Rhetoric*, x); and second, the appearance of a corpus of "'written' eloquence"—a "body of prose texts . . . on which to conduct the detailed, precise analysis of the verbal medium that is characteristic of rhetoric" (x). For Cole and Schiappa, knowledge as either "truth" or "information" is still something "outside" the knower and extricable from situations. Moreover, both knowledge and information can be evaluated by definitive, external measures: "truth" in the case of knowledge, and "accuracy" in the case of information. The result is a very disciplinary epistemology, defined primarily by a conception of subject matter, much the way Socrates, in the dialogue *Protagoras*, forces Hippocrates to define the instruction he expects to receive from the sophist.

That such a conception of knowledge might not tell the full tale of both rhētorikē and logōn technē is underscored by the failure of Cole and Schiappa even to raise the notion of paideia—despite its appearance in Protagoras, Isocrates, and Plato.[13] Paideia is not a strictly disciplinary model of knowledge; it is closely associated with imitation and the inculcation of habits and values. Identified with the construction of a certain type of subjectivity, paideia does not refer so much to knowledge that one "has" as it does to knowledge that one "is."[14] Moreover, whatever its ideological goals, paideia is evaluated primarily by its ability to engender a certain kind of social behavior, not to demarcate or represent either knowledge or truth. Rather than being extricated from culture, paideia is culture as knowledge. As Plato and Isocrates—and Jaeger—demonstrate, paideia can be trimmed to fit specific ideologies. However, the resistance of paideia to marking clear boundaries between subjectivity, knowledge, and culture at least resembles the logōn technē tradition as we have defined it. In focusing

---

rhētorikē was a useful label for Plato to use to stress the political aspects of Isocrates' training while diminishing the intellectual content. . . . Plato seems to have coined—or at least borrowed and defined—the new word rhētorikē as part of an effort to limit the scope and popularity of sophistic teaching, particularly that of his rival Isocrates" ("*Rhētorikē*," 10, 11).

[13] For paideia in Protagoras, see DK, 80 A 5.30, 80 A 21a.27, and 80 A 25.19.

[14] Similar descriptions of subjectivity may be found in Fish, "Consequences," and Bourdieu, OTP.

on rhētorikē as primarily the delimitation of the province of rhetoric, Cole and Schiappa underestimate the extent to which it signaled a difference in kind rather than degree. Once Plato succeeds in forcing the definition of logōn technē in terms of subject matter, rhetoric becomes an art with no meaningful, legitimate domain, and logōn technē becomes "teaching" with no valid ethical or epistemological standards.

Paideia, Logōn Technē, and Philosophia

One of the most explicit ancient definitions of paideia is found in Plato's *Protagoras*. At the beginning of the dialogue, the young Hippocrates announces his intention to become a student of Protagoras. His announcement elicits a tenacious round of questioning by Socrates, in which Hippocrates fails to specify in what capacity the sophist will serve as his teacher. According to W. R. M. Lamb's translation in the Loeb edition, Socrates makes the following query: "Perhaps it is not this sort of learning that you expect to get from Protagoras, but rather the sort you had from your language-master, your harp-teacher, and your sports-instructor; for when you took your lessons from each of these it was not in the technical way [*epi technēi*] with a view to becoming a professional [*dēmiourgos*], but for education [*paideiai*] as befits a private gentleman [*ton idiōtēn kai ton eleutheron*]" (312a–b). Guthrie's translation offers a slightly different perspective: "Perhaps then this is not the kind of instruction you expect to get from the schoolmasters who taught you letters and music and gymnastics. You didn't learn these for professional purposes, to become a practitioner, but in the way of liberal education, as a layman and a gentleman should."[15]

Though Hippocrates responds to Socrates in the affirmative, Socrates continues to press him to define the subject of which the sophist is a master, as well as the the "matter of his speeches" (312c–e). In frustration, Hippocrates finally concedes that he cannot answer Socrates' questions (313). Socrates calls the sophist a "merchant or peddler of the goods by which a soul is nourished" (312c) and gives Hippocrates the following warning: "If then you chance to be an expert in discerning which of them is good or bad, it is safe for you to buy knowledge from Protagoras or anyone else, but if not, take care

---

[15] The first translation cited is from the Loeb edition, and the second, from *Collected Dialogues*, ed. Hamilton and Cairns.

you don't find yourself gambling dangerously with all of you that is dearest to you" (313e–314). Such an expert would be a "physician of the soul" (313e), and by the dialogue's conclusion, Socrates makes it clear that only the philosopher qualifies as such an expert.

These brief excerpts invoke the terms and distinctions that underwrite Plato's paradigm of knowledge. True knowledge is contingent on the class status of the "knower." Paideia is instruction appropriate for the freeman, whose social role does not depend on a livelihood or profession. As we shall see, the specialization of function implied by Plato's notion of the professional is at the heart of his conception of social and political order. If Hippocrates had been able to define the subject matter of Protagoras's instruction (as sculpting is the subject matter of the sculptor), Socrates would have prescribed a function and social place for the technē, as well as its practitioner. For Plato, expertise is equivalent to function; and function determines one's place in the hierarchical order of the state. Though Plato generally depicts the philosopher as transcending that order, in the *Protagoras*, the philosopher is depicted as the "expert" in discerning good and bad; and that expertise defines the highest function in the state, to which all other specializations are subordinate. Finally, the substance of Plato's philosophy is the search for definitive measures of truth and goodness, what at the conclusion of the *Protagoras* Socrates calls "an art of measurement." Setting down the following proposition, Socrates asks Protagoras: "If now our happiness consisted in doing, I mean in choosing, greater lengths and avoiding smaller, where would lie salvation? In the art of measurement or in the impression made by appearances?" (356d). Socrates makes it clear that salvation resides in the art of measurement, the calculations of similarity and difference that guide dialectic. Thus, philosophy is a profession in that it requires expertise; philosophy is not a profession in that it is not practiced for earthly gain.

Isocrates sometimes uses *he tōn logōn paideia*, which could be translated as "the teaching of discourse," to refer to his *logōn technē*. It appears in the *Antidosis*, where it is translated by George Norlin as "the teaching of eloquence" (168) and "the art of discourse" (180). In the second case, Isocrates uses *he tōn logōn paideia* in one of the most explicit descriptions of the kind of training generally identified with paideia.[16] Two other terms are important in describing his paideia:

---

[16] See Isocrates, *Antid.* 171, 173, 304, and *Helen* 54.

epitēdeuma and *epimeleia*. "Epitēdeuma" is variously translated as "pursuit," "custom," and "way of life" (LSJ, 666). In its noun form, "epimeleia" denotes "attention, diligence" (LSJ, 645); in *Antidosis* 182, it is translated as "discipline." The verb *epimeleisthai* may mean to "take care of, have charge or management of" (LSJ, 645). In *Against the Sophists*, Isocrates criticizes sophistic instruction as "stuff and non-sense, and not as a true discipline [*epimeleian*] of the soul" (8). Isocrates redoubles his efforts at self-exculpation at 180 of *Antidosis*, asserting that the art of discourse, which trains the mind, and gymnastics, which trains the body, are "twin arts—parallel and complementary" (182). Their masters "prepare the mind to become more intelligent and the body to become more serviceable" (182). Both arts use "similar methods of instruction, exercise, and other forms of discipline [*epimeleias*]" (182). Isocrates offers the following comparison:

> For when they take their pupils in hand, the physical trainers instruct their followers in the postures which have been devised for bodily contests, while the teachers of philosophy impart all the forms of discourse in which the mind expresses itself. Then, when they have made them familiar and thoroughly conversant with these lessons, they set them at exercises, habituate them to work and require them to combine in practice the particular things which they have learned. (183–84)

Isocrates uses verbs related to epimeleia and paideia to describe what such a paideia may produce: "Watching over them [*epimelomenoi*] and training [*paideuontes*] them in this manner, both the teachers of gymnastic and the teachers of discourse are able to advance their pupils to a point where they are better men and where they are stronger in their thinking or in the use of their bodies" (185). The end of this instruction, which in 186 Isocrates calls "philosophia," should be "men" who can "excel in oratory or in managing affairs or in any line of work" (187). The student who submits to this training will "embody" the practices, "discourses," and values of his teacher; the only true test of that embodiment is the student's success in managing his own household and intervening in the affairs of the polis.

Though paideia for both Isocrates and Plato is concerned with the construction of a subject, their methods and ends contrast sharply. Isocrates offers exercises and practice; Plato offers the precise methodology of dialectic. Still, both Plato and Isocrates call their instruction philosophia and distinguish themselves from the sophists.

The ambiguities in their conceptions of philosophia are further complicated by specific references to Isocrates made by Plato and references by Isocrates that appear to be aimed at Plato. For example,
Socrates offers Isocrates the following praise at the conclusion of the
Phaedrus:

> Isocrates is still young, Phaedrus, but I don't mind telling you the future
> I prophesy for him. . . . It seems to me that his natural powers give him
> a superiority over anything that Lysias has achieved in literature, and
> also that in point of character he is of a nobler composition; hence it
> would not surprise me if with advancing years he made all his literary
> predecessors look like very small-fry—that is, supposing him to persist
> in the actual type of writing in which he engages at present—still more
> so, if he should become dissatisfied with such work, and a sublimer im-
> pulse lead him to do greater things. For that mind of his, Phaedrus, con-
> tains an innate tincture of philosophy. (278e–79a)

Isocrates will indeed take up the mantle of philosophy. Throughout
his defense in the *Antidosis*, Isocrates tries to identify himself with
Socrates, as another lover of wisdom wrongly accused of corrupting
youth. Insisting that what "some people call philosophy is not entitled to that name," Isocrates promises "to define and explain . . . what
philosophy, properly conceived, really is" (270–71).[17] Isocrates' explication of his philosophia, however, suggests that it resembles Plato's
only in name.

According to Isocrates in the *Antidosis*, the studies that truly deserve the name of philosophy are those "which will enable us to govern wisely both our own households and the commonwealth" (285).
Isocrates' description is evocative of Protagoras's definition of his
logōn technē: "The proper care of his personal affairs, so that he may
best manage his own household, and also of the state's affairs so as to
become a real power in the city, both as a speaker and man of action"
(*Protagoras* 318e–19). Isocrates specifically criticizes instruction in
"disputation [*eristikois logois*] and . . . astronomy and geometry" (*Antid.* 261). If we read "eristikoi logoi"—verbal wrangling or contentious
argument—as Isocrates' critical interpretation of Platonic dialectic,
then Isocrates has cited the precise curriculum set out by Socrates in

[17] For Isocrates' other uses of philosophia, see *Antid.* 30, 41, 304, and especially
176, where Norlin translates philosophia as "liberal education." See also *Panathenaicus.* 30–31.

the *Republic*.[18] While maintaining these subjects "do not injure" and may be worthy of praise, Isocrates observes that "most men see in such studies nothing but empty talk and hairsplitting; for none of these disciplines has any useful application either to private or public affairs" (261–62). He contends that "these disciplines are different in nature" (263); for the most part, they "only help us while we are in the process of learning" (264). These studies are useful in exercising and sharpening the mind—in preventing our "wits" from going "wool-gathering" (265); through them young men may enhance "their aptitude for mastering greater and more serious studies" (267). On the whole, however, they are a "gymnastic of the mind" and a "preparation for philosophy," according to Isocrates' definition (266–67).

That Plato identified such arguments with the sophists is apparent in a very similar evaluation of philosophy made by Callicles in the *Gorgias*:

> For philosophy, you know, Socrates, is a pretty thing if you engage in it moderately in your youth; but if you continue in it longer than you should, it is the ruin of any man. For if a man is exceptionally gifted and yet pursues philosophy far on in life, he must prove entirely unacquainted with all the accomplishments requisite for a gentleman [*kalon kagathon*] and a man of distinction. Such men know nothing of the laws in their cities, or of the language they should use in their business associations both public and private with other men. . . . And so when they enter upon any activity public or private they appear ridiculous, just as public men [*hoi politikoi*], I suppose, appear ridiculous when they take part in your discussions and arguments. (484c–e)

Callicles' perspective is virtually identical to that of Isocrates: both view dialectic as early training that prepares the student for participating in the more important affairs of the polis.

Doxa and *Epistēmē*

Plato, Protagoras, Aristotle, and Isocrates differ more in their attitudes toward than their definitions of *doxa* and *epistēmē*. "Doxa" is usually translated "opinion" and often marks a province of knowledge concerned with human affairs and behavior. "Epistēmē" generally

---

[18] For Plato's discussion of geometry, astronomy, and dialectic, see *Rep.* 521c–38a.

refers to scientific knowledge, and it is frequently associated with special skill or expertise. The contents of an epistēmē often rise above the contingencies of time and place. Thus, while doxa is contingent, mutable, and common, an epistēmē is transcendent, static, and specialized.[19]

The opposition of doxa to epistēmē is critical to Plato's differentiation of any art of discourse from philosophia. For Plato, doxa is opposed to truth (*alētheia*), as well as "science" (*epistēmē*); and it is identified with appearances (*phantasia*) and deception (*apatē*). By Socrates' account in the *Phaedrus*, knowledge consists in knowing "the truth about a given thing" (262a). This truth is the substance of an epistēmē and the product of philosophical inquiry. Socrates insists that those who give speeches in the court and in the Assembly aim only at making "the same thing appear to the same people now just, now unjust, at will" (261d). It is the nature of opinion to change and the nature of truth to remain the same; and only truth can be the subject of a "true" art.[20] Thus, Socrates bluntly concludes, "The art of speech [logōn . . . technēn] displayed by one who has gone chasing after beliefs, instead of knowing the truth, will be a comical sort of art, in fact no art at all" (262c).

In sharp contrast to any sense of knowledge as production or intervention, Platonic knowledge is a process of recollection. This conception of knowledge as the recovery of what the soul already knows is the doctrine of *anamnēsis* that appears in the *Phaedrus, Meno*, and the *Phaedo*.[21] In the *Phaedo*, Socrates explains that "we must always be born *knowing* and continue to know all through our lives, because 'to know' means simply to retain the knowledge which one has acquired, and not to lose it" (75d). Socrates explains anamnēsis another way in the *Meno*: "The soul, since it is immortal and has been born many times, and has seen all things both here and in the other world, has learned everything that is" (81c–d). A "man" can recover this knowledge, Socrates explains, provided "he keeps a stout heart and does not grow weary of the search" (81d). In the end, however, both "seeking and learning are in fact nothing but recollection" (81d).[22]

But what is the character of that knowledge? Socrates has made it

[19] Aristotle is not consistent in his use of epistēmē. In places, he uses epistēmē, much as he uses art elsewhere, to describe a rational, organized body of knowledge.

[20] See Plato, *Gorgias* 482b.

[21] See Plato, *Phaedo* 74a–76d, and *Phaedrus* 249e.

[22] For more on Platonic anamnēsis, see Guthrie, *History of Greek Philosophy*, vol. 4.

clear that it is neither changeable nor the product of sense impression. Again, matching subject type with type of knowledge, Socrates asks what kind of person will apprehend "the real nature of any given thing" (*Phaedo* 65d):

> Don't you think that the person who is likely to succeed in this attempt most perfectly is the one who approaches each object, as far as possible, with the unaided intellect, without taking account of any sense of sight in his thinking, or dragging any other sense into his reckoning—the man who pursues the truth by applying his pure and unadulterated thought to the pure and unadulterated object, cutting himself off as much as possible from his eyes and ears and virtually all the rest of his body, as an impediment which by its presence prevents the soul from attaining to truth and clear thinking? Is not this the person, Simmias, who will reach the goal of reality, if anybody can? (65e–66).

Simmias, of course, answers in the affirmative, and we know that the person will be a philosopher.

The rejection of sense impression is central to Plato's conceptions of imitation. While Platonic mimēsis is more complicated than many might wish it to be, there is little question that it is tied to Plato's Pythagorean roots.[23] Pythagorean geometry provided a model of perfect knowledge, a "changeless world of mathematics," as Guthrie puts it, that lay "behind the phenomenal world" (*History of Greek Philosophy*, 4:251). Mathematics and geometry serve as models of order throughout Plato's descriptions of knowledge, virtue, and the ideal state. They are invoked in the "art of measurement" that Socrates raises in Plato's *Protagoras*, and in the *Meno*, geometry plays an important role in explaining the teachability of virtue (82–87b). In the *Phaedo*, Socrates uses the calculation of equality to illustrate the concept of imitation. Referring to "sticks and stones," Socrates asks, "Is it not true that equal stones and sticks sometimes, without changing in themselves, appear equal to one person and unequal to another?" (74b). His interlocutor, Simmias, answers affirmatively. Socrates goes on to explain that the "approximate" equality that one recognizes is a "poor imitation." One is able to recognize equality, however, because one has "previous knowledge of that thing which he says that the other

---

[23] "Our present argument applies no more to equality than it does to absolute beauty, goodness, uprightness, holiness" (*Phaedo* 75d).

resembles, but inadequately" (74d–e). This knowledge consists of the ideas that the soul knew before birth.

Mathematics and geometry provide analogues of the highest knowledge of beauty and goodness; they also serve as propaedeutic for dialectic. In the *Republic*, geometry is subordinate only to dialectic, and even then in a rather complex way. Socrates explains that geometrical reasoning is "something intermediate" between opinion (doxa) and reasoning (*nous*) (511d). The immutable world of mathematics ensures the regularity of geometrical proofs. The practice of geometry, however, does not engage the highest form of reasoning for two reasons: it requires "hypotheses, underpinnings, footings, and springboards so to speak" (511b); and makes use of "images and likenesses" of geometric shapes (510e–11a). The aim of dialectic, according to Socrates, is to enable a kind of reasoning "which requires no assumption and is the starting point of all, . . . making no use whatever of any object of sense but only of pure ideas moving on through ideas to ideas and ending with ideas" (511b–c).

Plato uses the doxa/epistēmē distinction in a discussion in the *Republic* of the kind of knowledge that lies between "nescience" (or ignorance) and epistēmē: "Knowledge pertains to that which is and ignorance of necessity to that which is not, for that which lies between we must seek for something between nescience and science, if such a thing there be" (477a–b). Socrates makes it clear that there is such a thing, and it is that "which we call opinion" (477b). That distinction is not enough, however. Socrates goes on to insist that each type of knowledge has its own "faculty" (dynamis): "Opinion is set over one thing and science over another, each by virtue of its own distinctive power or faculty" (477b). Moreover, these faculties are unique to specific men. At the conclusion of book V, Socrates asks, "Shall we then offend their ears if we call them doxophilists rather than philosophers?" (480a). The word Plato coins is *philodoxos*, the "lover of opinion," who stands in sharp contrast to the *philosophos*, or "lover of wisdom."[24]

Plato's careful progression from types of knowledge, to unique faculties, and finally to specific kinds of people sets up the discussion that opens book VI concerning the appropriate leaders of the state. Socrates

---

[24] "To those who in each and every kind welcome the true being, lovers of wisdom [*philosophous*] and not lovers of opinion [*philodoxous*] is the name we must give" (*Rep.* 480a).

asks, "Since the philosophers are those who are capable of appre-
hending that which is eternal and unchanging, while those who are
incapable of this, but lose themselves and wander amid the multi-
plicities of multifarious things, are not philosophers, which of the two
kinds ought to be the leaders in a state?" (484b). The answer, of course,
is the philosophers, who form the guardian class of Plato's *Republic*.

Isocrates' evaluation of doxa stands in sharp contrast, if not direct
response, to two defining characteristics of Plato's true knowledge.
First, for Plato true knowledge is extricated from time and, therefore,
immune to change: "philosophy holds always to the same" (*Gorgias*
482a). For Isocrates, in contrast, it is the mark of an honest man to be
able to change his opinion when he is convinced of the justice of a
cause: "Honest men . . . do not remain fixed in opinions which they
have formed unjustly, but are in quest of the truth and are ready to be
convinced by those who plead a just cause" (*Antid.* 170). Second, in
Plato's republic, true knowledge is comprehensible solely to the small
circle of the ruling guardian class. Socrates insists that a "city established on principles of nature" would be "wise as a whole" only by
"virtue of its smallest class and minutest part of itself, and the wisdom that resides therein" (428e). He concludes that "these are by nature the fewest" who "partake of the knowledge which alone of all
forms of knowledge deserves the name of wisdom" (429). In contrast,
Isocrates declares that "if you compare me with those who profess to
turn men to a life of temperance and justice, you will find that my
teaching is more true and more profitable than theirs. For they exhort
their followers to a kind of virtue and wisdom which is ignored by the
rest of the world and is disputed among themselves; I, to a kind which
is recognized by all" (*Antid.* 84).

Protagoras outlines what is virtually an epistemology of "appearances." Placing the locus of knowledge in the two sources Plato re-
jected, the senses and opinion, Protagoras maintains that "every appearance [*phantasia*] is true" (Sprague, 11; DK, 80 A 15); and only that
which is apprehended through the senses may be said to exist: "All
things that appear to men also exist, but things which appear to no
man do not exist. . . (Sprague, 11; DK, 80 A 14.219). This faith in phantasia is at the heart of Protagoras's homo mensura doctrine.[25] Sextus
Empiricus explains:

[25] For more on Protagoras's man/measure doctrine, see Versenyi, *Man's Measure.*

Protagoras . . . will have it that of all things the measure is man [*an-thrōpon*], of things that are that they are, and things that are not that they are not, meaning by "measure" the standard of judgment, and using the word *chremata* rather than *pragmata* for "things." . . . And for this reason he posits only what appears to the individual, thus introducing relativity. . . . Now what he says is that matter is in a state of flux, and that as it changes there is a continuous replacement of the effluvia which it gives off; that, moreover, one's sensations undergo change and alteration in accordance with one's age and one's bodily condition. (Sprague, 10–11; DK, 80 A 14)

Protagoras is not referring to a secure form of empirical knowledge that depends on the standardization of either matter or human senses for its stability. Matter may be in "a state of flux," but the human senses are also mutable.

Protagoras's homo mensura doctrine is a singular example of a normative measure that resists decontextualized norms. Anthrōpos as measure is neither "man" in general nor archetypal, ideal man but rather anthrōpos (in the singular), situated in specific acts of perception. Sextus Empiricus's observation concerning Protagoras's use of "chrēmata" rather than "pragmata" further explicates Protagoras's theory of perception and value.[26] "Pragmata" generally refers to "things," including "matter[s], affair[s]" and "concrete reality" (LSJ, 1457). Though pragmata may refer to important matters (LSJ, 1457), it generally signals the kind of objectivity and distance associated with "concrete reality."[27] Chrēmata, in contrast, denotes *valuable* "things"; it may refer to things that "one needs or uses," "goods, property," "merchandise"—and even "money" (LSJ, 2004–5). In other words, *chrēmata* only denotes "things" in relation to their value either to individuals (for example, "use") or in a system of exchange. Edmunds makes a similar observation in his discussion of chrēmata in Pericles' funeral oration: chrēmata "means objects for use" (*Chance and Intelligence,* 39). One might compare the difference between pragmata and chrēmata to the difference between chronos and kairos. Time as chronos is abstract; it is time that is "extricated" from contingencies.

[26] For an interesting discussion of chrēmata and pragmata, see Untersteiner, *The Sophists,* excursus to chap. 3, 77–91.

[27] The singular *pragma,* for example, may refer to a "thing of consequence or importance," a "matter in hand, question"; the plural *pragmata* may denote "fortunes, cause, circumstances" (LSJ, 1457).

Kairos, on the other hand, is defined by contingency and perspective. Chronos contrasts with kairos in the way that "time" contrasts with "the opportune moment."

From this perspective, Protagoras's theory of knowledge *is* his theory of value; epistemology collapses into axiology. There are no decontextualized standards for evaluating either knowledge or value; what we know is what we find "worth knowing."[28] This fusion of knowledge and value is expressed in another way in Protagoras's discussion of truth, wisdom, and evil: "I think, when a man's soul is in an evil state, and so has thoughts which suit that state, then a good state of soul makes him think other thoughts, natural to that state, which some men ineptly call 'true,' whereas I call them better than the former kind but in no way truer" (Sprague, 14; DK, 80 A 21a). Protagoras's statement, which is taken from the *Theaetetus*, is a direct challenge to Plato's equation of goodness (or virtue) to absolute truth. Although Plato's equation, at one level, similarly bonds axiology to epistemology, it does so on the basis of absolute and decontextualized norms. In contrast, Protagoras replaces judgments of "the true" and "the good" with relative, situated assessments of "the better." Isocrates makes a similar point in what appears to be a direct response to Socrates' assertion that the mind of "our orator, the good and true artist" will always be "occupied with one thought, how justice may be implanted in the souls of the citizens and injustice banished, and how temperance may be implanted and indiscipline banished" (*Gorgias* 504d). Isocrates makes no such claims: "I consider that the kind of art which can implant honesty and justice in depraved natures has never existed and does not now exist. . . . But I do hold that people can become better and worthier if they conceive an ambition to speak well" (*Antid.* 274–75). Like Protagoras, Isocrates exchanges the absolute "good" for relative improvement.[29]

[28] Barbara Herrnstein Smith similarly argues the "attribution" of value is implicit in the act of perception in *Contingencies of Value*. For a specific discussion of rhetoric's relationship to the epistemology outlined by Smith, see *Pre/Text*, Special Issue on B. H. Smith, 10, 3–4 (1989).

[29] Isocrates agrees with the sophist when Socrates levels the following judgment on Callicles: "You are unaware that geometric equality is of great importance among gods and men alike, and you think we should practice overreaching [*pleonexian askein*] others" (*Gorgias* 508a). People can "become better and worthier," according to Isocrates, if they "become possessed of the desire to be able to persuade their hearers, and, finally, if they set their hearts on seizing their advantage [*pleonexias*]" (*Antid.* 275).

Protagoras's perspective on knowledge and value generously en-
franchises a "world" of discourse at two important points. First, Protagoras's theory of knowledge and value is relativistic without giving
way to either skepticism or solipsism. Though the extrication of value
from objects is precisely the move Protagoras's epistemology precludes, Protagorean relativism might be interpreted in the following
manner. For Protagoras the value and stability of "objects" of perception are "imposed"; however, they are not imposed in just any way. In
other words, relativity is not identical to radical arbitrariness. To say
that perception is an act embedded in a matrix of contingencies in-
volving both the world and the perceiver is not to say either that the
world is unknowable or that perception is only the experience of a
private self. It is to say that perceptions are situated acts of judgment,
open to question and challenge. The critical difference between Protagorean and Platonic epistemology and axiology is that in Protagoras's world these questions and challenges proceed from assessments
that, consciously and not, are based on standards embedded in our acts
of perception. Stoic epistemology bears some resemblance to that of
Protagoras in that it similarly binds perception to judgment, asserting
that "to know something is to have grasped or apprehended it in such
a way that one's grasp or apprehension cannot be dislodged by argument" (Long, *Hellenistic Philosophy*, 126). For Protagoras, however,
there is no such stopping point for argument. Moreover, while measures of value may never be fully explicit, they are not so tacit that
they cannot be revised. Protagoras's conception of wisdom and persuasion is based on the possibility of that revision. He gives the following definition of the wise man: "I call 'wise' precisely that man
who, by working a change in us, makes what is good appear and be to
any one of us to whom what is evil appears and is" (Sprague, 14; DK,
80 A 21). It is this power to institute alternative calculations of value
that is at the heart of the sophists' logōn technē as an art of making
the weaker argument appear the stronger.

Aristotle's perspective on doxa is worth raising here. Though in the
end his ideal state differs little from Plato's, in the world that is, Aristotle confers a legitimacy on doxa that Plato would have abhorred. For
Aristotle, doxa is fallible: "The states by virtue of which the soul possesses truth by way of affirmation or denial are five in number, i.e. art
[technē], knowledge, [epistēmē], practical wisdom [phronēsis], philosophic wisdom [*sophia*], and comprehension [nous]; for belief and
opinion [doxa] may be mistaken" (EN 1139b15–18). Although one may

be mistaken in opinion, doxa is still "legitimate" knowledge that is identified with practical wisdom. As if in direct response to Plato's assertions concerning the different faculties of doxa and epistēmē, Aristotle explains that of the "two parts of the soul that possess reason," practical wisdom is identified with "that part which forms opinions; for opinion [doxa] is about what can be otherwise, and so is practical wisdom [phronēsis] (EN 1140b25–28). Aristotle's willingness to confer legitimacy on doxa and the world of change is seconded in his defense of the rhetorical enthymeme:

> Since it is evident that artistic method is concerned with *pisteis* and since *pistis* is a sort of demonstration. . . , it is clear that he who is best able to see from what materials, and how, a syllogism arises would also be most enthymematic—if he grasps also what sort of things an enthymeme is concerned with and what differences it has from a logical syllogism; for it belongs to the same capacity both to see the true and [to see] what resembles the true. . . ; thus an ability to aim at commonly held opinions [*endoxa*] is a characteristic of one who also has a similar ability to regard to the truth [*sic*]. (Kennedy, 32–33; *Rhet.* 1355a3–18)

For Aristotle, the rhetor's world of doxa is not antithetical to the philosopher's world of certain knowledge. It is Plato who insists on the strict separation of the two.

Knowledge and Art in Plato's State

Technē is at the center of Plato's notions of social, political, and epistemological order, where it provides the principles that both separate other forms of knowledge from philosophy and subordinate other classes to the rule of philosopher. As with Plato's definitions of doxa and epistēmē, the relationship between art and social order is established by a series of equations: physis (nature) or faculty equals function equals place in the social order. One's function is identical to one's art, and virtue in the Platonic social order consists of fulfilling one's function. This depiction of technē contrasts sharply with earlier depictions in which technē marks and re-marks the contingent boundary between nature and culture. Instead, Plato's technē serves as an equal sign between nature and culture, effectively naturalizing a specific model of social order.

Plato's social order is rooted in Pythagorean harmonics and geometry. Pythagoras's contribution to harmonics was the determination of ratios that form an octave; these ratios, in turn, serve as geometric principles to define an "order of proportion," which amounts to an order of "unequal parts" (Wood and Wood, *Ancient Political Theory*, 162). This conception of hierarchical order, often called *harmonia*, corresponds to the ancient conception of proportional justice, described by Solon, whereby justice is a matter of distributing rights or resources according to one's merit or honor.[30] Proportional justice could still claim to protect equality; however, equality could be construed as "a relation between unequals" (Vlastos, "Equality," 156). Vlastos notes that this is precisely Solon's view of justice and order: equality obtained *within* classes, not *between* them (156). Similarly, as Vlastos points out, the model of democratic order in Thucydides VI.39 refers not "to the equal share of each and every citizen in the state but to the equal shares of the three 'parts' of the state (the rich, the wise, and the masses)" ("Isonomia," 354 n. 60).

Plato's conceptions of justice and order are at the heart of his frequent warnings to the sophists not to overstep boundaries. In the *Gorgias*, Socrates gives his most explicit judgment concerning the sophists' disregard for the state ordered by geometry:

> Wise men, Callicles, say that the heavens and the earth, gods and men, are bound together by fellowship and friendship, and order and temperance and justice, and for this reason they call the sum of things the 'ordered' universe, my friend, not the world of disorder or riot. But it seems to me that you pay no attention to these things in spite of your wisdom, but you are unaware that geometric equality is of great importance among gods and men alike, and you think we should practice overreaching [*pleonexian askein*] others, for you neglect geometry. (507e–508a)[31]

In a state bound by *harmonia*, "overreaching" is, indeed, a serious threat because each part must stay in its place or the integrity of the whole is compromised.[32]

---

[30] Wood and Wood, *Ancient Political Theory*, 162. Proportional justice is also called distributive justice. For another perspective, see Farrar, *The Origins of Democratic Thinking*.

[31] See also the interaction of Socrates with Thrasymachus in the *Republic*, in which harmonia is explicitly invoked in a discussion of the wise man who "will not wish to overreach [*pleonektein*]," (349d–50b).

[32] For a brief treatment of pleonexia, see Guthrie, *History of Greek Philosophy*, 4:309.

Plato details art's relationship to social order in the *Republic*, in which Socrates explains that "there is a specific virtue or excellence of everything for which a specific work or function is appointed" (353b). Function is a reliable determinant of social order for two reasons. First, each nature is assigned only one function: "It is impossible for one man to do the work of many arts well" (374a). Thus Socrates explains "that it is right for the cobbler by nature to cobble and occupy himself with nothing else, and the carpenter to practice carpentry, and similarly all others" (443c). Second, arts neither change nor merge their functions because "the benefit derived from each art is peculiar to it" (346c). Whereas Aristotle grounds technē in empeiria, Plato suggests that a technē is an innate function, independent of experience: "For it is not in respect of his sailing that he is called a pilot but in respect of his art and his ruling of the sailors" (341d). With art thus reduced to function and knowledge restricted to recollection, no meaningful place is left for invention.

In Plato's state, this functionalist perspective determines not only virtue but also advantage: "The art naturally exists for this, to discover and provide for each his advantage" (341d). The word for advantage here is *sympheron* rather than *pleonexia*; and while sympheron can be a synonym for pleonexia, it is clear that in this case advantage is defined as the submission to, rather than transgression of, boundaries of power and order.[33] In Plato's state, function provides both social order and the ties of human community. "The origin of the city . . . is to be found in the fact that we do not severally suffice for our own needs, but each of us lacks many things" (369b). Socrates explains that the "real creator" of the polis is "our needs" (369c–d). These "needs," in turn, further justify the "interdependent" and—for Plato—"hierarchical"—order of the state.

What is the function of the philosopher in such a state? In a note to

---

[33] Both pleonexia and sympheron can be translated "advantage." Though definitions of sympheron in LSJ tend to stress advantage within the bounds of what is "fitting," this qualification does not consistently distinguish sympheron from pleonexia. For example, Thrasymachus uses sympheron in the *Republic* in his discussion with Socrates of what becomes the "might makes right" doctrine: "I affirm that the just is nothing else than the advantage [sympheron] of the stronger" (338c). At the same time, Aristotle uses sympheron to describe one telos of deliberative discourse (*Rhet.* 1358b22). In these contexts, "sympheron" is frequently translated "expediency"; this is Roberts's translation of 1358b22. In his 1991 translation, George Kennedy uses "the advantageous." See also *Rhet.* 1362a18, 1363b7, 1375b13, 1376b29, and 1389a34.

Republic 421b, in the Loeb edition of the text, Paul Shorey maintains that the principle of "one man, one task," as he puts it, affirms that the state's order is neither arbitrary nor subject to whim (1:320). Socrates makes it clear that this principle of social order is distinctive. He asserts that the state is not a "festival," nor are its citizens "'happy' feasters" who can choose to take whatever they like (*Rep.* 421b). The happiness (*eudaimonia*) of the whole is what the guardian or philosopher class is both to create and to judge; and they do this by assigning the happiness that is appropriate to each class (421c).[34] While the goal of the republic is "not the exceptional happiness of any one class but the greatest possible happiness of the city as a whole" (420b), Socrates observes in reference to the life of the guardians that "it would not surprise us if these men thus living prove to be the most happy" (420b). Therefore the function of the philosophers is to be, literally, the crafters, or "dēmiourgoi," of the state (421c), defining (or inventing) both function and happiness for its various parts.[35]

The idea that the philosopher's function is to determine the functions of the rest of the state is similarly expressed in the *Statesman*. When the Stranger asks the young Socrates if there is an art "whose province is to decide whether or not we *ought* to learn any particular art" (304b), Socrates answers that there is indeed such an art—that of statesmanship (304d). Further, this higher-order art governs all arts, from rhetoric to warfare (304d–305a). It is a meta-art, or as Plato frankly admits, a "kingly art" (305e); and it is, of course, the rarest *technē*. As the Young Socrates affirms in the dialogue, "If the art of government is to be found in this world at all in its pure form, it will be found in the possession of one or two, or, at most, of a select few" (293a).[36]

[34] The notion of "share" in this passage is rendered by *metalambanein*, meaning to "have" or to "get a share of, partake" (LSJ, 1113).

[35] Socrates compares the guardian's task of assigning happiness to the artist's task of painting a statue: "It is as if we were coloring a statue and someone approached and censured us, saying that we did not apply the most beautiful pigments to the most beautiful parts of the image, since the eyes, which are the most beautiful part, have not been painted with purple but with black. We should think it a reasonable justification to reply, Don't expect us, quaint friend, to paint the eyes so fine that they will not be like eyes at all, nor the other parts, but observe whether by assigning what is proper to each we render the whole beautiful" (Rep 420c–d).

[36] "On this principle," according to the Stranger, "it is the men who possess the art of ruling and these only, whom we are to regard as rulers, whatever constitutional form their rule may take. It makes no difference whether their subjects be willing or unwilling" (*Statesman* 293b).

Plato's functionalist doctrine is designed to order hierarchically the diverse parts of the state. Ironically, however, the doctrine's distinction between external and internal justice, together with the attendant focus on specific purpose, autonomy, self-control, and "minding one's own affairs," produces a "sense" of self that is often appropriated as a general model of subjectivity. This issue arises toward the conclusion of book IV of the *Republic* in Socrates' distinction between internal and external justice.[37] External justice refers to the submission to function; it is the principle "that it is right for the cobbler by nature to cobble and occupy himself with nothing else, and the carpenter to practise carpentry, and similarly all others" (443c). Internal justice deals with "that which is within and in the true sense concerns one's self, and the things of one's self" (443d). In explaining this kind of justice, Socrates refers to the three principles of the soul—reason, appetite, and spirit—which are then related to Pythagorean harmonics. Socrates describes the man who seeks justice in the fullest sense:

> He . . . should dispose well of what in the true sense of the word is properly his own, and having first attained to self-mastery and beautiful order within himself, and having harmonized these three principles, the notes or intervals of three terms quite literally the lowest, the highest, and the mean, and all others there may be between them, and having linked and bound all three together and made of himself a unit, one man instead of many, self-controlled [*sōphrona*] and in unison. (443d–e)[38]

Only after attaining this state of harmony is a man ready to turn to "the getting of wealth," the care of the body, "political action" (*politikon*), or "private business" (*ta idia*) (443e). Even then, the plumb line, of sorts, for justice is the preservation of this internal "state." This man must believe "the just and honourable action to be that which preserves and helps to produce this condition of soul, and . . . the unjust action to be that which ever tends to overthrow this spiritual constitution" (443e–44a). Moreover, "wisdom" (sophia) is the science (epistēmē) that will maintain this state, and "opinion" (doxa) the ignorance that allows it to be overthrown (443e–44a). Though in different terms, a similar emphasis on autonomy is found in book X of

---

[37] At places in the *Republic* Plato uses *dikaiosynē* rather than *dikē*; see 433a and 443b–45e.

[38] For more on *sōphrosynē*, see *Rep.* 430d–32b; *Phaedrus* 68c, 237e; and *Charmides* 433a–b. See also Guthrie, *History of Greek Philosophy*, 4:166, and North, *Sophrosyne*.

the *Laws*. There, the soul is defined as "the motion which can set itself moving"—or "self-movement" (896a). Just as the parts of the state are hierarchically defined by different functions, souls are hierarchically defined by different types of movement. Motion that is "induced by something else" must "come second in the scale, or as low down as you please to put it"—even a "truly soulless body" (896b).

A briefer discussion of internal justice appears in book IX of the *Republic*. Socrates explains that the man guided by internal justice will "keep his eyes fixed on the constitution in his soul" (*Rep.* 591e). Glaucon observes that the city they have described "can be found nowhere on earth" (592a–b). Socrates agrees but suggests that "there is a pattern of it laid up in heaven for him who wishes to contemplate it and so beholding to constitute himself its citizen" (592b). That being the case, "it makes no difference whether it exists now or ever will come into being" (592b); for this polis can be the philosopher's own private "state": "The politics of this city only will be his and of none other" (592b). The same sentiment is expressed in book IV, when Socrates puts forth the proposition that "the having and doing of one's own and what belongs to oneself would . . . be justice" (434a).

Plato's predilection for resolving the problems of the polis in the mind of the philosopher points to two important characteristics of his conception of art, politics, and social order. First, social order and ties of community are primarily defined as vertical hierarchies of function. "Needs" create the state, according to Socrates. Diverse arts exist to meet those needs (*Rep.* 369b–c); and the order of the polis resides in citizens' fidelity to their respective functions. Plato's conception of both community and art contrasts sharply, as we shall see, with that of Protagoras, who maintains that respect (aidōs) and justice (dikē) create bonds of philia and order in the polis. Moreover, as Socrates describes it, the internal state of justice is defined in reference to the self rather than to the community. Though commonsense wisdom would affirm that one must attend to the order of one's soul before one can attend to the order of the state, one might question the capacity of Plato's internal state of justice to provide a general model of citizenship. In one sentence, Guthrie points to both the implicit political quietism of such an idea and its usefulness to Christian religious traditions. Referring to Socrates' admission at 592a–b that the republic they have described will likely hold a citizenry of one, Guthrie concludes, "The search is less for a city than for personal righteousness" (*History of Greek Philosophy*, 4:486).

Second, though Socrates prescribes internal justice for all members of the state (*Rep.* 443d–e), it would seem unlikely that all citizens—from cobblers to guardians—would be equally free to attend to the matters of the soul that this internal harmony requires. At points, it appears that the relationship Plato posits between the individual and the state is one of direct transfer. Socrates explains: "We supposed that, if we found some larger thing that contained justice and viewed it there, we should more easily discover its nature in the individual man" (434d).[39] As Guthrie suggests, the "next step" would appear to be "to transfer our findings to the individual" (*History of Greek Philosophy*, 4:473). The one connection between the individual and the state that Socrates is most anxious to make, however, is that between the soul's three principles and the state's three classes. Indeed, just before Socrates raises the relationship between the individual and the state, he insists on clarifying one more time both justice and injustice. Justice is "this principle of doing one's own business" (*Rep.* 433b); and injustice is "the interference with one another's business . . . of three existent classes, and the substitution of the one for the other" (434b). Consequently, as "the city was thought to be just because three natural kinds existing in it performed each its own function," one should "expect the individual also to have these same forms in his soul" (435b–c). While the "whole" of the state should exist in each of its parts, those parts can still differ in kind—and certainly in importance.

The tension between Plato's normative ideal of justice and his hierarchical, functional state gives way to a number of suspicious "default" modes that preserve the normative force of the ideal, while exempting certain members of the state from its demands, as well as its rewards. In further exploring the relationship between external and internal justice, Socrates seems to admit as much when he describes internal justice as virtually a form of private property: "it is better for everyone to be governed by the divine and the intelligent, preferably indwelling and his own" (590d–e). "In default of that," however, such governance can be "imposed from without" (590d). Similarly, sōphrosynē, which Shorey translates as "soberness," is described as a virtue all citizens should possess—both "the rulers and the ruled" (431e). It is characterized as "a kind of concord and harmony"—a "beautiful order" that results when a man has become the "'master of himself'" (430e). Still, sōphrosynē itself has different functions

---

[39] See also *Rep.* 435a–b.

depending on one's role in the state. "Concord" is, indeed, the fruit of sōphrosynē because the "unanimity" it engenders is "the concord of the naturally superior and inferior as to which ought to rule both in the state and the individual" (432a).

Plato's careful description of internal as well as external order amounts to a prescription according to which subjects both acquiesce to and reproduce the relations of power crafted by the guardians. In a note on 370a in the *Republic*, Shorey aptly observes that Plato "anticipates the advantages of the division of labour as set forth in Adam Smith" (151). In turn, Anthony Arblaster describes how Smith posits the individual's acquiescence to function in such a state:

> He observed that he had 'never known much good done by those who affected to trade for the public good,' while on the other hand the individual (Smith uses this term) who seeks 'his own advantage . . . and not that of the society' discovers that 'the study of his own advantage naturally, or rather necessarily, leads him to prefer that employment which is most advantageous to the society.' Although 'He generally, indeed, neither intends to promote the public interest nor knows how much he is promoting it.' Yet 'he is in this, as in many other cases, led by an invisible hand to promote an end which was no part of his intention. Nor is it always the worse for the society that it was not part of it. By pursuing his own interest he frequently promotes that of the society more effectually than when he really intends to promote it.' (*Western Liberalism*, 34; Arblaster's ellipses)

Like Plato, Smith asserts that "advantage" resides in fulfilling one's function in the state (*Rep.* 341d). The problem lies in the tautological relationship between function and advantage. That one would fare better in a society by submitting to a prescribed function might just as easily bear witness to the intractability of a class system as it does to the intrinsic value of "finding one's place."

In Plato's case, the hand that guides subjects toward their respective functions is not so invisible since this "guidance" is the explicit task of the guardians. Though all members have a function in Plato's state, it is clear that not all functions are equally valuable. Socrates admits that if a cobbler, for example, pretended to another function, he would pose "no great danger to the state" (421a). Guardians who do not fulfill their function, however, are capable of destroying it (421a–e). Indeed, according to Socrates, guardians should not be allotted happiness that might "make them anything but guardians" (420d). One could try to reassign happiness to other classes. "We could make," as Socrates explains, the "potters recline on couches from left to right before the fire drinking toasts and feasting with their wheel alongside to potter with when they are so disposed" (420e).[40] Such action might challenge the form of the polis, but it does not pose the same threat as confusing the happiness and function of the guardians.

Given the differences in both function and happiness, it would seem unlikely that the normative standard of "internal justice" will be achieved by all. As we shall see, Aristotle outlines a similar state of internal equilibrium in his concept of eudaimonia. Never for a moment, however, does he suggest such a "state" would be attained by anyone outside the philosopher/ruler class. Indeed, this "state" of subjectivity would appear to be the philosopher's construction and his reward. The "individual" in Plato's state is likely to be, as Arblaster puts it, "the exceptional individual" (*Western Liberalism*, 48).

Protagoras's Prometheus Narrative

Many of the issues raised thus far reach something of a climax in Plato's *Protagoras*. The dialogue contains encounters between Socrates and Protagoras that demonstrate the incommensurability of their paradigms of knowledge, subjectivity, and social order.[41] It includes one more version of the Prometheus narrative—and all this in the context of a debate concerning the teachability of virtue.[42]

The dialogue begins with Socrates' interrogation of the young Hippocrates, who has announced his intention to meet Protagoras. Hippocrates and Socrates engage in a brief round of dialectic, in which Socrates pushes the younger man, unsuccessfully, to define the subject matter of the instruction he expects to receive from Protagoras. Both men go to the house of Callias to meet the sophist, and Socrates raises the discussion he has had with Hippocrates. Protagoras gives

---

[40] "We could clothe the farmers in robes of state and deck them with gold and bid them cultivate the soil at their pleasure" (*Rep.* 420e).

[41] For other interpretations of these issues, see Adkins, "*Aretē, Technē*, Democracy and Sophists," and Nehamas, "Eristic, Antilogic, Sophistic, Dialectic."

[42] For one approach to the dialogue, see Maguire, "Protagoras . . . or Plato?" For more on Protagoras, see Schiappa, *Protagoras and Logos*, and Morrison, "Protagoras in Athenian Public Life."

two initial responses to Socrates' question concerning what Hippocrates will receive from the sophist. Protagoras replies directly to Hippocrates: "Young man, if you come to me, your gain will be this. The very day you join me, you will go home a better man, and the same the next day. Each day you will make progress toward a better state" (*Protag.* 318a). Socrates presses Protagoras in the same way he did Hippocrates: "Toward what, Protagoras, and better at what?" (318d). Protagoras's second reply could serve as something of a standard definition of the logōn technē tradition: "The proper care of his personal affairs, so that he may best manage his own household, and also of the state's affairs so as to become a real power in the city, both as a speaker and a man of action" (318e–19). Socrates asks in response if Protagoras is referring to "the art of politics [*tēn technēn politikēn*], and promising to make men good citizens [*politas*]" (319a). Protagoras responds in the affirmative.[43]

Socrates then launches into a critique of the democratic conception of political art, which explicates the observation in the *Republic* that the state is not a festival and citizens "happy feasters" who may take what they want. Socrates observes that when Athens begins a building project, architects are called; when ships are needed, shipbuilders are solicited (*Protag,* 319b). Moreover, if someone who is not an expert (or craftsman) in these arts should attempt to give Athens expert advice, that person would be ridiculed and even ejected from the Assembly (319c). It is only in regard to matters of state that "the man who gets up to advise them may be a builder or equally well a blacksmith or a shoemaker, merchant or shipowner, rich or poor, of good family or none" (319d). Socrates then concludes, perhaps with irony, that since no one is ever criticized for not being an "expert" in the art of statesmanship, Athenians must "not think this is a subject that can be taught" (319d).

Protagoras responds with his version of the Prometheus narrative, but the incommensurability between Socrates' and Protagoras's conceptions of knowledge and subjectivity is firmly established early in the dialogue. Socrates asks "what"; Protagoras answers "who." Socrates raises dialectical concerns of definition and analysis; Pro-

---

[43] For treatments of Protagoras's conception of the teachability of virtue, see Adkins, "*Aretē, Technē,* Democracy, and Sophists," and Roseman, "Protagoras and the Foundations of His Educational Thought." For a perspective on philosophers, sophists, and teaching, see Blank's "Socratics versus Sophists on Payment for Teaching."

tagoras responds with stories and descriptions of general opinion. That the two are dealing with largely irreconcilable paradigms might be inferred by the negotiation, which at one point gives way to conflict, over the "rules of argument." Before Protagoras begins the Prometheus narrative, he asks Socrates if he should give his explanation as a story or a reasoned argument. The audience invites Protagoras to choose, and the sophist then relates the Prometheus myth. Approximately halfway through the dialogue, however, Socrates protests that he cannot tolerate Protagoras's extended responses (334c–d). He tries to insist that Protagoras follow the rules of dialectic and respond to Socrates' questions with brief answers (335a). Observing that Protagoras will "not of his own free will continue in the role of answerer," Socrates prepares to leave (335a–b). Their audience intervenes, and a compromise of sorts is reached, which clearly favors Socrates' wishes. The rules of dialectic will govern their discussion; Protagoras is simply allowed to ask questions first.[44]

In many ways, Protagoras's Prometheus narrative holds little in common with those of Hesiod and Aeschylus. Prometheus's technē is not really tied to wily intelligence, and his personality and struggle receive no meaningful treatment. The strongest shaping force on Protagoras's version is its service as a response to Socrates' discussion of political art. Consequently, Protagoras's narrative shares with the others concerns with apportionment (moira) and the defining characteristics of human community.[45]

Protagoras begins his version with the creation of mortal creatures, who are brought to Epimetheus and Prometheus to be allotted their distinctive features and powers. Epimetheus persuades Prometheus to give him the task (320d). Epimetheus distributes these characteristics and abilities so that creatures that are given strength are not allotted speed, and those allotted speed lack strength: "To those that he endowed with smallness, he granted winged flight or a dwelling underground; to those which he increased in stature, their size itself was a protection" (320e). His mode of distribution is intended to prevent any one species from either dominating or being destroyed (320e–21). He then equips them with appropriate protection from the elements and

[44] For more on Platonic dialectic, see Nehamas, "Eristic, Antilogic, Sophistic, Dialectic."

[45] For other approaches to Protagoros's Great Speech, see McNeal, "Protagoras the Historian"; Moore, "Democracy and Commodity Exchange"; and Kerferd, "Protagoras' Doctrine of Justice."

similarly assigns to each a form of sustenance, again in such a way that no one species could cause the extinction of another (321b–c). With typical absence of forethought, however, Epimetheus dispenses all the powers given him to the animals, leaving humankind "naked, unshod, unbedded, and unarmed" (321c).

Protagoras observes that Prometheus has already lost "the right of entry to the citadel where Zeus dwelt" (321d). But "by stealth" he penetrates the "dwelling shared by Athena and Hephaestus, in which they practiced their art, . . . and carrying off Hephaestus' art of working with fire, and the art of Athena as well, he gave them to man" (321d–e). Protagoras claims that Prometheus's theft gave humankind "a share in the portion of the gods [*theias moiras*]," which led not only to kinship with the gods but also to the discovery of other technai (322a). Protagoras's list of the arts resembles that of Aeschylus: "By the art which they possessed, men soon discovered articulate speech and names, and invented houses and clothes and shoes and bedding and got food from the earth" (322a).

The most important part of Protagoras's version, however, is still to come. The technai do provide humankind with "the means of life" (322a). In sharp contrast to Plato's republic, however, these arts do *not* form the bonds of the polis. Humankind seeks safety from wild beasts by "coming together and founding fortified cities" (322b). But not even the need for safety creates viable ties of community: "When they gathered in communities they injured one another for want of political skill [*politikēn technēn*], and so scattered and continued to be devoured" (322b–c). To save humankind from extinction, Zeus sends Hermes to distribute "the qualities of respect for others [*aidō*] and a sense of justice [*dikēn*], so as to bring order into our cities and create a bond of friendship [*desmois philias*] and union" (322c).[46] When Hermes asks if respect and justice should be distributed like the other arts "on the principle that one trained doctor suffices for many laymen, and so with other experts," Zeus replies that they must be distributed to all: "Let all have their share. There could never be cities if only a few shared in these virtues" (322d). Thus Protagoras concludes that Athenians do not call experts in matters of political wisdom because they also believe that "everyone must share in this kind of virtue; otherwise the state could not exist" (323).

Before turning over the discussion to Socrates, Protagoras makes

[46] See also Cairns, *Aidōs*.

several more arguments from doxa. He points out that people willingly acknowledge ignorance of many arts (his example is flute playing), but it would be considered madness for people to proclaim publicly their deficiencies in civic virtue (323a–b). He also contends that we do not punish those who by chance or nature are weak or ill formed, but we do punish those who commit acts contrary to civic virtue. This argument makes two points for Protagoras. Because we punish those who commit public vices, we must expect public virtues from all. Moreover, our willingness to punish bears witness to our conviction that public virtue may be taught, for "punishment is not inflicted by a rational man for the sake of the crime that has been committed . . . but for the sake of the future, to prevent either the same man or, by the spectacle of his punishment, someone else, from doing wrong again" (324b). In a similar vein, Protagoras points to the care people take in raising their children as further proof that civic virtue can be taught. The education he describes from 325a through 326e is a paradigmatic description of one form of paideia. Mother, father, nurse, and tutor all pay diligent attention to the child's behavior, "instructing him through everything he does or says, pointing out, 'This is right and that is wrong, this honorable and that disgraceful, this holy, that impious; do this, don't do that'" (325d). Protagoras goes on to compare the modeling of the writing master to that of a state's laws:

> You know how, when children are not yet good at writing, the writing master traces outlines with the pencil before giving them the slate, and makes them follow the lines as a guide in their own writing; well, similarly the state sets up the laws . . . and compels the citizens to rule and be ruled in accordance with them. Whoever strays outside the lines, it punishes, and the name given to this punishment both among yourselves and in many other places is correction, intimating that the penalty corrects or guides. (326c–e)

Protagoras concludes that virtue is "something in which no one may be a layman [*idiōteuein*] if a state is to exist at all" (327a).

The focus shifts abruptly when Socrates reenters the dialogue. He immediately turns to the dialectical problem of defining virtue—in particular, the question of virtue's unity. As many scholars have observed, the discussion is filled with problems.[47] Guthrie describes it

---

[47] For recent treatments of Plato's conception of virtue and the dialogue *Protagoras*, see Irwin, *Plato's Ethics*, chaps. 3 and 6.

as a "labyrinth of petty and sometimes fallacious argument through which Socrates leads Protagoras" (*History of Greek Philosophy*, 4:222). Socrates begins with the analogy of parts of virtue to the parts of the face: "Is virtue a single whole" like the "parts of a face ... mouth, nose, eyes, and ears—or like the parts of a piece of gold which do not differ from one another or from the whole except in size?" (329c–d). For Socrates, the face is an image of the relationship of functional parts to the whole, analogous to Plato's state. Eventually, Socrates secures Protagoras's assent to the proposition that happiness is directly tied to the avoidance of evil and pain. The dialectical distinctions that follow appear designed to demonstrate that only a very careful calculus can accurately evaluate the means/end relationships that bring about either happiness or pain. Socrates then asks Protagoras: "If now our happiness consisted in doing, I mean in choosing, greater lengths and avoiding smaller, where would lie salvation? In the art of measurement or in the impression made by appearances?" (356d). The argument has been crafted so that Protagoras, in the end, wearily agrees that only Socrates' art of measurement can assure a "good life." It is clear that in the second half of the dialogue the terms and rules of argument can only nullify Protagoras's epistemology. His own doctrine of measurement, that "anthrōpos" is the measure of all things, is not even raised.

The first half of the dialogue, however, clearly establishes the distinctive features of Protagoras's logōn technē. First, it is inextricably tied to the affairs of the polis. It is not only an art that allows one to change one's share, or moira; it is an art in which all citizens must have a share. Second, like Plato's instruction, its end is also virtue; Plato's and Protagoras's conceptions of virtue, however, hold little in common. Protagorean virtue is constitutive of social and political ties, not an internal state of justice. Indeed, in the existent Protagorean texts it is difficult to find any discussions of the internality of the subject similar to Plato's internal justice. Third, though Protagoras does not mark out a self-contained subject, his paideia has far more to do with the construction of a subject than with the delineation of subject matter, an art, or knowledge per se. Though his curriculum includes music, poetry, and "panegyrics of the good men of old," they are included "so that the child may be inspired to imitate them and long to be like them" (326a). That subject is not defined by its own coherence but by action in personal and public affairs.

The conflicts raised in the *Protagoras* appear in different forms in the *Gorgias* and the *Phaedrus*. In the *Gorgias*, a dispute similar to that in the Protagoras arises when Socrates presses the sophist to define the epistēmē of rhētorikē (449d–e). The sophist responds with the word "logos," here translated as "words" (449e). Socrates points out that each art "is concerned with words that have to do with its own subject matter" (450b).[48] At one point, they appear to agree on the definition of rhetoric as "the art which secures its effect through words" (450e). Like Protagoras, however, Gorgias is led down a dialectical path where he will assent to Socrates' definition of rhetoric as "a creator of a conviction that is persuasive but not instructive about right and wrong" (455a). Socrates' proposition is designed to bring Gorgias one step closer to placing rhetoric outside Plato's domain of true knowledge in the province of empeiria—and thus appearances—where it "produces gratification and pleasure," but not true knowledge (462c–d). No one can define a subject matter for the art of discourse that meets Socrates' epistemological requirements. In the *Republic*, Socrates explains that "a particular science of a particular kind is of some particular thing of a particular kind" (438c). This is a standard rhetoric can never meet—it is the crux of the incommensurability between Plato's philosophy and Protagoras's technē.

Marking the Boundaries of Fate

The Myth of Er, which concludes Plato's *Republic*, deals in part with the same issues of distribution and varying abilities found in the Prometheus and prehistory accounts of technē.[49] In Plato's myth, however, technē is conspicuously absent, and what is at issue is not distribution but "judgment" and "choice." By depicting choice as an individual faculty, Plato in effect universalizes a specific model of virtue and subjectivity. As we have seen, however, that model is a serviceable ideal to only a few.

Er is a slain warrior who revives on his funeral pyre twelve days after his own death, and his story details the events of those twelve days. The warrior describes dispensations of judgments, punishments, and blessings and then relates the manner in which new lives are allotted. He explains that the dead are brought to a meadow where they behold

---

[48] What is translated here as "subject matter" is *pragma*.

[49] See Kirk et al., *The Presocratic Philosophers*, 259.

a light stretched like a pillar between two extremities. This light is the "girdle of the heavens"; and, as the story goes, "from the extremities was stretched the spindle of Necessity, through which all the orbits turned" (616c). Eight whorls are in orbit, like "boxes that fit into one another" (616d). The spindle turns on "the knees of Necessity," and eight Sirens stand near the rim of each whorl, uttering a single note (617b). Enthroned by Necessity as well are her daughters, the three Fates, who also sing: "Lachesis singing the things that were, Clotho the things that are, and Atropos the things that are to be" (617c).

Lachesis announces that the group has come to the place "where birth is the beacon of death"; however, this time "no divinity shall cast lots for you, but you shall choose your own deity [*daimona*]" (617e). In other words, lives will not be *assigned* to the group; each will choose his or her own life from a large pool of "patterns of lives before them on the ground, far more numerous than the assembly" (618a). The lot will determine only in what order they will choose; and the warrior is careful to explain that there are enough "extra" lives that "even for him who comes forward last, if he make his choice wisely and live strenuously, there is reserved an acceptable life, no evil one" (619b). The lives are many—lives of men and women, as well as animals. They include lives of tyranny, penury, and exile, as well as lives famous for beauty, strength, and virtue (618a–b). "Souls," however, are not included with these lives: "But there was no determination of the quality of soul, because the choice of a different life inevitably determined a different character" (618b). Thus, the narrative recounts the "strange, pitiful, and ridiculous spectacle" of watching souls select their lives (619e–20).

What is at stake, as Socrates makes clear, is finally to discover the type of teacher who could give one "the ability and the knowledge to distinguish the life that is good from that which is bad, and always and everywhere to choose the best that the conditions allow" (618c). Socrates enumerates some of these conditions in what, at points, seems a cold-blooded eugenic experiment. He ponders the effects of "beauty commingled with poverty or wealth" and "of high and low birth . . . and strength and weakness and quickness of apprehension and dullness" (618c–d). The critical difference here is that "necessity" is posterior to choice: "Let him to whom falls the first lot first select a life to which he shall cleave of necessity [*ex anankēs*]. . . . The blame is his who chooses. God is blameless" (617e).

One important question is raised by this experiment: How is the soul shaped to make a choice? Through myth, Plato constructs a place outside of time, where choice, supposedly, can be extricated from situation. It is there that one may choose one's own condition—indeed, choose one's fate, the very action that by definition "fate" disallows. Socrates would appear to point to his own contradiction when he admits that decisions tend to be made on the basis of "habits in former lives"; and thus he acknowledges, to some extent, that souls are products of conditions. For the most part, however, the narrative transforms *choice* into both a standard of judgment and unit of measure: choosing the worse life will make the soul more unjust; choosing the better life will make it more just (618e).

The problem is that to choose one's own condition is not only to mitigate fate and necessity but also virtually to deny their existence. For the most part, moira referred to the constraints embedded in conditions—one's given share. As we know from numerous textual sources and studies, many Greek traditions insisted that virtue and "conditions"—which is to say "class"—were synonymous.[50] Thus, Plato's association of virtue with moira is not exceptional; his introduction of choice is. Such a depiction of individual choice would have seemed ludicrous in many predemocratic traditions, where the single uncontestable fact of life was that one begins with an allotted portion that may or may not differ significantly from those apportioned to others. In certain historical situations, that portion might be questioned, contested, and adjusted; but however unfair an allotted portion might be, there was no denial that one's lot was clearly tied to one's definition of the self and one's role in the culture. Subjectivity remained tied to systems of power, resources, and distribution, which could never be put in the background. More important, as long as these systems were *not* denied, they were subject either to renegotiation or to overthrow. One may be given a poor lot in life; and for that reason one may be seen as possessing very little virtue.[51] At the same time, one is not held responsible—or blamed—for the meagerness of one's allotted portion. At the heart of most myths of fate and necessity is precisely this sense of assignation—or fate—and not choice.

In contrast, Plato's Myth of Er places choice at the center of virtue,

[50] See Marrou, *Education in Antiquity*, especially chap. 4, and Vlastos, *"Isonomia."*
[51] See Edmunds's translation and discussion of WD 686: "for wretched mortals, their goods are their life" (*Chance and Intelligence*, 40).

a relocation with ambiguous consequences. One clear point of the myth is to separate aretē from birth, which might appear to make virtue more accessible—even "democratic." The obfuscation of conditions in individual choice, however, creates the familiar twentieth-century conception of a "level playing field." If no individual is "forcibly" denied the power of "choice" in a democracy that places supreme value on individual self-determination, then democracy's work is assumed to be finished. In other words, such liberal democracies assume the stage of Plato's Myth of Er: to confer democratic citizenship is to allow citizens to choose their own lives.

The significance of Plato's fissure between subjectivity and conditions is easy to underestimate and difficult to explain, for what is at stake is the control and reproduction of limits by which fate, necessity, virtue, and subjectivity are defined. The extrication of subjectivity from contexts opens the way for conceiving the subject as a standard, interchangeable unit, defined—as Plato depicts it—by personal choice.[52] Such a model of subjectivity assumes that human choice may transcend matrices of obligations, rewards, roles, habits, and activities. In his critique of this conception of subjectivity, Bourdieu suggests that limits are, for good and ill, constitutive of "subjectivity." In other words, "finding our place" in culture is a matter of hitting a mark between aiming too high and aiming too low; however, this process is not done in isolation—and it certainly is not "a choice." As Bourdieu puts it, mechanisms of socialization exist not only "to engender aspirations and practices objectively compatible" with agents' conditions but also to exclude "improbable practices" (OTP, 77). Bourdieu gives the following description of the kind of "practical calculation" by which subjects find their place in the "world":

> Unlike the estimation of probabilities which science constructs methodically on the basis of controlled experiments from data established according to precise rules, practical evaluation of the likelihood of the success of a given action in a given situation brings into play a whole body of wisdom, sayings, commonplaces, ethical precepts ("that's not for the likes of us") and, at a deeper level, the unconscious principles of the *ethos* which . . . determines "reasonable" and "unreasonable" conduct for every agent subjected to those regularities. (77)

---

[52] See the preface to Bourdieu, LP, especially p. 22.

As Bourdieu observes, the same point was made succinctly in eighteenth-century Scotland: "'We are no sooner acquainted with the impossibility of satisfying any desire,'" says Hume in *A Treatise of Human Nature*, "'than the desire itself vanishes'" (OTP, 77).

The acts of exclusion by which agents reconstitute limits take a number of forms. What is practically calculated as "unlikely" may be dismissed "without examination as *unthinkable*" (OTP, 77). In other words, it is possible to recreate a doxic relationship to the world by repositioning what is "unlikely" in the domain of the "unthinkable." Thus, acts of exclusion involve agents in a strange complicity with the conditions that made the attainment of certain goals unlikely in the first place—a "double negation," according to Bourdieu, "which inclines agents to make a virtue of necessity, that is, to refuse what is anyway refused and to love the inevitable" (OTP, 77).

Such acts of exclusion may be described as the embodiment of limits. This sense of "embodiment" functions much like Stanley Fish's description of "belief," which he contrasts with "theory":

> A theory is a special achievement of consciousness; a belief is a prerequisite for being conscious at all. Beliefs are not what you think *about* but what you think with, and it is within the space provided by their articulations that mental activity—including the activity of theorizing— goes on. Theories are something you can have—you can wield them and hold them at a distance; beliefs have *you*, in the sense that there can be no distance between them and the acts they enable. . . . [B]eliefs . . . cannot be the object of my attention, because they are the content of my attention. . . . Beliefs affect behavior—not because they are consulted when a problem presents itself, however, but because it is within the world they deliver that the problem and its possible solutions take shape. ("Consequences," 116–17)

The two points on which Bourdieu and Fish would clearly agree is that beliefs are contingent on specific conditions and that they are incalculably powerful. We do not *have* to believe in the law of gravity to keep from floating out of our chairs, nor do we *have* to believe that the earth is round in order to have a satisfying life. However, the strong belief that the earth is flat could do more than convince us not to attempt a long sea voyage; it could prevent us from ever even imagining the possibility. As Fish makes clear, beliefs do more than define how we think *about* the world and the problems and opportunities it presents. Instead, beliefs construct—or deliver—the world as we know it, with its problems and opportunities already formed.

The often dark magic at work here is twofold. At one level, the most effective limits preclude imagining the possibility of their transcendence. At another level, if imagining the transcendence of limits is *possible*, but actually transgressing those limits is highly *improbable*, then agents often, as Bourdieu puts it, "make a virtue of necessity" and refuse to attempt what appears to be doomed to failure. In other words, when the possibility of transcending a situation by any number of personal acts of will remains highly unlikely, the one act of will guaranteed to be successful is that of refusing to play the game. The more inevitable certain limits appear, the more staunchly their transcendence may be refused. The staunch refusal of what is already denied is precisely the alchemy that transforms social contingency into necessity. Put more simply, as long as "nothing succeeds like success," then "nothing will fail like failure."

In this context, the two apothegms "Necessity is the mother of invention" and "Making a virtue of necessity" take on new significance. In the one case, to call necessity the parent—indeed the mother—of invention is to say that necessity gives birth to its own undoing, for invention will change or deform a limit once seen as "necessary." In the other case, to make a virtue of necessity is to do more than to acquiesce; it is to ascribe a positive social value to an intractable limit, which for a time is likely to ensure the reproduction of that limit. Moreover, the limits reproduced by agents who have acquiesced to boundaries are perhaps the most impenetrable because they are "embodied." The more limits are "embodied," the less likely are agents to question the principles by which they are marked and the forces by which they are maintained. In sum, rational subjectivity requires the experience of limits; what is at stake, however, are the forces that determine those limits and the "available means" of transgressing and renegotiating them.

The question raised by Plato's myth differs little from the question raised by Strauss. Why doesn't every subject choose to ascend the ladder of virtue? Strauss similarly claims that the state depends on virtue, and virtue depends on the inculcation of reason and wisdom. By Strauss's account, however, reason and wisdom are the peculiar property of aristocracy.[53] Education in Strauss's state is the means by

---

[53] See the discussion in Chapter 1; references are taken from Strauss, *Liberalism Ancient and Modern*, see especially pp. 4–5.

which mass democracy is transformed into democracy proper; and true democracy is simply a broadened aristocracy. In other words, a democracy supposedly provides the stage of the Myth of Er, on which every subject has the opportunity to choose to be an "exceptional" subject. The absence of technē in the Myth of Er illustrates the distance between Plato's conception of virtue and traditions of technē—such as that of Protagoras—according to which technē is a means of challenging, mitigating, and even changing, one's fate.

6 Aristotle and the Boundaries of the Good Life

> A subject is never the condition of possibility of language or the cause of the statement: there is no subject, only collective assemblages of enunciation. Subjectification is simply one such assemblage and designates a formalization of expression or a regime of signs rather than a condition internal to language. Neither is it a question of a movement characteristic of ideology, as Althusser says: subjectification as a regime of signs or a form of expression is tied to an assemblage, in other words, an organization of power that is already fully functioning in the economy, rather than superposing itself upon contents or relations between contents determined as real in the last instance. Capital is a point of subjectification par excellence.
>
> —Gilles Deleuze and Félix Guattari, *Thousand Plateaus*

Much of the history of Western rhetoric has been the story of attempts to transform the art into some form of either philosophy or ethics/politics. As we shall see in the next chapter, Aristotle's division of knowledge into the theoretical, practical, and productive has been invoked as the authority for both transformations. For Aristotle, what we now call philosophy was theoretical knowledge; it was the "highest knowledge" and encompassed the study of metaphysics, mathematics, and the natural sciences. Practical knowledge consisted of the study of ethics and politics and was explicitly directed toward the end of *eudaimonia*, variously translated as "happiness" or "the good life." These transformations of rhetoric into either theoretical or practical knowledge were possible only by dismissing the third category in Aristotle's epistemological taxonomy, productive knowledge. This domain incorporated all the important technai—architecture, navigation, medicine, and, as I shall argue, rhetoric.

Consequently, Aristotle plays a complex role in the transformation of the logōn technē tradition. Many of the ancient connotations associated with technē are reinscribed in Aristotle's domain of productive knowledge. In contrast, rhetoric is anything but an art of intervention and invention when it is revised to meet the criteria of Aristotle's categories of theoretical and practical knowledge. The problem of rhetoric's place in Aristotle's divisions of knowledge becomes even more tangled in the nineteenth and twentieth centuries, when post-Enlightenment perspectives on knowledge fostered the binary opposition of theory to practice, which only further obscured the place of Aristotle's productive knowledge.[1]

To argue that rhetoric is a productive art, outside Aristotle's domains of theoretical and practical knowledge, is to challenge a number of assumptions and interpretive traditions.[2] Generally, it has been somewhat easier to extricate rhetoric from Aristotle's category of theoretical knowledge since its defining characteristic (it is static knowledge that serves no earthly end) is clearly ill suited to an art concerned with the everyday affairs of the polis. But defining rhetoric's relationship to practical knowledge presents another set of problems. Do we really want to argue that rhetoric is distinct from ethics? Do we want to teach a rhetoric that does not aim at the good life?

I hope to show that there is good reason for rescuing rhetoric from Aristotle's domain of practical knowledge as well. Theoretical and practical knowledge intersect in Aristotle's concept of eudaimonia, and for Aristotle eudaimonia was a very specific model of subjectivity and social and political order. Aristotle appears to conclude that eudaimonia is a *hexis*, or "state," that is one with the contemplation of the highest knowledge, which consists of the first principles of theoretical knowledge.[3] More important, subjectivity in this hexis undergoes a kind of apotheosis by virtue of its ability to appropriate the highest objects of knowledge. Indeed, as Aristotle describes it, subjectivity itself becomes a form of private property.

Although Aristotle outlined a very specific model of subjectivity in his concept of eudaimonia, he also maintained that this subject was

[1] For related critiques of the theory/practice opposition, see Ball, "Plato and Aristotle."

[2] For interpretations of the relationship of rhetoric to philosophy, see Ijsseling, *Rhetoric and Philosophy in Conflict*, and Grassi, *Rhetoric as Philosophy*.

[3] The complicated relationship between first principles and ends impinges on Aristotle's concepts of actuality, potentiality, and formula. See one discussion in *Phys.* 199a30–200a30.

the product of a distinct set of class relations. In no way did eudaimonia serve as a general model of either the knowing subject or the citizen of the polis. Aristotle directly asserts that this hexis will be attained only by the philosopher; in other words, only philosophers win the ambiguous title of "subject." That "subject" is defined primarily in terms of knowledge, and it is depicted as solitary and self-possessed. Perhaps it is even "self" conceived as "possession."

In sum, while it may seem strange to praise rhetoric for failing either to consist of the highest knowledge or to be driven by the end of the "good life," Aristotle's greatest contribution to rhetoric may have been his willingness to allow it these two failures. In this chapter I explore Aristotle's taxonomy of knowledge, his concept of eudaimonia, and his views of rhetoric and philosophy as they contrast with those of Isocrates.

Theoretical, Practical, and Productive Knowledge

One of the greatest stumbling blocks to understanding Aristotle's concept of productive knowledge is the modern opposition of theory to practice. John Burnet's discussion of Aristotle's taxonomy of knowledge in the introduction to his commentary on the *Nicomachean Ethics* illustrates the theory/practice opposition at work: "Thought has only two forms; it is always either (1) theoretical or (2) practical and productive, and the difference between these is that the former has to do with things which are either immovable or have their source of motion in themselves, while the latter deals with such things as require an external cause to set them in motion" (xxi). Burnet refers to a discussion in book VI, chapter 2 of the *Nicomachean Ethics*, where Aristotle sets out three kinds of intellect: "contemplative . . . practical . . . productive" (1139a27–28). As Burnet explains, Aristotle makes the distinction between the contemplative intellect which "moves nothing" and intellect "which aims at an end and is practical; for this rules the productive intellect as well" (1139a35–b). Very soon after, however, Aristotle emphatically asserts that "making and acting are different" (1140a–2). In other words, "the reasoned state of capacity to act is different from the reasoned state of capacity to make" (1140a3–5), and Aristotle goes on to give examples from the technē of architecture (1140a6–10). Thus, while productive knowledge and practical knowledge share the characteristic of being concerned with things that do not contain their own "efficient cause," both types of knowledge still retain their distinctive capacities—or forms of intellection. The distinction to which Burnet points between things that are self-moved and things that are not receives some of its most detailed treatment in the *Physics*, where it is central to understanding Aristotle's teleological system and the operations of physis. The distinction does not, however, adequately elucidate Aristotle's taxonomy of knowledge—as Aristotle himself goes on to explain in the *Nicomachean Ethics*. What Burnet's discussion demonstrates is the tendency throughout modern Aristotelian scholarship to make the theory/practice distinction override the theoretical/practical/productive triad.

Part of the confusion concerning productive knowledge may be due to the absence of any statement in the Aristotelian corpus that specifically details its "subdisciplines." There are no concise summaries of the constituents of productive knowledge comparable to that of theoretical knowledge in the *Metaphysics*: "There must, then, be three theoretical philosophies, mathematics, natural science, and theology" (1026a18–19). Still, both productive knowledge and art appear throughout the Aristotelian corpus, and most scholars raise the category, even if it is only to argue for its insignificance. Abraham Edel, for example, organizes the largest part of his *Aristotle and His Philosophy* according to the theoretical/practical/productive triad, placing rhetoric and poetics clearly within the domain of productive knowledge.[4] Edel goes on to point out that Aristotle's concept of physis is absolutely dependent on his concept of art, observing, "It is ironic that the craft model that comes from production should provide the concepts for theory, for of the triad theory, practice, and production, production was lowest in Aristotle's scale of value" (69). Even this recognition of productive knowledge, however, is more the exception than the rule.[5]

This triad did not originate with Aristotle. The divisions are found in a Pythagorean tradition, predating Aristotle by at least a century,

[4] Exploring rhetoric's complex relationship to poetics is beyond the scope of this study. The classic treatment is Baldwin, *Ancient Rhetoric and Poetic*. Berlin takes on the political significance of the opposition of rhetoric to poetics in "Rhetoric, Poetic, and Culture."

[5] For another discussion of rhetoric's classification as an art, see Barnes, "Is Rhetoric an Art?" McKeon's classification of rhetoric as an architectonic productive art claims much of the territory associated with theoretical or philosophical knowledge; see his "Uses of Rhetoric in a Technological Age."

called the Doctrine of Three Lives—the Theoretic, the Practical, and the Apolaustic:

> There are three kinds of men, just as there are three classes of strangers who come to the Olympic Games. The lowest consists of those who come to buy and sell, and next above them are those who come to compete. Best of all are those who simply come to look on [*theōrēin*]. Men may be classified accordingly as lovers of wisdom [*philosophoi*], lovers of honour [*philotimoi*], and lovers of gain [*philokerdeis*]. (Burnet, *Greek Philosophy*, 42)

Aristotle himself recalls these distinctions in a discussion of the lowest type of life—the life that identifies goodness with pleasure:

> To judge from the lives that men lead, most men, and men of the most vulgar type, seem (not without some reason) to identify the good, or happiness, with pleasure; which is the reason why they love the life of enjoyment. For there are, we may say, three prominent types of life—that just mentioned, the political and thirdly the contemplative life. (EN 1095b14–19)[6]

Again, these orders of knowledge were social as opposed to conceptual. They referred to walks of life rather than to relationships between concepts.

In his study of the theory/practice opposition, Nicholas Lobkowicz explains that to the Greeks, "theory" was "a particularly sublime way of life which was less shallow than that of mere pleasure-seekers and less hectic than that of 'politicians'" (*Theory and Practice*, 7). It was a life characterized by independence from external concerns. Pythagoras, for example, insists that the "spectator" is the only "truly free man" (*Theory and Practice*, 7). Because theoretical knowledge transcends time, its contemplation was also believed to lift the thinker above mortality.

> Placed between an ever-changing but nevertheless everlasting Nature, on the one hand, and gods who never grew old, on the other hand, man

---

[6] For Plato's version, see *Rep.* 376a–b: "I set apart and distinguish those of whom you were just speaking, the lovers of spectacles and the arts, and men of action, and separate from them again those with whom our argument is concerned and who alone deserve the appellation of philosophers or lovers of wisdom."

was the only mortal being in a cosmos of immortal reality. In the philosopher's contemplation of the eternal this human condition somehow was transcended; since the only activity conceivable in the gods was contemplation, a man who lived the 'theoretical' life had to be considered dearest to the gods and therefore happiest. (7)

It is precisely this kind of contemplation that informs Aristotle's notion of eudaimonia.

If it is difficult to find any serious treatment of productive knowledge, it is even harder to find any discussion of its relationship to rhetoric. Edward M. Cope, a nineteenth-century commentator on the *Rhetoric*, acknowledges that art must be a form of productive knowledge. Still, he suggests this is something of a mistake in Aristotle's thought and contends that rhetoric is more appropriately characterized as practical knowledge. William M. A. Grimaldi, on the other hand, completely dismisses the domain of productive knowledge and makes a detailed case for rhetoric's classification as theoretical, or philosophical, knowledge.[7] One of the few references to rhetoric's relationship to productive knowledge is made by Lobkowicz, who simply notes in passing that in the *Topics* rhetoric is compared to medicine as a kind of productive knowledge—"faculties" of "doing of that which we choose with the materials that are available" (*Theory and Practice*, 38–39 n. 105; *Top.* 101b5).

Without making the connection to Aristotle's productive knowledge, recent rhetorical scholarship has explored the significance of the discipline's classification as a technē. Janice Lauer and Richard Young, in particular, have argued that art is a meaningful model of knowledge that should shape rhetoric's disciplinary identity. Similarly, Calvin Schrag has contended that the concept of art challenges foundationalist interpretations of both rhetoric and philosophy, whereas Barbara Biesecker has pointed toward technē as a heuristic for refiguring a postmodern rhetoric.[8]

Judgments concerning Aristotle's classification of rhetoric, however, require returning to the Aristotelian corpus. The most explicit treatments of Aristotle's domains of the theoretical (*epistēmē*), the practical (*praxis*), and the productive (*poiēsis*) are found in chapters 2–7

[7] The interpretations of Cope and Grimaldi will be discussed in detail in Chapter 7.

[8] See Lauer, "Issues in Rhetorical Invention"; Richard Young, "Arts, Crafts, Gifts, and Knacks"; and Schrag, "Rhetoric Resituated at the End of Philosophy," Schrag, *Communicative Praxis*, and Biesecker's "Coming to Terms."

of book VI of the *Nicomachean Ethics* and chapters 1–3 of book 1 of
the *Metaphysics*. It is important to acknowledge at the outset that the
three categories are not airtight. As in Burnet's example above, a specific principle of classification may bring together two domains of
knowledge that are expressly distinguished elsewhere. Moreover,
Aristotle is not always consistent in using epistēmē to refer only to
theoretical knowledge or technē to refer only to productive knowledge.

In book I, chapter 2 of the *Nicomachean Ethics*, for example, politics is described as "the most authoritative art and that which is most
truly the master art [*architektonikēs*]" (1094a26–27). Aristotle provides the following explanation for giving politics this designation:

> It is this that ordains which of the sciences should be studied in a state,
> and which each class of citizens should learn and up to what point they
> should learn them; and we see even the most highly esteemed of capac-
> ities to fall under this, e.g. strategy, economics, rhetoric [*rhetorikēn*];
> now, since politics uses the rest of the sciences [*epistēmōn*], and since,
> again, it legislates as to what we are to do and what we are to abstain
> from, the end of this science must include those of the others, so that
> this end must be the good [*agathon*] for man. (1094a28–b7)

In this passage, politics and rhetoric are referred to as both arts and sciences. Moreover, Aristotle's declaration that because politics uses
these other sciences (including rhetoric) it must incorporate their
ends has been construed as a defense of rhetoric's classification as
practical knowledge. Such statements, however, must be placed in the
context of Aristotle's other treatments of both rhetoric and the epistemological taxonomy. For example, after using the ambiguous term
paraphues, which Kennedy translates as "offshoot," to describe
rhetoric's relationship to dialectic and politics, Aristotle accuses:
"Thus, too, rhetoric dresses itself up in the form of politics, as do those
who pretend to a knowledge of it, sometimes through lack of education, sometimes through boastfulness and other human causes"
(Kennedy, 39; *Rhet.* 1356a27–30).

Despite such apparent contradictions and terminological inconsis-
tencies, Aristotle's theoretical, practical, productive distinctions are
some of the most stable concepts in the corpus, and their stability is
due largely to their close relationship to Aristotle's conception of teleology. In the most thorough discussions of the taxonomy, each domain

is marked according to its relationship to Aristotle's four causes: formal, efficient, material, and final.

Theoretical knowledge is the very contemplation of the notion of an "end," or telos. For Aristotle, the principles of a telos are tied to the principles of origination, which Aristotle called first principles. First principles and ends consist of the "belief about things that are universal and necessary" (EN 1140b31–32). Aristotle explains that "the first principle of what is known cannot be an object of knowledge, of art, or of practical wisdom; for that which can be known can be demonstrated, and art and practical wisdom deal with things that can be otherwise" (EN 1140b33–41a). The distinction between that which can be demonstrated and that which can be otherwise is of key importance. The knowledge of first principles is governed by logical necessity and exists apart from temporal contingencies: "It is eternal; for things that are of necessity in the unqualified sense are all eternal; and things that are eternal are ungenerated and imperishable" (EN 1139b23–24).

Theoretical knowledge is concerned with what exists and acts "by necessity." It is also the highest knowledge, an essential constituent of true wisdom:

> Wisdom must plainly be the most finished of the forms of knowledge. It follows that the wise man must not only know what follows from first principles, but must also possess truth about the first principles. Therefore wisdom must be comprehension combined with knowledge—knowledge of the highest objects which has received as it were its proper completion. (EN 1141a16–20)

Aristotle is very precise in distinguishing theoretical knowledge from any knowledge concerned with action or production—even from any knowledge that is not about the "best." He expressly excludes politics from the domain of theoretical knowledge because "it would be strange to think that the art of politics, or practical wisdom, is the best knowledge, since man is not the best thing in the world" (EN 1141a20–22). Theoretical knowledge is associated with contemplation of the "highest objects." The soul even retains a specific faculty "by which we contemplate the kind of things whose principles cannot be otherwise" (EN 1139a6). In its most "finished form," theoretical knowledge is actual knowledge that is identical with its object: "Thought is itself thinkable in exactly the same way as its objects are.

For in the case of objects which involve no matter, what thinks and what is thought are identical; for speculative knowledge and its object are identical: (*De An.* 430a5–7).[9]

The most significant distinguishing characteristic of theoretical knowledge is that it is pursued for no practical end. To reinforce the importance of this distinction, Aristotle offers a brief "history" of the development of theoretical knowledge:

> It is owing to their wonder that men both now begin and at first began to philosophize; they wondered originally at the obvious difficulties, then advanced little by little and stated difficulties about the greater matters, e.g. about the phenomena of the moon and those of the sun and the stars, and about the genesis of the universe. And a man who is puzzled and wonders thinks himself ignorant. . . ; therefore since they philosophized in order to escape from ignorance, evidently they were pursuing science in order to know, and not for any utilitarian end. (*Met.* 982b12–21)

Theoretical knowledge is not only belief about the first principles of movement but also a "self-moved," or "self-directed," way of life. Theoretical knowledge is a "free science" that "alone exists for itself" (*Met.* 982b28). Aristotle admits that this knowledge can exist only when mundane needs have been satisfied:

> For it was when almost all the necessities of life and the things that make for comfort and recreation were present, that such knowledge began to be sought. Evidently then we do not seek it for the sake of any other advantage; but as the man is free, we say who exists for himself and not for another, so we pursue this as the only free science, for it alone exists for itself. (*Met.* 982b23-28)

Aristotle's philosopher bears a strong resemblance to Plato's ideal ruler: his life of contemplation is secured by social boundaries that make his epistēmē "free."

In sum, theoretical knowledge is concerned with ends, without being directed toward any utilitarian end; though change is part of its study, it is itself immutable. Aristotle's theoretical knowledge retains the sense of theōria as the observation of spectacle; it also illustrates

---

[9] For a further discussion of the relationship of actual knowledge to objects, see *De An.* 430a20–25 and 431a1–5.

once again the ancient equation between social and epistemological orders.[10]

Practical knowledge, in contrast, is concerned with action and—what is far less than perfect—human behavior. Aristotle offers a definition of practical knowledge by describing the man who possesses it:

> Now it is thought to be a mark of a man of practical wisdom to be able to deliberate well about what is good and expedient for himself, not in some particular respect, e.g. about what sorts of thing conduce to health or to strength, but about what sorts of thing conduce to the good life in general. This is shown by the fact that we credit men with practical wisdom in some particular respect when they have calculated well with a view to some good end which is one of those that are not the object of any art. (EN 1140a25–30)

In other words, practical knowledge, or wisdom, is "a reasoned and true state of capacity to act with regard to human goods" (EN 1140b20). In contrast to theoretical knowledge, practical knowledge is never concerned with "the necessary," because "it is impossible to deliberate about things that are of necessity" (EN 1140b1). Practical knowledge differs from productive knowledge on the basis of their different "ends": "For while making has an end other than itself, action cannot; for good action itself is its end" (EN 1140b5–7).

Practical knowledge has one well-defined telos—eudaimonia. An important treatment of eudaimonia is found in book X of the *Nicomachean Ethics*, where Aristotle defends the premise that happiness is the "highest" end. His argument is relatively simple: "Everything that we choose we choose for the sake of something else—except happiness, which is an end" (EN 1176b30–31).

There is no serious deliberation about an alternative to eudaimonia

[10] Lobkowicz details the early association of theōria with "gaze": "It is well known that the expression 'theōros' means 'spectator at games'; 'theōria' then, would mean what a spectator at games does, namely watching" (*Theory and Practice*, 6). He points out that "theōros" also signified both the envoy sent to consult an oracle and the official title of state ambassadors to sacral festivals (6). Thus, "philotheorōs" meant "lover of contemplation" (6). Vernant discusses the relationship of theōria to spectacle, pointing out that even technology in ancient Greece was associated with spectacle. The achievements of early Greek science were "objects to be marvelled at, . . . thaumata made to astonish people" (MT, 283). As Vernant explains, "Their value and interest lie not so much in their usefulness as in the admiration and pleasure that they arouse in the spectator" (283).

as the telos of practical knowledge. But Aristotle admits that the appropriate hierarchy of means and ends that lead to eudaimonia is subject to deliberation. He finally assigns this task to the political philosopher. In the *Nicomachean Ethics*, Aristotle maintains that "the study of pleasure and pain belongs to the province of the political philosopher; for he is the architect of the end, with a view to which we call one thing bad and another good without qualification" (1152b1–3).[11] Though politics and ethics are closely identified, politics is clearly privileged: "In all sciences and arts the end is a good, and the greatest good and in the highest degree a good in the most authoritative of all—this is the political science of which the good is justice, in other words, the common interest" (*Pol.* 1282b14–18). Ironically, Aristotle's statement about politics and "common interest" introduces his defense of a slightly attenuated version of Plato's functionalist justice.[12] Again, Aristotle is brutally clear about his understanding of the difference between rhetoric and the art of politics: "But those of the sophists who profess the art (of politics) seem to be very far from teaching it. For, to put the matter generally, they do not even know what kind of thing it is nor what kinds of things it is about; otherwise they would not have classed it as identical with rhetoric or even inferior to it" (EN 1181a12–15).[13]

Productive knowledge contrasts with the contemplation associated with theoretical knowledge and the action associated with practical knowledge. Productive knowledge is defined by three characteristics: its concern with the contingent, its implication in social and economic exchange, and its resistance to determinate ends. Aristotle offers the following summary definition of art:

> Art [technē] is identical with a state of capacity to make, involving a true course of reasoning. All art is concerned with coming into being, i.e. with contriving and considering how something may come into being

[11] "The whole concern both of excellence and of political science is with pleasures and pains; for the man who uses these well will be good, he who uses them badly bad" (EN 1105a10–13).

[12] Aristotle's discussion of proportional/functional justice invokes Protagoras's example of the gifted flute player that we find in Plato's *Protagoras*. While Aristotle's defense of distributive justice appears throughout the corpus, an important discussion begins in the *Politics* at 1282b14 and extends to 1284a2.

[13] For alternative readings of the relationship of rhetoric to *phronesis* (practical knowledge or prudence), see Garver, *Aristotle's Rhetoric*, and Nussbaum, *Fragility of Goodness*. See also Arnhart, *Aristotle on Political Reasoning*.

which is capable of either being or not being, and whose origin is in the maker and not in the thing made; for art is concerned neither with things that are, or come into being, by necessity, nor with things that do so in accordance with nature (since these have their origin in themselves). (EN 1140a10–16)

"What can be otherwise" is Aristotle's version of contingency. Because art is concerned with the contingent, it can never claim, as does theoretical knowledge, to transcend time. Indeed, the ability to seize the appropriate moment, to exploit time rather than transcend it, is one of the defining features of technē.[14] The capacity for an object or activity to be "otherwise" is particularly important in distinguishing art from nature. As Aristotle explains above, only nature develops "of necessity," in an immutable and unchanging fashion.

Despite the often ambiguous status of productive knowledge, many scholars observe that Aristotle's concept of art is at the heart of his teleological perspective: "Of things that come to be some come to be by nature, some by art, some spontaneously. Now everything that comes to be comes to be by the agency of something and from something and comes to be something" (*Met.* 1032a12–14). Nature is the exemplar of teleological activity: "Nature does nothing in vain. For all things that exist by Nature are means to an end, or will be concomitants of means to an end" (*De An.* 434a31–32). Art is governed by the same teleological principles. Indeed, it appears that the very "discovery" of this principle in nature is possible only because it was first understood in the operation of human production:

Where there is an end, all the preceding steps are for the sake of that. Now surely as in action, so in nature; and as in nature, so it is in each action, if nothing interferes. Now action is for the sake of an end; therefore the nature of things also is so. Thus if a house, e.g., had been a thing made by nature, it would have been made in the same way as it is now by art; and if things made by nature were made not only by nature but also by art, they would come to be in the same way as by nature. The one, then, is for the sake of the other; and generally art in some cases completes what nature cannot bring to a finish, and in others imitates nature. If, therefore, artificial products are for the sake of an end, so clearly also are natural products. (*Phys.* 199a8–18)

[14] On kairos, see Kinneavy, "Translating Theory into Practice in Teaching Composition," and Wilhoit, "Kairos Revisited."

Aristotle reinscribes Plato's functionalism in a teleological system in which each function is part of a higher purpose. Because "not every stage that is last claims to be an end, but only that which is best" (*Phys.* 194a32–33), one key objective of intellectual inquiry is to distinguish means from ends. But herein resides one critical problem of the teleological perspective: What principle outside the system allows one to evaluate means and ends? Further, on what basis are intermediate ends hierarchized? To a great extent, Aristotle's categories of knowledge are an attempt to answer these questions by marking different domains in which different standards for evaluating means and ends apply.

Productive knowledge is clearly purposeful knowledge; it is always "for the sake of" another end.[15] But productive knowledge is also always implicated in exchange. Its first principle is always in a producer and its end in a user, or receiver.[16] Aristotle explains that "from art proceed the things of which the form is in the soul" (*Met.* 1032a–32b). Productive knowledge always remains in exchange because its end is in the user as opposed to the artistic construct. The user is so privileged in Aristotle's system that he insists the user is the most appropriate judge of an artistic product:

> There are some arts whose products are not judged of solely, or best, by the artists themselves . . . for example, the knowledge of the house is not limited to the builder only; the user, or in other words, the master, of the house will actually be a better judge than the builder, just as the pilot will judge better of a rudder than the carpenter, and the guest will judge better of a feast than the cook. (*Pol.* 1282a18–24)

Because the first principle of productive knowledge is in the producer and the end is in the user, productive knowledge can have no "ends in itself."

Because productive knowledge has no "ends in itself," it can never be "self-moved," which is particularly important in Aristotle's teleological system. Only nature has its own principle of movement. In the *Physics*, Aristotle defines nature itself as "a principle of motion and change" (200b12–13). Art, however, requires both an external mover

---

[15] Aristotle offers the saw as an example of something that could never be an end in itself: "For instance, why is a saw such as it is? To effect so-and-so and for the sake of so-and-so" (*Phys.* 200a10).

[16] See EN 1140a5–15.

and material at hand, "since anything which is produced is produced by something . . . and from something (and let this be taken to be not the privation but the matter . . .)" (*Met.* 1033a24–26). An art's source of change or motion is always different and always split between producer and user; in other words, neither producer nor user is capable of determining productive knowledge. In sharp contrast to theoretical knowledge, which is described as an inalienable "state," productive knowledge is defined by an act of exchange.

In various places, Aristotle directly applies the criteria of productive knowledge to the art of rhetoric. For example, one of the art's defining features is its concern solely with things that can be "otherwise." Aristotle explains that the subjects of rhetorical deliberation can only be those that "seem to be capable of admitting two possibilities" (Kennedy, 41; *Rhet.* 1357a4–5). Aristotle iterates in book I that rhetoric "does not belong to a single defined genus of subject" (1355b8). Indeed, when Aristotle defines rhetoric as "an ability, in each [particular] case, to see the available means of persuasion" (36; 1355b26–27), he underscores the extent to which rhetoric can never be a static body of knowledge; rhetorical knowledge is always subject to the contingencies of context, time, and history. Because rhetoric must conform to the key criterion of productive knowledge—the capacity to be "otherwise"—Aristotle's description of the art has overtones of sophistic rhetoric: "One should be able to argue persuasively on either side of a question" (34; 1355a29–30). He goes on to explain that this ability to reason "in opposite directions," like the sophistic dissoi logoi, is certainly not the aim of rhetoric (34; 1355a34). Indeed, Aristotle maintains that "the underlying facts are not equally good in each case; but true and better ones are by nature always more productive of good syllogisms and, in a word, more persuasive" (35; 1355a36–38).[17] Aristotle makes it very clear, however, that rhetoric's place in the epistemological taxonomy is *not* determined by the truth or falsity of its subject matter but rather its indeterminacy with regard to knowledge and value. Regarding knowledge, if the propositions of an argument are too specific, they have moved beyond the boundary of rhetoric: "The more [speakers] fasten upon [the subject matter] in

---

[17] The notion of "underlying facts" has been much disputed. See, for example, Grimaldi, *"Rhetoric" I*, 30. See also LSJ, 1457 and 1884. Cope, as well as LSJ, stresses that *hypokeimena pragmata* refers as much to "subject matter" and "states of affairs" as it does to "underlying facts."

its proper sense, [the more] they depart from rhetoric or dialectic" (1358a24–25). With regard to value, Aristotle insists that the deliberative orator's aim is *sympheron* (which Roberts translates as "utility" and which Kennedy translates as the "advantageous"): "The deliberative orator's aim is utility: deliberation seeks to determine not ends but the means to ends, i.e. what it is most useful to do" (1362a17–20).

The relationship of rhetoric to productive knowledge is particularly explicit in relation to social exchange. As Aristotle explains, "A speech [situation] consists of three things: a speaker and a subject on which he speaks and someone addressed, and the objective [*telos*] of the speech relates to the last (I mean the hearer)" (Kennedy, 47; 1358a37–b2).[18] Because the first principles and ends of productive knowledge are always situated in some form of social exchange, art can never be concerned with determinate knowledge or value. Determinate knowledge remains in the domain of the theoretical, whereas the one calibrator of the good—eudaimonia—remains in the domain of practical knowledge. Much like Protagoras's theory of value, productive knowledge has no external arbiter, no final judge, but only "makers" and "users" who change with every exercise of an art.

Eudaimonia and Subjectivity as Private Property

With regard to politics, Plato and Aristotle shared a number of assumptions. The idea that all "men" could be self-directed knowers would have seemed preposterous to both. They both admitted that the philosophical life was tied to class privilege and disposition, made possible only by subordinating other classes to fulfill various social and economic functions in the state. If we believe that self-direction is the defining characteristic of the "individual," then Plato and Aristotle would have agreed with Anthony Arblaster that "'the individual' really means 'the exceptional individual'" (*Western Liberalism*, 48).

One problem in addressing the political thought of Plato and Aristotle is that both outlined ideal and compromise states. In Plato's ideal republic, the philosopher/king rules, whereas his compromise state is

[18] See also *Rhet.* 1356b28.

ruled by laws. Similarly, Aristotle's ideal state is an aristocracy, but his compromise state is a polity—a mixed constitution that confers most political responsibility on the middle class.[19] We focus here on the social order to which they generally gave the most attention— their ideal states.

The differences in their perspectives are complex. As we saw, for Plato the various technai, with their corresponding "functions," define the hierarchical order of the state. Plato's functionalism is comparable to Aristotle's teleology. In Aristotle's case, however, eudaimonia displaces the technai as the basis of the state's order. The telos of Aristotle's state is clearly established in the *Politics*. Using *eu zēn*, literally "good life" instead of eudaimonia, Aristotle asserts that "the end of the state is the good life" (1280b39–40). But the parts of the state, according to Aristotle, are like parts of the body; they "are defined by their function and power" (1253a23–24).[20] By this analogy Aristotle means that the parts of the whole that make up the state are different: "The elements out of which a unity is to be formed differ in kind" (1261a28–29). As with Plato's technai, these "differences in kind" become the basis for the hierarchization of parts. According to Aristotle, "the excellence [*aretē*] of a thing is relative to its proper function" (EN 1139a18). In other words, the aretē of an element of Aristotle's state resides in its adaptation to a hierarchized function. Like Plato, Aristotle maintains that each element of the state should partake of "the excellences of character," (*Pol.* 1260a18). This does not mean, however, that all elements are capable of achieving the same kind and level of virtue. Aristotle explains that "all should partake of them, but only in such manner and degree as is required by each for the fulfilment of his function" (1260a18–20). Functions can provide a stable order for the state because each part is assigned only one function. Referring to the "elements" of the state, Aristotle observes that "every instrument is best made when intended for one and not for many uses" (1252b3–5). For example, quoting Sophocles, Aristotle observes that silence is the special excellence assigned to a woman (1260a30). Similarly, "a slave is useful for the wants of life, and therefore he will obviously require only so much excellence as will prevent him from failing in his function" (1260a34–37).

[19] For Aristotle's discussion of democracies governed by a large middle class, see *Pol.* 1295a25–96b12.

[20] For another perspective on Aristotle's eudaimonia, see Irwin, "Moral Science and Political Theory in Aristotle."

Aristotle's view of function concurs with Solonian timocracy; equality can hold within classes, not between them.[21] Equal claims within a part of the state do not translate into equal claims to the state as a whole. As Aristotle explains, "Those who are equal in one thing ought not to have an equal share in all, nor those who are unequal in one thing to have an unequal share in all" (1283a28). In other words, "all men have a claim in a certain sense, . . . but not all have an absolute claim" (1283a30). "If we take into account a good life," Aristotle insists, "education and excellence have superior claims" (1283a24–25).

Aristotle's teleological view of the state leaves him with the same problem confronted by Plato: How does one distribute rights, benefits, and honors in a state in which both order and value are defined by class function? Are benefits given according to a principle of the most labor—those who work hardest in the state deserve the most reward? Aristotle maintains that in an aristocracy, his ideal state, "honors are given according to excellence and merit" (1278a20–21). But Aristotle frames this principle of distribution in a complex argument concerning the boundaries of the state.

To maintain the coherence of his teleological system, Aristotle makes a part/whole distinction that rationalizes the exclusion of rewards to those who provide the subsistence of the state. He does this by comparing the state to an organic compound: "As in other natural compounds the conditions of a composite whole are not necessarily organic parts of it, so in a state or in any other combination forming a unity not everything is a part which is a necessary condition" (1328a24–25). Directly applied to citizenship, the principle means "that we cannot consider all those to be citizens who are necessary to the existence of the state" (1278a2–3). Regarding the artisan class, composed of slaves and foreigners, Aristotle explains:

> The best form of state will not admit them to citizenship; but if they are admitted, then our definition of the excellence of a citizen will not apply to every citizen, nor to every free man as such, but only to those who are freed from necessary services. The necessary people are either slaves who minister to the wants of individuals, or mechanics and labourers who are the servants of the community. (1278a8–12)

---

[21] Vlastos, "Solonian Justice," 78–82; see also *Pol.* 1301b29–1302a8.

Later in the *Politics*, Aristotle makes a similar distinction between the internal parts of the state and those who provide the state's "necessary" conditions: "Farmers, artisans, and labourers of all kinds are necessary to the existence of states, but the parts of the state are the warriors and councillors" (1329a36–39).

Consequently, when Aristotle insists that "the best life, both for individuals and states, is the life of excellence," he is not only restricting eudaimonia but also conferring the status of "individual" on a very restricted group (1323b40–41). Aristotle is hardly subtle concerning the unequal distribution of eudaimonia in the polis. He contrasts his own perspective with that of Socrates, who believed, according to Aristotle, that the "legislator ought to make the whole state happy" and, further, that "the whole cannot be happy unless most, or all, or some of its parts enjoy happiness" (1264b17–18). Aristotle counters that "in this respect happiness is not like the even principle in numbers, which may exist only in the whole, but in neither of the parts" (1264b19–22). He goes on to assert that "if the guardians are not happy, who are? Surely not the artisans, or the common people" (1264b22–23). Aristotle contends that the inability of the many to achieve eudaimonia accounts for different forms of government: "Whereas happiness is the highest good, being a realization and perfect practice of excellence, which some can attain, while others have little or none of its, the various qualities of men are clearly the reason why there are various kinds of states and many forms of government" (1328a37–28b).

If we accept that the good life is restricted to a few, we still might question whether eudaimonia could be a kind of benevolent rule that acknowledges that happiness and equality for all is a noble objective seldom achieved in reality. At one point in the *Politics*, Aristotle provides the following description of eudaimonia in the state: "The state is the union of families and villages in a perfect and self-sufficing life, by which we mean a happy and honourable life. Our conclusion, then, is that political society exists for the sake of noble actions, and not of living together" (1281a1–4). As Aristotle depicts it, the life that aims at *eudaimonia* is far more concerned with the vertical trajectory of self-sufficiency than the horizontal bonds of friendship in the polis.[22]

---

[22] This statement is part of Aristotle's argument that in his state a citizen's claim would be based on political excellence (*politikē aretē*) rather than either money or noble birth (*Pol.* 1281a4–9). At the same time, Aristotle is aware that excellence seldom thrives where money and power are scarce.

Aristotle's conception of eudaimonia poses problems for his taxonomy of knowledge. One paradox over which he puzzles is whether eudaimonia is an activity or a state. This problem arises to a large extent because eudaimonia has been defined as the end of practical knowledge; and practical knowledge is identified with praxis, or acting. How then can the end of practical knowledge be anything other than an action? Still, when Aristotle describes the good life, he often defines it as a contemplative state. This contradiction is acute even for Aristotle: it makes "no small difference," he insists, "whether we place the chief good in possession or in use, in state or in activity" (EN 1098b31–33). He introduces the discussion of eudaimonia in the *Nicomachean Ethics* by defining happiness as "an activity of soul in accordance with complete excellence" (1102a5). At another point in the discussion, however, eudaimonia is described as both a state and an action: the happy man is one who "will do and contemplate what is excellent" (1100b19–20). In one extreme characterization of eudaimonia as an inactive state, he goes so far as to say that "possession of excellence seems actually compatible with being asleep, or with lifelong inactivity" (1095b32–33). A compromise regarding the status of eudaimonia is suggested by Aristotle's definition of happiness as an "activity" that is contemplative (1177a17–18). It is "the realization and perfect exercise of excellence" (*Pol.* 1332a9–10). Aristotle explains that the tension between eudaimonia as a state, or "hexis," and an activity can be resolved because *eudaimonia* consists in a continuous activity of contemplation, "since we can contemplate truth more continuously than we can *do* anything" (EN 1177a21–22). Thus, while contemplation is a kind of action, the fact that it is continuous makes it immune to accidents of time.

The chief characteristic of eudaimonia, as a continuous activity of contemplation, is self-sufficiency, which occurs on at least two levels. First, it is self-sufficiency of thought: "The self-sufficiency that is spoken of must belong to the contemplative activity" (EN 1177a27–28). Thoughts, themselves, are self-sufficient. In the *Politics*, Aristotle states that the ideas associated with happiness are "independent and complete in themselves" (1325b20). But the self-sufficiency of eudaimonia occurs at another level. A man can attain eudaimonia only when he has been "sufficiently equipped" with "the necessaries of life" (EN 1177a28–29). Here Aristotle blurs the boundary between theoretical and practical knowledge by describing the activity of eudaimonia as identical to the theoretical life of speculation. Like theoretical knowledge, eudaimonia is an activity that must be "loved for its own sake" (1177b1); and like the theoretical life, eudaimonia "depend[s] on leisure" (1177b5). Aristotle thus summarizes the contemplation of eudaimonia:

> The activity of intellect, which is contemplative, seems both to be superior in worth and to aim at no end beyond itself, and to have its pleasure proper to itself (and this augments the activity), and the self-sufficiency, leisureliness, unweariedness (so far as this is possible for man), and all the other attributes ascribed to the blessed man are evidently those connected with this activity. (1177b18–23)

This contemplation is not the thoughtful consideration of a body of knowledge. For Aristotle, contemplation is the actualization of knowledge in the mind. He explains that "speculative knowledge and its object are identical"; thus "actual knowledge is identical with its object" (*De An.* 430a20). Both passages are from Aristotle's treatise *De Anima* (*On the Soul*), a complicated text that outlines Aristotle's theories of perception and knowledge. The text is particularly challenging because, to a large extent, it must unify Aristotle's teleological system by explaining how we know the complex relationships between induction and deduction, potentiality and actuality. But the identification between speculative thought and its object is also made in the *Metaphysics*: "Thought and the object of thought are not different in the case of things that have not matter, they will be the same, i.e. the thinking will be one with the object of its thought" (*Met.* 1075a2–4). In his commentary on *De Anima*, W. D. Ross defines the first type of apprehension—that is, passive intellect—as the "apprehension of universals which are actually present in individual perceptible things" (46). According to Ross, this faculty is "rightly called reason" as opposed to sense perception, "since it is the awareness of universals" (46). At the same time, it *is* contingent on experience. It is called "passive intellect" because "it is the awareness of something actually given in experience" (46). Ross affirms, however, that Aristotle does indeed describe this type of perception as "reason's *becoming* its objects" (46). Active intellect, on the other hand, apprehends universals "not present in perceptible things," such as geometrical universals (46). This intellect is active because it must "*divine* the existence of perfect squareness and perfect circularity" and consequently must "make" these relationships or "think them into existence" (46).[23]

The distinction between passive and active intellect is important only if the mind's "becoming its objects" is clearly associated with the speculative life. Aristotle makes that association explicit in *De Anima*:

> When thought has become each thing in the way in which a man who actually knows is said to do so (this happens when he is now able to exercise power on his own initiative), its condition is still one of potentiality, but in a different sense from the potentiality which preceded the acquisition of knowledge by learning or discovery: and thought is then able to think of itself. (429b6–9)

As Ross points out, this condition is equivalent to a kind of "godlike status"—the virtual apotheosis of self-sufficiency (42).

Aristotle's affection for self-sufficiency would seem to be odds with the description of the individual and the state in book I, chapter 2 of the *Politics*. There Aristotle maintains that "the state is by nature clearly prior to the family and to the individual, since the whole is of necessity prior to the part" (1253a19–20). Aristotle goes on to assert, "The proof that the state is a creation of nature and prior to the individual is that the individual, when isolated, is not self-sufficing (1253a25–26).[24] In the same passage, however, Aristotle also asserts that "things are defined by their function and power" (1253a23). Moreover, the entire discussion precedes Aristotle's treatment of the household, which includes such famous statements as "a slave is a living possession" (1253b32).

Other statements about the individual that appear to refer to a general conception of "human nature" almost always apply to only a few. Two sets of terms create these ambiguities—the individual and the state, on the one hand, and functions, rulers, and the ruled, on the other. As with Plato's sōphrosynē, the need for community by some parts of the polis must be satisfied by their submission to rule: "Na-

---

[23] The passage in *De Anima* is generally interpreted, R. D. Hicks explains, as distinguishing two types of apprehension, passive and active intellect (*Aristotle "De Anima,"* 498). Active intellect clearly bears a significant relationship to productive knowledge. As Hicks notes, active intellect is *ho poiētikos nous*, productive comprehension or wisdom. For further discussion, see 498–99.

[24] See also *Pol.* 1278b19–30.

ture herself has provided the distinction when she made a difference between old and young within the same species, of whom she fitted the one to govern and the other to be governed" (1332b36–38). Put another way, "In the world both of nature and of art the inferior always exists for the sake of the superior" (1333a21–23). Elsewhere in the *Politics*, Aristotle makes the following circular argument: "The ruling class should be the owners of property, for they are citizens, and the citizens of a state should be in good circumstances; whereas artisans or any other class which is not a producer of excellence have no share in the state. This follows from our first principle, for happiness cannot exist without excellence, and a city is not to be termed happy in regard to a portion of the citizens but in regard to them all" (1329a18–25). The statement is confusing and appears to contradict his assertion that eudaimonia will *not* be found in all parts of the state. What is clear, however, is that Aristotle is not offering to change the equation between aretē and eudaimonia in order for happiness to exist "in regard to them all." Instead, he will change the boundaries of the state so that those without excellence will not contaminate the eudaimonia of the best. The same problem arises in Aristotle's discussion of the distribution of aretē. All members of the state must have a share of these excellences; those shares will differ, however, both in kind and quantity. This is what Aristotle means when he asserts that "the excellence of the part must have regard to the excellence of the whole" (1260b14–15). In sum, many constituents of the polis and the oikos simply never achieve the status of "individual."

In contrast to Plato, Aristotle demonstrates a peculiar affection for private property.[25] Aristotle believes that the state plays a role in protecting private property and clearly distinguishes his politics from anything resembling democratic reform. He maintains that the redistribution of property is not an appropriate objective for the state.[26] "The beginning of reform," he insists "is not so much to equalize property as to train the nobler sort of natures not to desire more, and to prevent the lower from getting more; that is to say, they must be kept down, but not ill-treated" (1267b5–8). In the *Politics*, Aristotle

[25] The following excerpt is situated in a direct response to Socrates. For a full discussion, see *Pol.* 1260b25–67b20.

[26] Aristotle further argues that equal distribution is an inappropriate objective because "where there is equality of property, the amount may be either too large or too small" (*Pol.* 1266b24–26).

begins an apology for private property by arguing that it is the prerequisite for the virtue of liberality. But he also defends private property as a form of self-love:

> It is clearly better that property should be private, but the use of it common; and the special business of the legislator is to create in men this benevolent disposition. Again, how immeasurably greater is the pleasure, when a man feels a thing to be his own; for surely the love of self is a feeling implanted by nature and not given in vain, although selfishness is rightly censured; this, however, is not the mere love of self, but the love of self in excess, like the miser's love of money. (1263a37–63b)[27]

Aristotle's description of private property suggests that there is an interdependent, if not mutually constitutive, relationship between the love of self and the love of property.

Ernest Barker's discussion of property in book 2 of the *Politics* may be a case of overinterpretation; however, it demonstrates the uses to which Aristotle's conception of private property so easily lends itself. According to Barker, Aristotle is suggesting that "the sense of personality and its concomitant virtue of self-respect (*philautia*)" is the "ultimate foundation of property" (*Political Thought*, 393). Barker describes a mutually constitutive relationship between property and the self: "Each of us must have *his own*, just because he is *himself*" (393). Indeed, Barker goes so far as to identify the "annexation" of personal property with the growth of the self:

> The very sense of self, the feeling of a personality, is conditional upon possessing something which makes its expression possible. I cannot know myself, unless I can express my will (which is myself) in action; I cannot express it in action, unless I have a medium for such expression. I come to know myself, through what I have made my own: my property is a mirror, which reflects myself to me. (393)

Whether or not we concur in full with Barker's explication of *Politics* 1263, his interpretation is a stunning example of the extent to which Aristotle's normative ideal of subjectivity is embedded in specific social and economic relations. Private property is the means of both self-

---

[27] For Aristotle's discussion of liberality, see *Pol.* 1263b7–14 and 1265a31–38.

expression and self-knowledge; knowledge of the self would be impossible without the procurement of private property.[28] The subject and object distinction, usually made in the context of epistemology, is relocated at the center of the notion of private property.

What is unique about Aristotle's normative ideal is that it in no way obscures the social and economic conditions of its possibility; indeed, he could hardly be more explicit that the relations that secure the subject's self-sufficiency are social, economic, and political.

The subjects of theoretical and practical knowledge, however, remain in contrast to the subjects of productive knowledge. Aristotle's productive knowledge invokes the senses of technē found in Homer and Hesiod. There technē is a valuable possession—indeed, a kind of commodity—but its transfer always redefines the subjects involved by effecting some shift in power or status. In the domain of productive knowledge, subjects are "users," not "knowers"; and every different use of a technē defines the subject differently. Subjects of productive knowledge are defined by social exchange rather than private possession, and just as a technē can never be a form of private property, neither can the makers and users with which it is identified be private, stable entities. Thus, productive knowledge poses a stumbling block for those who attempt to invoke Aristotle to authorize either a philosophical or an "ethical" rhetoric. Rather than embodying culture's highest value, the subjects of productive knowledge are better characterized as the very nexus of competing standards of value; rather than securing boundaries of either knowledge or subjectivity, productive knowledge is more likely to be implicated in their transgression and renegotiation.

Technē and Philosophy according to Isocrates and Aristotle

I began by suggesting that the ancient rhetorical tradition is largely incommensurable with philosophical traditions that are guided by static models of subjectivity, value, and knowledge. That incommensurability is foregrounded in the contrasting definitions of philosophy outlined by Aristotle and Isocrates.

---

[28] See Aristotle's discussion of the limits of the art of acquiring wealth and the unlimited character of exchange by currency in *Pol.* 1256b40–58a19.

In the *Antidosis*, Isocrates reframes the prehistory narrative of technē to describe the peculiar power of the art of discourse:

> We ought, therefore, to think of the art of discourse just as we think of the other arts, and not to form opposite judgments about similar things, nor show ourselves intolerant toward that power which, of all the faculties which belong to the nature of man, is the source of most of our blessings. For in the other powers which we possess . . .[29] we are in no respect superior to other living creatures; nay, we are inferior to many in swiftness and in strength and in other resources; but, because there has been implanted in us the power to persuade each other and to make clear to each other whatever we desire, not only have we escaped the life of wild beasts, but we have come together and founded cities and made laws and invented arts [*technas heuromen*]; and, generally speaking, there is no institution devised by man which the power of speech has not helped us to establish. (253–55)

A very similar prehistory account, which also depicts the art of discourse as the source of civilization, occurs almost verbatim in *Nicocles* 5–6.

As Cole points out, the *Panegyricus* and the *Panathenaicus* also contain two versions of the narrative. According to Cole, however, in these versions "Athens" has replaced the power of speech (*Democritus*, 7). Cole argues that Isocrates' use of the account is evidence that it has become a sophistic topos: "The *Panegyricus* (28–40) and later the *Panathenaicus* (119–48) celebrate Athens as the bringer of technology, culture, and law; and in almost identical passages of the *Nicocles* (5–6) and *Antidosis* (253–54) the same role is assigned to oratory" (7). But Cole's description of the *Panegyricus*, in particular, is misleading. His statement that Athens has simply replaced oratory depends on ending the prehistory account at 40. In fact, Isocrates continues his pseudo-historical account of the benevolent, civilizing power of Athens by discussing three more contributions of the Hellenes: trade, the Olympic Games, and *philosophia*. Isocrates insists that it is "philosophy . . . which has helped to discover and establish all these institutions, which has educated us for public affairs and made us gentle towards each other, which has distinguished between the misfortunes that are due to ignorance and those which spring from necessity [*ex anankēs*]"

---

[29] Here Isocrates notes that he has used the same narrative in Nicocles.

(*Panegyricus* 47). Athens receives more praise because she "has honoured eloquence. . . ; for she realized that this is the one endowment of our nature which singles us out from all living creatures, and that by using this advantage [*pleonektēsantes*] we have risen above them in all other respects as well" (48).[30] Isocrates clearly signals the end of his account and a shift of subject at 51, rather than 40.[31] By ending the passage at 40, however, Cole accomplishes several purposes. First, in contrasting these two uses of the myth in the *Antidosis* and *Nicocles*, on the one hand, and the *Panegyricus* and the *Panathenaicus*, on the other, Cole can point to evidence in Isocrates of either contradiction or insincerity—typical accusations for rhetors. By refusing to acknowledge that the prehistory account in the *Panegyricus* includes the art of discourse, Cole is able to dismiss Isocratean *philosophia*. Isocrates has appropriated the story as an epideictic topos, deployed for "a narrower purpose" (Cole, *Democritus*, 6). The subtext is clear and familiar. In Isocrates' hands, the narratives are a rhetorical topos—no less, no more; and his hands are those of a rhetor (that is, not a philosopher)—no less, no more.

Aristotle also offers a prehistory account, which includes but does not focus on technē. In the *Metaphysics*, Aristotle explains that animals "live by appearances and memories, and have but little of connected experience"; however, anthrōpoi live "by art and reasonings" (980b25–28). As we know from the earlier discussion in Chapter 3, humans distinguish themselves by using memory and reasoning to make experience the basis of art. At another level, artists are distinct from "men of experience," and their knowledge is of a higher order because "men of experience know that the thing is so, but do not know why, while the others know the 'why' and the cause" (*Met.* 981a24–30).

The terminus of Aristotle's evolutionary account is clearly philosophy. Art is only the midpoint between the experience of particulars and knowledge that is divorced from the senses; indeed, it is the halfway mark between a life driven by basic "necessity" and a life of leisure.[32]

---

[30] My argument is not intended to question the obvious imperialist designs of *Panegyricus* but rather to suggest that in this text Isocrates makes the "glory" of eloquence at least co-equal to the "glory" of Athens.

[31] "But in order that I may not appear to be dwelling at length on the details . . . because I lack ground for praising her conduct in war, let what I have said suffice for those who glory in such services" (Isocrates, *Panegyricus* 51).

[32] It is precisely such midpoints that have earned Aristotle the title of the patriarch of a middle class.

At first he who invented any art that went beyond the common perceptions of man was naturally admired by men, not only because there was
something useful in the inventions, but because he was thought wise
and superior to the rest. But as more arts were invented, and some were
directed to the necessities of life, others to its recreation, the inventors
of the latter were always regarded as wiser than the inventors of the former, because their branches of knowledge did not aim at utility. Hence
when all such inventions were already established, the sciences which
do not aim at giving pleasure or at the necessities of life were discovered, and first in the places where men first began to have leisure. This
is why the mathematical arts were founded in Egypt; for there the
priestly caste was allowed to be at leisure. (*Met.* 981b12–25)

Because philosophy could be sought only when "almost all the necessities of life and the things that make for comfort and recreation were
present" (982b22–24), technē is a part of both cultural and economic
evolution. These orders of knowledge continue to reflect a social order—a hierarchy of the "mind" that places the "man" who is occupied
with philosophy at the highest level: "The man of experience is
thought to be wiser than the possessors of any perception whatever,
the artist wiser than the men of experience, the master-worker than
the mechanic, and the theoretical kinds of knowledge to be more of
the nature of wisdom than the productive" (*Met.* 981b30–82a).

In sum, arguments that Aristotle elevates rhetoric to the status of
philosophy and ethics must be based on a very selective reading of the
Rhetoric. For example, if one looks to the text for a thoroughly worked-
out argument distinguishing rhetoric from what Plato called the dangerous art of appearances and deception, one will be disappointed. Aristotle's treatment of deception (*apatē*) is confined to the appearance of
the term in various rhetorical topics. Apatē appears in a treatment of
forensic topics in book I: "Look to see whether the contract is contrary
to any written or common laws and in the case of written laws either
those of the city or foreign ones, then [whether it is contrary] to other
earlier or later contracts; for later contracts take precedence, or else the
earlier ones are authoritative and the later ones fraudulent [*ēpatēkasin*],
whichever argument is useful" (Kennedy, 115; *Rhet.* 1376b24–28). In
this instance, apatē is a strategy to be used to break or invalidate an
oath; it is quite explicitly an instrument in the rhetor's toolbox.

It is apparent that Isocrates and Aristotle had vastly different conceptions of philosophy. It also seems fairly obvious that Aristotle won

the definitional contest for philosophy. But just how different were their conceptions of rhetoric? Isocrates' definition of philosophia is not obscure; in fact, what is painfully clear is just how inextricable it is from—if not identical to—his art of discourse. The critical value of Aristotle's taxonomy is that it *did* leave room for art; to a large extent it preserved the sophistic tradition by placing rhetoric in the domain of technē rather than in that of philosophy. What is lost in the taxonomy, however, is the sense of the art of rhetoric as a valued mode of intervention into existing conditions and a means for the invention of new possibilities.[33]

[33] Aristotle gives us plenty of reason to be confused about rhetoric's relationship to politics and about politic's relationship to eudaimonia. In the opening passages of the *Nicomachean Ethics*, Aristotle appears to ascribe to politics the same authority given to philosophy; moreover, many have used the same passage to place rhetoric as a sub-discipline of politics. In a discussion over what discipline would examine the difference between the "chief good" and things that we choose "for the sake of something else," Aristotle asserts: "And politics appears to be of this nature; for it is this that ordains which of the sciences should be studied in a state, and which each class of citizens should learn and up to what point they should learn them; and we see even the most highly esteemed of capacities to fall under this, e.g. strategy, economics, rhetoric; now, since politics uses the rest of the sciences, and since, again, it legislates as to what we are to do and what we are to abstain from, the end of this science must include those of the others, so that this end must be the good for man" (EN 1094a27–b8).

7 Aristotle's *Rhetoric* and the Theory/Practice Binary

> Politics begins, strictly speaking, with the denunciation of this tacit contract of adherence to the established order which defines the original doxa; in other words, political subversion presupposes cognitive subversion, a conversion of the vision of the world.
> —Pierre Bourdieu, *Language and Symbolic Power*

In Hesiod's *Theogony*, technē plays a curious but significant role in a narrative that describes the conception and birth of the Titans. According to the story, Earth (Gaia) has lain with Heaven (Ouranos) and given birth to Oceanus, Coeus, Crius, Hyperion, Iapetus, Theia, Rhea, Themis, Mnemosyne, Phoebe, and Tethys. The next child born is Cronos, who is described as wily [ankulomētēs], terrible, and filled with hatred for his "lusty sire" (137–39). After Cronos, Earth gives birth to the Cyclopes and then three more sons—Cottus, Briareos, and Gyes—each possessing one hundred arms and fifty heads (150–51) and described as "presumptuous children" (149), with "irresistible" and "stubborn strength" (153). According to the story, the three were so hated "from the first" by their father that "he used to hide them all away in a secret place of Earth so soon as each was born, and would not suffer them to come up into the light: and Heaven rejoiced in his evil doing" (156–57).

As M. L. West observes, at this point the wording of the myth turns "conveniently ambiguous" (Commentary on *Theogony*, 214). What is translated by H. G. Evelyn-White as "secret place of Earth" is *gaiēs en keuthmōni* (Hesiod, *Theog.* 158). The third-declension noun *keuthmōn* can refer to a "hiding place, hole," or "hollows" (LSJ, 944). Liddell, Scott, and Jones translate the noun phrase from Hesiod as "the nether world" (944):

And he used to hide them all away in a secret place of Earth so soon as each was born and would not suffer them to come up into the light. . . . But vast Earth groaned within, being straitened, and she thought a crafty [*doliēn*] and an evil wile [*technēn*]. Forthwith she made the element of grey flint and shaped [*teuxe*] a great sickle, and told her plan to her dear sons. And she spoke, cheering them, while she was vexed in her dear heart: 'My children, gotten of a sinful father, if you will obey me, we should punish the vile outrage of your father; for he first thought of doing shameful things.' (*Theog.* 158–66)

The sons are afraid, and only "Cronos the wily" responds to his mother's plea. Earth then hides her son, puts a "jagged sickle" in his hands, and reveals to him the plot (*dolos*) (175). This part of the story concludes:

And Heaven came, bringing on night and longing for love, and he lay about Earth spreading himself full upon her. Then the son from his ambush stretched forth his left hand and in his right took the great long sickle with jagged teeth, and swiftly lopped off his own father's members and cast them away to fall behind him. (176–82).

Like most early narratives, this one is troubled by problems of strict logic. Equipped with such tools of scholarly discourse as personification, metaphor, and "myth," scholars continue to haggle over whether Earth's children are still in the "womb" or simply hidden in the hollows of the earth. West's own euphemistic conclusion betrays a disconcerting masculinist perspective: "The Titans were kept in Gaia's womb by Uranos' unremitting embrace: that is why she is so distressed (159–60), and why castration solves the problem" (Commentary on *Theogony*, 214).

The story might seem an unlikely exemplar of technē as a model of knowledge, but it contains many of the characteristics of technē that I have attempted to trace. Earth's technē is an act of intervention—to say the least; it deploys the kind of cunning intelligence (ankulomētēs) that is the only viable weapon against the force (bia) and brute strength (kratos) of Ouranos. Her technē is both a plan and a trick (dolos). Moreover, as the grandmother of Prometheus, Earth devises a crafty "wile" (technē) that requires foresight; she must imagine a future that is different from the present, and her plan requires lying in wait until the opportune moment for seizing the advantage over Ouranos. Her technē is exchanged from herself to Cronos, and once deployed, it brings about a new order among the gods—Earth included. Thus, her cunning art "produces" alternative relations of power and a "different" Earth.

Hesiod's treatment of technē in the myth of Gaia provides an interesting contrast to his two accounts of technē in the Prometheus narratives. Whereas Pandora is depicted as a deceitful work of art, Hephaestus's artistic "product," Gaia herself, is the artificer—the one who conceives the plan and masterminds its execution. Whereas the Prometheus narratives stress the "product" dimension of technē—Prometheus's trick offering and Pandora—Gaia's story emphasizes the more temporal notions of plan and intervention. What both stories bear in common is the depiction of technē as "productive" of alternative possibilities and lines of power.

Such brutal but decisive senses of the power of technē are worth remembering as we examine the fate of "art" in nineteenth- and twentieth-century interpretations of rhetoric. The art that Plato compared to boxing and Tacitus called "an associate of sedition" becomes in Cope's hands a managerial art, ready for service in an emerging industrial culture. For Grimaldi, rhetoric is both mirror and prism, reflecting a kind of immanent truth and justice in the world that is not apparent to the naked eye. Though in different degrees, for both commentators rhetoric functions in service to interpretation rather than to invention; it is a hermeneutic rather than a heuristic art.

Theory/Practice and Productive Knowledge

The modern history of rhetoric has virtually been determined by the theory/practice binary.[1] The distinction between theoretical and practical rhetorics becomes even more complicated when Aristotle's *Rhetoric* itself becomes an institutional exemplar in the hands of classicists rather than rhetors. When the distinction between the theoretical and the practical is used to secure either the canonicity of the *Rhetoric* and or the respectability of the discipline, it frequently ceases

---

[1] See Kennedy's division of rhetoric into three categories: technical, sophistic, and philosophical (*Classical Rhetoric*, 16–17). Though the classifications of rhetoric by Cope and Grimaldi exemplify this conflict, a thorough discussion of the opposition is beyond the scope of this paper. For a survey of the conflict between theoretical and practical rhetorics, see Sutton, "The Death of Rhetoric and Its Rebirth in Philosophy."

to refer to two distinct domains of inquiry. Instead, theory and practice are arranged in a conceptual hierarchy whereby theory either
governs or reflects rhetorical practice. This is precisely the form in
which Aristotle's divisions of knowledge appear in the work of two
English-language commentators on the *Rhetoric*. For both commentators, to some extent, the theory/practice binary demarcates the
"practice" of rhetoric as an object of study. Both Cope and Grimaldi
institute rhetoric as a formal discipline only by suppressing the very
contingencies of time and circumstance by which rhetoric was once
defined.

The theory/practice binary resides at the heart of epistemological
foundationalism. In the simplest terms, a foundationalist conception
of theory consists of two interdependent claims. First, foundationalist theory claims to provide the general principles that mirror, interpret, or govern an activity or object. As Stanley Fish would say, theory
in the "strong" sense promises to be a general hermeneutic, guided by
principles that are immutable because they rise above the particular-
ities of time and circumstance.[2] Another description of epistemological foundationism is found in Richard Rorty's discussion of the goals
of traditional philosophy: "Philosophy's central concern is to be a general theory of representation, a theory which will divide up culture
into the areas which represent reality well, those which represent it
less well, and those which do not represent it at all" (*Philosophy and
the Mirror of Nature*, 3). Fish uses Chomskian linguistics as an example of foundationalist principles: "They have their source not in culture but in nature, and therefore they are *abstract* (without empirical
content), *general* (not to be identified with any particular race, location, or historical period but with the species), and *invariant* (do not
differ from language to language). As a system of rules, they are 'independent of the features of the actual world and thus hold in any possible one'" ("Consequences," 108).

In rhetoric's disciplinary history, theory is often characterized as
mirroring rhetorical practice. To represent rhetoric by invariable rules,
however, rhetorical practice must be depicted as a virtually immutable behavior, more like a natural process than a social activity. In
other words, rhetorical practice must have a basis other than culture—

---

[2] For discussions of foundationalist theory, see Mitchell, *Against Theory*. Fish's description of "strong" theory is found on pages 106–8 of "Consequences." See also
Rorty, *Philosophy and the Mirror of Nature*.

in either biological nature or "human" nature. In both cases, rhetorical behavior is extricated from its social and historical contexts. Foundationalist theory's second claim, closely related to this rift between nature and culture, is that the very practices of interpreting and theorizing escape the forces of time and circumstance. Both objects of interpretation and "interpreters" may be excised from culture and history. Thus, epistemological foundationalism is characterized by its demarcation of an unsituated, dehistoricized object of study, over which an equally decontextualized observer may exercise interpretive mastery.

Fish offers a succinct explanation of the fallacy inherent in this proposed relationship between unsituated interpreters and interpretations. According to Fish, foundationalist theory can never achieve its aim of exhaustive description because "the primary data and formal laws necessary to its success will always be spied or picked out from within the contextual circumstances of which they are supposedly independent" ("Consequences," 110). Put another way, "The objective facts and rules of calculation that are to ground interpretation and render it principled are themselves interpretive products: they are, therefore, always and already contaminated by the interested judgments they claim to transcend" (110).

Pierre Bourdieu takes the analysis of the interpreter's perspective one step further, maintaining that the very perspective of distance on a practice or object of study is a social as well as an epistemological stance. The premise of Bourdieu's *Outline of a Theory of Practice*, a detailed critique of the theory/practice opposition, is that the position from which an interpreter views practical activity as "*an object of observation and analysis*" betrays both a social and an epistemological break (OTP, 2). According to Bourdieu, the "social conditions of objective apprehension" reflect a social hierachy in which the scientific perspective is privileged by those who control "dominant systems of classification" (OTP, 178, 169). Quite explicitly Bourdieu contends that the theoretical perspective is the distinguishing mark of a particular class, a perspective won against "the conditions of existence and the dispositions of agents who cannot afford the luxury of logical speculation" (OTP, 115).[3] Bourdieu argues, in effect, that epistemological

---

[3] "The practical privilege in which all scientific activity arises never more subtly governs that activity (insofar as science presupposes not only an epistemological break but also a *social* separation) than when, unrecognized as privilege, it leads to an implicit theory of practice which is the corollary of neglect of the social conditions in which science is possible" (OTP, 1).

orders are inextricably tied to social orders. This is precisely the sense of "orders of knowledge" that appears in Pythagorean traditions, reinscribed from Plato to Aristotle.

Productive knowledge, for Aristotle, is concerned with "making," a *poesis* that is characterized by both epistemological and ethical indeterminacy. In the *Nicomachean Ethics*, Aristotle explains: "All art is concerned with coming into being, i.e. with contriving and considering how something may come into being which is capable of either being or not being" (1140a11–13). The end of productive knowledge, in contrast to theoretical and practical knowledge, is always "outside itself," residing not in the "product" but in the use made of the artistic construct by a receiver or audience. Just as in the art of architecture, the master of the house is the best judge of the art; so also in the art of rhetoric, the audience of the speech determines its "end" or *telos* (Kennedy, 47; *Rhet.* 1358b1–2). Productive knowledge is concerned with the indeterminate and the possible—and that which presents us, as Aristotle explains in the *Rhetoric*, with alternative possibilities (41; 1357a4–5). In contrast to theoretical knowledge, productive knowledge is decisively instrumental and uncompromisingly situated. Instead of rising above the contingencies of time and circumstance, productive knowledge is consumately dependent on them.

Throughout the Aristotelian corpus, rhetoric consistently conforms to the criteria that distinguish productive knowledge. Aristotle maintains that the end of rhetoric is outside itself—in the "hearer" (Kennedy, 47; *Rhet.* 1358b1–2). The insistence, moreover, that rhetoric is "not concerned with any special or definite class of subjects" (35, 37; 1355b8–9, 31–34) iterates another important criterion of productive knowledge: its concern with that which can be otherwise. Consequently, rhetoric is exempt from the epistemological determinacy of theoretical knowledge and the ethical determinacy of practical knowledge. The characteristics that foundationalist theory tries to efface are the distinguishing features of rhetoric as productive knowledge: its implication in an exchange, the value of which is both social and economic; its resistance to determinant epistemological and axiological ends; and its consummate dependence on time and circumstance. The modern reformulation of the theory/practice binary clearly contrasts with the ancient relationship between the theoretical and the practical. For Cope and Grimaldi, the theory/practice binary transforms rhetoric from a situated social exchange into a static object—or stable activity—grounded in nature. Whether rhetoric is defined either as a "practical art" or as philosophy, "theory" performs the function of guiding and interpreting the "practice" of rhetoric.

Edward M. Cope and Rhetoric as Practical Knowledge

E. M. Cope wrote *An Introduction to Aristotle's "Rhetoric"* and his commentary on the *Rhetoric* at Trinity College in the mid–nineteenth century, in the midst of England's industrial transformation. Cope's interpretation of Aristotelian technē reflects both associationist psychology, current in England at the time, and a concern with predicting and improving the efficiency of human behavior. Though he finally argues that rhetoric does not belong in the domain of productive knowledge, Cope is unique in that he seriously confronts rhetoric's relationship to productive knowledge—so much so that he is compelled to offer a detailed defense of his reclassification of rhetoric as a "practical art."

In the end, Cope does not reconstruct rhetoric as discipline secured by the precepts of epistemological foundationalism in the most restricted terms. In contrast to Grimaldi, Cope does not argue for a mimetic relationship between rhetorical theory and rhetorical practice. Instead, he focuses on Aristotle's discussions of the relationship between rhetoric and politics, with the goal of identifying rhetoric as a subdiscipline of politics and thus reclassifying it as a type of practical knowledge. Though the domain of practical knowledge does not, as does theoretical knowledge, utterly efface rhetoric's social and temporal contingencies, this identification associates rhetoric with "action" over "production" and finally reconstructs rhetoric as a science of human behavior—or what we might call a subdiscipline of "political science."

Cope's case for rhetoric's identification with practical knowledge begins with a discussion of two epistemological taxonomies that recur throughout the corpus: the theoretical/practical/productive triad, and the distinction between probable and certain knowledge. Cope reviews the epistemological triad as it is presented in the *Metaphysics*, acknowledging that the "division of philosophy and knowledge into *theōrētikē, praktikē*, and *poiētikē*, defined severally by their *telē* or objects, truth, practice, and production, 'speculative' 'practical' and 'productive,' is set forth at length in the Metaph E. I. and assumed elsewhere as the only true and natural classification" (*Introduction*, 18 n. 1.). One of the most explicit articulations of the triad is found in the *Metaphysics*, where Aristotle asserts that "all thought is either practical or productive or theoretical" (1025b25). Regarding the triad as "the only true and natural classification," Cope references Hermann Bonitz's note on 1025b18. Cope does not, however, go on to review the extensive discussions of the triad found throughout *Metaphysics*. Instead, he points to another distinction found in Aristotle's discussions of knowlege, what he calls a "two-fold division of objects of knowledge," which is based, he maintains, on book I, chapter 2 of the *Nicomachean Ethics:* "(1) things which are entirely independent of human action and human power, which are the objects of speculative philosophy, and (2) things whose origin does depend upon human will impulse and action, whether they terminate in the action or *energeia* itself or are carried on to an *ergon*, the production of something permanent and concrete, as in art proper" (*Introduction*, 18 n. 1). In Cope's discussion of the passage, rhetoric is defined in terms of the opposition of certain (or "scientific") to probable knowledge. Rhetoric is concerned with "human actions characters and motives," which are, Cope insists, "by their very nature only contingent and probable; nothing can be *predicted* of them with certainty" (10).[4] Certain knowledge, in contrast, can be defined in terms of "necessary" laws and conclusions. Cope offers the following description of rhetoric's distinguishing features: "Rhetoric with few exceptions excludes the universal and necessary, and deals only with the probable; and this is the *essential* difference between it and the scientific or demonstrative processes" (10). Thus Cope identifies the distinction between that which submits to and that which resists human intervention with the distinction between certainty and probability.

The discussion Cope references in the *Nicomachean Ethics* is less concerned with certainty and probability than it is with the elevation of politics as the "most authoritative art and that which is most truly the master art" (EN 1094a26–27). Still, Cope's treatment of the opening passages of the *Nicomachean Ethics* serves several purposes. First, it allows him to identify rhetoric with politics. As Cope observes, in these passages Aristotle asserts that it is the role of the art of politics

---

[4] Rhetoric further contrasts with certain knowledge in that like dialectic it is "indifferent to the truth of its conclusions, so far as it is considered as an art" (Cope, *Introduction*, 9).

to determine what subjects should be studied in the state. Rhetoric is included with strategy and economics as one of the most "highly esteemed" subjects of study (EN 1094b2–3). This identification of rhetoric with politics also enables Cope to associate rhetoric with praxis, or acting, as opposed to poesis, or making. The result is the occlusion of the domain of practical knowledge and the reduction of the epistemological triad to the binary distinction between theory and practice. As we shall see, Cope finally identifies praxis with empeiria; and rhetoric becomes a "practical art" that manages "experience" in the positivist sense.

It is only fair to note that Cope acknowledges that the two taxonomies are guided by different principles. He observes that the triad is demarcated according to the final cause, or telos, of each domain. The two-part taxonomy, in contrast, is based on the classification of "the origin or cause to which the objects upon which the speculation is exercised owe their existence" (*Introduction*, 18 n. 1). This description appears to refer to Aristotle's concept of formal causality; however, Cope goes on to assert that the "origin or cause" is what "gives rise to a two-fold division of objects of knowledge" (18 n. 1). Consequently, the character of the objects of knowledge—in other words, their "material cause"—determines their classification as either probable or certain knowledge.[5]

The cost of privileging Aristotle's material cause, however, is the effacement of final causality and, hence, the domain of productive knowledge. To reduce the three-part taxonomy to the single distinction between certainty and probability, Cope must make two arguments. First, he must contend that the distinction between productive and practical knowledge is not central to Aristotle's taxonomy of knowledge. Referring to Aristotle's discussion of productive knowledge in *Nicomachean Ethics*, book VI, chapter 4, Cope goes so far as to suggest that the passage in which Aristotle "*seems* . . . to confine the term 'art' to rules and practice which end in production" is of questionable authorship; indeed, Cope attributes it to Eudemus (*Introduc-*

---

[5] This focus on material causality is not hard to defend within the corpus. As Cope notes, a frequent refrain throughout the corpus is that any treatment of a subject will "be considered sufficient if its distinctness and exactness be only in proportion to its subject matter (or materials)" (*Introduction*, 11). "Our discussion will be adequate if it has as much clearness as the subject-matter admits of; for precision is not to be sought for alike in all discussions, any more than in all the products of the crafts" (EN 1094b13).

tion, 16 n. 2). Cope goes on to maintain that the definition of productive knowledge in the *Nicomachean Ethics* could apply only to "art in its strictest sense" (16 n. 2). Cope asserts that rhetoric cannot be productive knowledge because it "does not result in the production of something permanent and concrete, as in art proper" (18 n. 1). He finally marshals Quintilian's relatively unsatisfactory resolution of the dilemma in the *Institutio Oratoria*, in which Quintilian insists that rhetoric is "concerned with action," in contrast to such arts as painting (II.xviii.2). Quintilian concludes that "since it is with action that its practice is chiefly and most frequently concerned, let us call it an active or administrative art" (II.xviii.5). Cope then amends Quintilian's classification by calling rhetoric a "practical art" (*Introduction*, 19).

Cope's redefinition of rhetoric as a "practical art" necessitates a second argument regarding the relationship of rhetoric to Aristotle's concept of technē. Cope confronts this problem by allying the "practical" character of rhetoric not only with "acting" but also with "experience." This conception of experience, however, is grounded in the positivist orientation of nineteenth-century associationist psychology. Such an alliance would seem to be at odds with Cope's classification of rhetoric as a "subordinate branch of *politikē*" (*Introduction*, 17). But politics can become a kind of "science" when human behavior is interpreted as being governed by "natural laws."

Cope makes the association between nature and rhetoric/politics through his interpretation of empeiria. He uses Aristotle's discussion of thought and perception in the opening passages of the *Metaphysics* to identify "experience" with acting. Cope's paraphrase of 980a27–81a2 is consistent with Ross's translation:[6] "Sensation of some kind is the distinctive mark of *animal* life: from sensation, in *some* animals, arises memory, and in proportion to the strength of this faculty is the force of intellect and the power of acquiring knowledge. In man, memory, by repetition of the same impression, gives rise to experience, *empeiria*, and from it proceed art, and ultimately science" (*Introduction*, 20). Cope interprets both sensation and memory in the terms of nineteenth-century psychology, then called "mental philosophy." Art is a "process of generalisation from experience" (20). According to Cope's translation of *Metaphysics* 981a5–7, art is produced "when from many mental impressions arising from experience a

---

[6] Ross's translation is found in Barnes, *Complete Works.*

single universal conception is formed about their common properties"
(20).

This identification of "mental impressions" with empeiriai reflects
nineteenth-century associationist psychology. Grounded in the work
of John Locke, it offered an empirical account of human behavior and
thought by locating the source of ideas in sense data. According to this
theory, the ideas generated by sense data were reorganized in the mind
by such laws of association as contiguity and similarity. Associationist psychology, as William Woods points out, bears traces of Aristotle's
theories of perception and memory.[7]   The empirical orientation of
Cope's depiction of sense perception, however, is probably more indebted to Francis Bacon and John Locke. Aristotle's notions of sense
data and perception do not maintain the same empirical cast. Regarding Aristotle's theories of sensation, G. E. L. Owen has argued that Bacon's conception of empirical facts is based on a distinction between
phainomena (observed facts) and *endoxa* (common conceptions on the
subject) that is not consistently maintained by Aristotle.[8] The "fac-
ticity" of sense experience found in associationist psychology was
used by the utilitarians to make ethics an exact and even predictive
science by depicting human behavior according to laws of nature. For
example, in *System of Logic*, John Stuart Mill asserts that such a science could predict human behavior in the same way that the physical
sciences predicted natural events (bk. VI, Chap. 2).

Similarly, rhetoric's usefulness as a discipline, according to Cope,
resides in its potential to predict and control natural behavior. Cope
refers to *Rhetoric* 1355b25 to make connections between human behavior, the laws of nature (which were the laws of association), and
rhetoric. This passage defines the field of study as "the faculty of observing in any given case the available means of persuasion"
(1355b25). According to Cope's interpretation, "the available means of
persuasion" are the constraints embedded in empeiria that govern
rhetorical performance. Empeiria, Cope explains, "is an *irrational* procedure; manifests itself in a merely mechanical mode of operation,

---

[7] Woods, 21–22. For discussions of the impact of associationist psychology on
rhetorical theory, see Woods, "Nineteenth-Century Psychology and the Teaching of
Writing," and Crowley, "Invention in Nineteenth-Century Rhetoric."

[8] For a full discussion, see Owen, *"Tithenai ta phainomena,"* in *Logic, Science, and
Dialectic,* 239–51. Both Owen and Martha Nussbaum suggest that the boundary between empirical fact and dialectical material in Aristotelian thought, if it existed at all,
was indefinite and permeable. See also Nussbaum, *Fragility of Goodness,* 1986, 245–51.

working like a machine, and displaying a skill which results from nothing but habit and association, and is acquired by mere repetition; . . . it deals only with individual cases, and never rises to general conceptions or rules" (*Introduction*, 22). By Cope's account, rhetoric is useful because it resembles and improves on the operations of nature: rhetoric "acts in combining and generalising and reducing to rule and system, and so making applicable, the scattered and desultory observations of phenomena already noted and existing in various departments of nature and human speculation" (26). Aristotle's conception of "the available means of persuasion," according to Cope, is designed "to withdraw the notion of the art in some degree from the exclusively practical application of it encouraged by the sophistical school, and to fix attention rather upon its theory and method" (34). As a consequence, the art of rhetoric is dependent "in no respect upon the result, but only on the method employed" (33). Cope maintains that this is a "more scientific treatment of the subject" (34). Though Cope insists that rhetoric resides in the domain of probability, his theory explicating rhetorical behavior has distinctly scientific overtones: rhetoric's purpose is to be more effective than the "natural" laws of association at predicting and controlling experience. On the one hand, Cope acknowledges that rhetorical theory is instrumental in managing experience; still, he maintains that its value resides in its potential to "*predict* results" (23). Method thus functions like modern scientific theory. It is capable of predicting human behavior because it reflects the natural laws that govern behavior.

Cope's analysis falls under the jurisdiction of epistemological foundationalism at the point that it attempts a match between "method" and nature. While Cope does not explicitly claim that rhetorical method mirrors or represents the laws of nature, the suggestion remains that the legitimacy of rhetorical method resides in its resemblance to stable, natural processes. Experience is thus limited by the closed set of laws that memory uses to combine sense impressions. The laws that explain perception are still rooted in a detemporalized conception of nature. Cope is not interested in rhetoric as a situated, social exchange. His purpose is to define principles that explain rhetoric as a form of human behavior constrained by laws of nature. In this context, an academic account of rhetoric will be evaluated largely by the standards by which "theory" itself is assessed— standards such as coherence and economy. The more these principles are formalized, the more stable rhetoric becomes as an object of study.

William Grimaldi and Rhetoric as Theoretical Knowledge

Designed to secure epistemological and ethical legitimacy for rhetoric, Grimaldi's commentaries on the *Rhetoric*, volumes 1 and 2, and *Studies in the Philosophy of Aristotle's "Rhetoric"* are finely crafted examples of epistemological foundationalism. Grimaldi's objective is to bring both ethics and philosophy under the aegis of rhetoric, a goal he seeks to accomplish through formalist interpretations of elements of Aristotelian rhetoric. In the broadest terms, Grimaldi argues that Aristotle sets out formal conceptions of both discourse and rhetorical proof. Those formal structures (primarily the enthymeme, but also the three proofs of *ēthos, logos,* and *pathos*) are stable and valid because they reflect natural forms of intellectual and moral reasoning. Thus, like Cope, Grimaldi uses "nature" to validate his interpretation of rhetoric. Unlike Cope, however, Grimaldi does not seriously confront rhetoric's relationship to Aristotle's productive knowledge.

Grimaldi's interpretation of rhetoric's relationship to philosophy and ethics is strongly indebted to structuralist linguistics. The "underlying principles of discourse" provide rhetoric with "philosophical" subject matter: "Rhetoric is the art which presents man with the structure for language, and, by way of structure, enables language to become an effective medium whereby man apprehends reality" (*Studies*, 8). For Grimaldi, to investigate the art of discourse is to explore the communication and apprehension of reality. He explains, "The heart of the problem of rhetorical study as seen in Aristotle is that all significant human discourse is structured language, an organic whole, which communicates effectively man's reflection on and articulation of, reality" (8).

Grimaldi's construction of Aristotelian rhetoric turns largely on his interpretation of the rhetorical syllogism, or enthymeme. Grimaldi maintains that the enthymeme is a formal structure that organizes the elements of rhetoric (its various appeals and topoi), but it is also a "general method of reasoning," a "methodology of deductive and inductive inference" (*Studies*, 49, 103). The enthymeme not only reflects the workings of the mind, its also unites the three rhetorical proofs of ēthos, pathos, and logos. It is this unification of the proofs that Grimaldi's insists brings ethics under the aegis of rhetoric. As "the integrating structure of rhetorical discourse," the enthymeme unites reason and emotion; it "incorporates . . . all of the elements demanded by language as the vehicle of discourse with another: *reason, ethos, pathos"* (16–17). The result, according to Grimaldi, is that Aristotle's "art of logos" brings "together the results of the activity of the speculative intellect and those of the practical intellect" (53–54).

Grimaldi's argument that rhetoric subsumes philosophy or theoretical knowledge takes another, more complicated turn. Grimaldi focuses on what he calls the "material" causes of the enthymeme— probabilities, signs, and topics. These are complicated elements in Aristotle's thought as a whole, and it is impossible to do justice to Grimaldi's equally complex discussion. Though his end of Grimaldi's argument is the claim that rhetoric is equivalent to philosophy, what is at issue in this specific context is the probative, or demonstrative, force of enthymemic materials. In the simplest terms, Grimaldi's discussion consists of two major arguments: (1) The enthymemic "materials" of signs and probabilities are sufficiently "grounded in the real order" to confer on rhetoric the function of representing both reality and truth. (2) The "if, then" structure of the enthymeme is a form of inferencing that mirrors the "natural ways in which the mind thinks" (*Studies*, 131, 130). Aristotle's most detailed discussion of probabilities (*eikota*), non-necessary signs (*sēmeia anōnyma*), and necessary signs (*tekmēria*) is found in the *Prior* and *Posterior Analytics*. Grimaldi maintains that, according to the *Analytics*, both necessary and nonnecessary signs, hold "a stronger demonstrative force than *eikos*" (111). Sēmeia are necessary signs so closely tied to Aristotelian logic that their demonstrative force is not even questioned. The interpretation Grimaldi must vigorously defend, however, is that probabilities can be sufficiently rooted in objective reality to make "an inference from *eikos* . . . an eminently reasonable guaranty that the conclusion represents the objective fact" (109).

Grimaldi admits that probabilities are not bound by the relations of "internal necessity" that characterize sēmeia and tekmēria in syllogistic demonstration (*Studies*, 111). However, he insists that *eikota* can have demonstrative force not only by virtue of their relationship to "objective fact," but also because they are "permanent and stable" and thus capable of expressing "a reasonable and stable aspect of the real order" (108, 109).[9] Grimaldi summarizes his argument: "*Eikos* is

---

[9] Grimaldi's conception of "probability" contrasts with the sophistic notion of probability argument. For sophists, such as Protagoras, the probable marked a distinct epistemological domain; it was not simply the attenuation of certain knowledge.

that which the generality of men think, or may think, and as such it carries persuasive force to the mind. Aristotle's *eikos* and the knowledge which comes from it is rooted in the real order and it is this existential aspect of it which makes it a legitimate source for further knowledge" (110).

Having grounded probabilities and signs in a stable reality, Grimaldi goes on to argue that Aristotle's twenty-eight common topics, or *koinoi topoi,* are both "general axiomatic propositions" and "valid forms of inference" that reflect "natural" processes of reasoning (*Studies,* 130). The twenty-eight topics divide into three "inferential and logical patterns": antecedent-consequent (also cause-effect), more-less, and a form of relation (131). As Grimaldi explains them, these topics are "ways in which the mind naturally and readily reasons, and they are independent, in a way, of the subject to which they are applied, and may be said to be imposed as forms upon this material in order to clarify and determine it further" (134). Eikota and sēmeia provide the "premises of enthymematic reasoning"; and the rhetor may find those materials in both general and particular topics.[10] In enthymemic reasoning, the koinoi topoi are "applied to the subject-matter," which, according to Grimaldi, are "presented by" the special topics, or the *"eide"* (130). The three modes of inference function much like Cope's laws of association, grounding the operations of rhetoric in nature. Grimaldi admits that his argument leads him to claim two functions for the enthymeme. If, on the one hand, the enthymeme is a form of reasoning, then its function is inventional. According to Grimaldi's argument, however, this act of invention is also a mode of proof. He explains, "The scientific syllogism is . . . basically . . . an instrument for the acquisition of knowledge which takes apparently separate and independent concepts and puts them into a structure which leads to new knowledge. In the same way the enthymeme gives structure to the sources which contribute to belief or conviction. In both instances the scientific syllogism and the rhetorical syllogism, as structural form, stand apart from their sources. . . . The only permanent element in 'syllogism' is its structure as a form of inference. Its apodeictic, dialectical, rhetorical character is determined by its content, or the source material it uses" (137).

---

[10] Grimaldi is largely responsible for articulating definitive distinctions between general and specific topics. See the discussion found on 115–35 of *Studies.*

Grimaldi concludes that by virtue of its universality, enthymemic form is capable of representing not only reality, but also truth and justice. More specifically, the enthymeme functions heuristically to determine the most effective proofs and philosophically and ethically to determine the "best" proofs. This argument is explicit in Grimaldi's commentary on *Rhetoric* 1355a21–25, a passage that W. Rhys Roberts translates as follows: "Rhetoric is useful because things that are true and things that are just have a natural tendency to prevail over their opposites, so that if the decisions of judges are not what they ought to be, the defeat must be due to the speakers themselves, and they must be blamed accordingly."[11] Grimaldi's alternative translation goes much further in claiming an epistemological and axiological function for rhetoric: "Rhetoric is useful because truth and justice are naturally stronger than their opposites; and so, if judgements are not made as they should be, it follows necessarily that truth and justice are defeated by their opposites (untruth and injustice). And this merits censure" (*"Rhetoric" I*, 27). Grimaldi concludes: "Implicit in this statement, and worthy of note, is that rhetoric prevents us from making wrong judgements, and in doing so it protects truth and justice. To defend the usefulness of rhetoric on this ground, as A. [Aristotle] does, is to attribute to rhetoric an important and significant position. For what A. is quite pointedly saying is that rhetoric is mimesis and that it is supposed to re-present the real (i.e., truth and justice) in any situation for an auditor. Rhetoric does this the only way it can: through language. . . . If truth and justice are defeated, it is because rhetoric has failed in its function as mimesis" (27). For Grimaldi, the rhetorical enthymeme is able to both determine and represent truth and justice in the world.

Grimaldi's depiction of rhetoric's province comes up against Aristotle's two assertions that rhetoric is "not concerned with any special or definite class of subjects" (*Rhet.* 1355b5) and that the subjects of rhetorical deliberation must present us with "alternative possibilities" (1357a 1–5, 20). In many ways Grimaldi refuses to confront Aristotelian rhetoric on its own terms, refashioning it instead to fit a model of knowledge and ethics which, in many ways, is more foundationalist than the most conservative interpretations of Aristotelian philosophy. According to this paradigm, rhetoric can conform to

---

[11] Roberts's translation is found in Barnes, *Complete Works.*

the most rigorous epistemological and axiological standards. What rhetoric can no longer be, however, is a valuable, transferable technē, which, instead of reflecting reality, is capable of creating new versions of the real and the valuable.

8 · Arts of Virtue and Democracy

Arts of Intervention versus Sciences of Representation

The significance of containing rhetoric within the theory/practice binary resides in its transformation of an art of intervention into a discipline of representation. From this perspective, rhetoric is far more prone to reproduce the given than to invent new possibilities. Invention is always constrained. As Aristotle observed, we can work only with "the available means" of situations and of art. What could it mean at the turn of the millennium to intervene in such a way as to "invent" alternative futures? I would suggest that it can mean several things.

One of my objectives has been to extricate rhetoric and technē from "normalizing" traditions that work against interventions of any kind. One of the most powerful normalizing strategies is that of description. In other words, to imagine the invention of other possibilities, we must try to examine how "what is" has been invented and reproduced. In this context, one of Bourdieu's contributions is to explore the influences on our estimations of the given, the probable, and the possible. On the normative force of description, Bourdieu explains that "even the most strictly constative scientific description is always open to the possibility of functioning in a prescriptive way, capable of contributing to its own verification by exercising a theory effect through which it helps to bring about that which it declares" (*Language and Symbolic Power*, 134). "Theory effect" refers to the rhetorical force inherent in any socially authorized account of "what is":

The specific force of official representations is that they institute the principles of a practical relation to the natural and social world in words, objects, practices, and especially in collective, public events, such as the major rituals, deputations and solemn processions (the Greeks called them *theories* . . .), of which our processions, rallies and demonstrations . . . are the secularized form. . . . Officialization is the process whereby the group (or those who dominate it) teaches itself and masks from itself its own truth, binds itself by a public profession which sanctions and imposes what it utters, tacitly defining the limits of the thinkable and the unthinkable and so contributing to the maintenance of the social order from which it derives its power. (LP, 108).

Description not only creates the world but also who we are engaging that world.

Description may even be more powerful than prescription in eliciting compliance to limits of behavior and desire, particularly when the source of those descriptions is accorded a high degree of cultural authority. In this case, "seeing what others see" is a decisive criterion of group membership. In other words, not to see what appears to be "self-evident" to many—especially those who are in possession of significant social authority—is to define oneself as "outside" the group, as either an aberration (a "crazy") or as one who has spurned group membership.[1] In contrast, prescription in whatever form—legal, social, religious—"tips its hand" as a form of compulsion and, as such, leaves itself open to competing forces seeking similar control. Put more simply, in many cases it is far easier to challenge a prescriptive order or law than an accepted account of "reality."

One "reality" that I have attempted to question is the self-evidence of a normative model of subjectivity, particularly one defined by self-determination and "choice." Plato had to create the mythical land of Er in order to question the standards that govern individual choice. His experiment seems to confirm Bourdieu's contention that "only in imaginary experience (in the folk tale, for example), which neutralizes the sense of social realities, does the social world take the form of a universe of possibles equally possible for any possible subject" (LP, 64). In other words, for most agents the world seldom presents itself as a smorgasbord of options, limited only by ignorance or indolence. Agents are more likely, as Bourdieu suggests, to "'cut their coats according to their cloth'" (65); or, put another way, to "shape their aspi-

[1] See also LP, 109.

rations according to concrete indices of the accessible and the inaccessible" (64). Ancient philosophers frankly admitted that the sage and the philosopher-king were gender- and class-specific. Their states were composed of parts that differed in "kind," and nothing would have appeared more foolish to them than to judge the mouth according to the functions of the eye. So what are we to make of liberal arts traditions that hold to normative conceptions of "virtue"—which, in the end, are inextricably tied to historically (as well as socially and economically) specific conceptions of subjectivity? Surely to fail according to standards that in no way embody one's interests, values, or history is to experience the most bitter kind of failure. Those standards do more than effect failure and exclusion. They provide the basis for rationalizing the unequal distribution of "virtue," together with its social and economic rewards. The notion that education is a process of "attitude adjustment" to specific values and patterns of distribution goes back at least to Aristotle, who insisted that "it is not the possessions but the desires of mankind which require to be equalized, and this is impossible, unless a sufficient education is provided by the laws" (*Pol.* 1266b29–32).

From this perspective, the often virulent responses to changes in the canons and demographics of the academy are not overreactions. Canon changes are not minor adjustments; neither is the admission of diverse constituencies in the academy simply a matter of opening the doors a little wider. These changes have brought to light the contingent character of the values, norms, and ideals on which the humanities were founded. By putting into question the normative ideals of the liberal arts, their founding mission has, indeed, been threatened. But to question the normative values of an institution is not to question the importance of norms and values per se. In the same way, to understand that knowledge is historically contingent is not to say that meaningful knowledge is impossible.

If Protagoras, Isocrates, and Cicero were appointed deans and chancellors of universities today, I doubt that they would institute a curriculum based on principles of radical democracy. For the most part, the early rhetors enabled the already advantaged to seize even more. I bring them discursively into the academy to recall their conceptions of knowledge as intervention and invention. Part of my purpose in outlining the tradition of technē has been to use it heuristically to suggest alternative models of knowledge and value. In particular, I have attempted to depict the ways in which technē interacted with fate—

or, to use Bourdieu's allusion, the way it confronted the allotment of cloth rather than the pattern of the coat.

To refigure rhetorical studies as an art of intervention and invention is to create a very different classroom.[2] When the focus of instruction is intervention in specific rhetorical contexts, both students and teachers must grapple with the material realities of genre and access. What forums are available and what must be invented to enable the kind of political agency that was once the primary aim of rhetorical instruction? In this context, what is at stake for teachers is less the transmission of specific material than the renegotiation of students' own symbolic capital. The skills involved in such a process include the appropriation of a habit of vigilance that is alert for indeterminacies and points of intervention in existing systems of classification. Enabling students to "seize the advantage" in specific rhetorical contexts amounts to inviting them to be a part of constructing standards of value and advantage in their cultures.

Inventing Arts of Respect and Justice

Toward the conclusion of Protagoras's prehistory account, the sophist describes the failure of humankind to live together peacefully in cities: "When they gathered in communities they injured one another for want of political skill [*tēn politikēn technēn*]" (Plato, *Protagoras*, 322b). To prevent the race from self-destruction, Zeus sends Hermes "the qualities of respect for others and a sense of justice, so as to bring order into . . . cities and create a bond of friendship and union" (322c). Hermes asks Zeus how he should apportion these gifts of aidōs and dikē. Should they be distributed according to the same principle of compensation that guided the apportionment of the arts—so that "one trained doctor suffices for many laymen and so with other experts" (322c)? Or, asks Hermes, should right and respect be dealt to all? Zeus responds, "Let all have their share. There could never be cities if only a few shared in these virtues" (322d).

According to Protagoras, political technē consists of these two qualities: "aidōs," which is generally translated "respect," and "dikē," here translated "right" and often translated "justice." As we have

---

[2] For one vision of a very different classroom, one that uses the African metaphor of "crossroads" (rather than "border politics") for refiguring power and difference, see Handel Kashope Wright, "(Re)conceptualising Pedagogy."

seen, Greek conceptions of justice take a number of forms, forms that generally serve particular interests. We observed in Chapter 2, for example, the role played by Solonian reforms in severing political justice from economic justice. As such disputes bear witness, different definitions of justice become rhetorical strategies in service to specific social, economic, and political goals.

To some extent, however, there is less room for disagreement concerning the meaning of aidōs—not because it is more simple but because it is more of an emotion than an idea, a posture of the body and the heart rather than an idea in the mind. In his book-length study of the term, Douglas Cairns notes that the Greek concept of aidōs was an attitude toward oneself and others that was tied to both a sense of shame and a sense of honor: "The feeling of *aidōs*, entailing concentration on the self and one's own status, is prompted by and focuses on consideration of the status of another" (*Aidōs*, 3). In his discussion of Protagoras's Prometheus narrative, Cairns observes that aidōs appears as "the social virtue par excellence," retaining its traditional meaning of a "valued disposition or trait of character encompassing a sense of the ways in which one's own honour and status are bound up with those of others" (356). Aidōs is thus an attitude of respect toward others that is inextricably tied to the respect one can expect for oneself. This attitude is neither silent nor passive. As Cairns explains, aidōs is also an "inhibitory emotion" that influences one's behavior (2). Herein lies the relationship between aidōs and shame:

> The notions of shame and respect are not totally unrelated; to feel inhibitory shame (*aidōs* is always prospective and inhibitory in the earliest authors) is to picture oneself as losing honour, while to show respect is to recognize the honour of another. . . . [T]o be concerned with one's own honour is to envisage oneself as one among others, also bearers of honour; thus to limit one's own claim to honour is to accept one's status *vis-à-vis* others, to inhibit self-assertion is to recognize how such conduct would impinge upon the honour of others. (13)

The image of the "limit" appears again, but this time the limit is the product of both an attitude and a relationship. The attitude of aidōs assumes that one does not have all the answers—that one's perspective is, by definition, partial.

Though aidōs is a kind of self-limitation, it differs from compliance in two important ways. First, compliance is not constitutive of a relationship. Aidōs assumes that communication and conviction occur only within the bonds of trust and obligation. Indeed, the attitude of aidōs may be one of the best illustrations of an active, good-faith invitation to form a relationship. Because purely authoritarian discourse is concerned solely with strengthening an already rigid position, it is an almost ceremonial rejection of a relationship. The most dangerous authoritarian discourses may not even be those which reject a relationship but those which refuse even to acknowledge the possibility of relationship. According to Jean-François Lyotard, the most serious injustices turn on the failure either to address or to be addressed by the other—a failure that amounts to the refusal of a relationship.[3] Purely heretical discourse may similarly renounce a relationship by addressing the other only in ways that require the other's self-negation. Aidōs is both the means to and the end of a relationship; compliance bears witness to the failure of a relationship. Aidōs also differs from compliance in that—at least according to Protagoras—it is inextricably tied to justice. Respect requires a good-faith effort toward a relationship from all parties, and good-faith efforts are difficult when the stakes and resources of each party are unequal. The posture of aidōs has a right to expect justice in return; justice and respect would seem to be inextricably tied.

Unfortunately, we live in a world bound by many bad-faith contracts—laws, policies, and institutions based on negotiated settlements that protect all sides from having to form relationships. We can choose, however, either to labor to create paths for new relationships or to live in solitude and fear. If common experience is the requisite for common agreement, it is likely that we will live in a very contentious world. If we have to see the same reality before we can begin to talk, we will live in a world with very little dialogue. Difference can no longer be the anomaly, the enemy, or the problem to be solved. Difference is the condition.

I would like to imagine that we could approach the social world the way Aristotle did the natural world, believing that the delights of the senses bear witness to our desire to know, and that our desire to know consists in the pleasure of bringing differences to light.

---

[3] See Lyotard, *The Differend*.

Bibliography

Ackrill, J. L., ed. *A New Aristotle Reader*. Princeton: Princeton University Press, 1987.

Adkins, A. W. H. "*Aretē, Technē*, Democracy, and Sophists: Protagoras 361b–328d." *Journal of Hellenic Studies* 93 (1973): 3–12.

———. *Merit and Responsibility*. Oxford: Oxford University Press, 1960.

Alford, C. Fred. *The Self in Social Theory: A Psychoanalytic Account of Its Construction in Plato, Hobbes, Locke, Rawls, and Rousseau*. New Haven: Yale University Press, 1991.

Apostle, Hippocrates. *Aristotle's "Metaphysics."* Translated with Commentaries and Glossary. Bloomington: Indiana University Press, 1966.

———. *Aristotle's "Physics."* Translated with Commentary and Glossary. Indiana University Press, 1969.

Arac, Jonathan, ed. *Postmodernism and Politics*. Theory and History of Literature, vol. 28. Minneapolis: University of Minnesota Press, 1986.

Arblaster, Anthony. *Democracy*. Milton Keynes: Open University Press, 1987.

———. *The Rise and Decline of Western Liberalism*. Oxford: Blackwell, 1984.

Arnhart, Larry. *Aristotle on Political Reasoning: A Commentary on the "Rhetoric."* DeKalb: Northern Illinois University Press, 1981.

Baldwin, Charles Sears. *Ancient Rhetoric and Poetic*. New York: Macmillan, 1924.

Ball, Terence. "Plato and Aristotle: The Unity versus the Autonomy of Theory and Practice." In *Political Theory and Praxis: New Perspectives*, ed. Terence Ball. Minneapolis: University of Minnesota Press, 1977.

Balsdon, J. P. V. D. "*Auctoritas, Dignitas, Otium*." *Classical Quarterly* 10 (1960): 43–50.

Barbu, N. I. "*De Ciceronis humanitate*." *Latinitas* 16 (1968): 9–21.

Barker, Ernest. *The Political Thought of Plato and Aristotle*. New York: Dover, 1959.

——. _The "Politics" of Aristotle: Translated with an Introduction, Notes, and Appendixes._ 1946. Reprint, London: Oxford University Press, 1958.

Barnes, Jonathan. "Is Rhetoric an Art?" _DARG Newsletter_ 2, 2 (1986): 2–22.

Baron, Hans. "Leonardo Bruni: 'Professional Rhetorician' or 'Civic Humanist'?" _Past and Present_ 36 (1967): 21–37.

Bellah, Robert Neeley. _The Good Society._ New York: Knopf, 1991.

——. _Habits of the Heart: Individualism and Commitment in American Life._ Berkeley: University of California Press, 1985.

Benhabib, Seyla. _Critique, Norm, and Utopia: A Study of the Foundations of Ancient Philosophy._ New York: Columbia University Press, 1986.

——. _Feminism as Critique: Essays on the Politics of Gender in Late-Capitalist Societies._ Cambridge: Polity, 1987.

Berlin, James. _Rhetoric and Reality: Writing Instruction in American Colleges, 1900–1985._ Carbondale: Southern Illinois University Press, 1987.

——. "Rhetoric, Poetic, and Culture: Contested Boundaries in English Studies." _The Politics of Writing Instruction: Postsecondary,_ ed. Richard Bullock and John Trimbur, 21–38. Portsmouth, N.H.: Boynton/Cook, 1991.

——. _Writing Instruction in Nineteenth-Century American Colleges._ Carbondale: Southern Illinois University Press, 1984.

Bernal, Martin. _Black Athena: The Afroasiastic Roots of Classical Civilization._ 2 vols. New Brunswick: Rutgers University Press, 1987–91.

Biesecker, Barbara. "Coming to Terms with Recent Attempts to Write Women into the History of Rhetoric." _Philosophy and Rhetoric_ 25, 2 (1992): 140–61.

Blank, David. L. "Socratics versus Sophists on Payment for Teaching." _Classical Antiquity_ 4 (1985): 1–49.

Bourdieu, Pierre. _Distinction: A Social Critique of the Judgement of Taste._ Trans. Richard Nice. Cambridge: Harvard University Press, 1984.

——. _Language and Symbolic Power._ Trans. Gino Raymond and Matthew Adamson. Ed. John B. Thompson. Cambridge: Harvard University Press, 1991.

——. _The Logic of Practice._ Trans. Richard Nice. Cambridge: Polity, 1990.

——. _Outline of a Theory of Practice._ Trans. Richard Nice. Cambridge: Cambridge University Press, 1977.

Bové, Paul. _Intellectuals in Power: A Genealogy of Critical Humanism._ New York: Columbia University Press, 1986.

Bowles, Samuel, and Herbert Gintis. _Democracy and Capitalism: Property, Community, and the Contradictions of Modern Thought._ New York: Basic, 1986.

Burckhardt, Jacob. _The Civilization of the Renaissance in Italy: An Essay._ Trans. S. G. C. Middlemore. 4th ed. New York: Phaidon, 1951.

Burn, Andrew Robert. _The World of Hesiod: A Study of the Greek Middle Ages c. 900–700 B.C._ New York: Benjamin Blom, 1966.

Burnet, John. _Early Greek Philosophy._ 4th ed. London: Black, 1930.

——. _The "Ethics" of Aristotle Edited with an Introduction and Notes._ London: Methuen, 1900.

——. *Greek Philosophy: Thales to Plato* New York: St. Martin's, 1962.

Burtt, Shelley. *Virtue Transformed: Political Argument in England, 1688–1740.* Cambridge: Cambridge University Press, 1992.

Bury, J. B. *A History of Greece to the Death of Alexander the Great.* New York: Modern Library, 1913.

Buxton, R. G. A. *Persuasion in Greek Tragedy: A Study of Peitho.* Cambridge: Cambridge University Press, 1982.

Cairns, Douglas L. *Aidōs: The Psychology and Ethics of Honour and Shame in Ancient Greek Literature.* Oxford: Clarendon, 1993.

Campana, Augusto. "The Origin of the Word 'Humanist.'" *Journal of the Warburg and Courtauld Institutes* 9 (1946): 60–73.

Castoriadis, Cornelius. *Crossroads in the Labyrinth.* Trans. Kate Soper and Martin H. Ryle. Cambridge: MIT Press, 1984.

Charlton, William. "Greek Philosophy and the Concept of an Academic Discipline." In *Crux: Essays in Greek History Presented to G. E. M. de Ste. Croix,* ed. P. A. Carledge and F. D. Harvey. London: Duckworth, 1985.

Cixous, Hélène, and Catherine Clement. *The Newly Born Woman.* Trans. Betsy Wing. Theory and History of Literature, no. 24. Minneapolis: University of Minnesota Press, 1986.

Cmiel, Kenneth. *Democratic Eloquence: The Fight over Popular Speech in Nineteenth-Century America.* Berkeley: University of California Press, 1990.

Coates, Willson H., Hayden V. White, and J. Salwyn Schapiro. *The Emergence of Liberal Humanism.* New York: McGraw-Hill, 1966.

Cohen, David. *Law, Sexuality, and Society.* Cambridge: Cambridge University Press, 1991.

Cole, Thomas. *Democritus and the Sources of Greek Anthropology.* Philological Monographs, no. 25. Cleveland: Western Reserve University Press for American Philological Association, 1967.

——. *The Origins of Rhetoric in Ancient Greece.* Baltimore: Johns Hopkins University Press, 1991.

Conacher, D. J. *Aeschylus' "Prometheus Bound": A Literary Commentary.* Toronto: University of Toronto Press, 1980.

Conley, Thomas M. *Rhetoric in the European Tradition.* New York: Longman, 1990.

Cope, Edward M. *An Introduction to Aristotle's "Rhetoric."* London: Macmillan, 1867.

——. *The "Rhetoric" of Aristotle, with a Commentary.* Ed. John Sandys. 3 vols. Cambridge: Cambridge University Press, 1877.

Cornford, F. M. *From Religion to Philosophy.* 1912. Reprint, New York: Harper, 1957.

Crane, R. S. "The Idea of the Humanities." In *The Idea of the Humanities and Other Essays Critical and Historical.* Volume I, 3–15. Chicago: University of Chicago Press, 1967.

——. "Shifting Definitions and Evaluation of the Humanities from the Renaissance to the Present." In *The Idea of the Humanities and Other*

Essays Critical and Historical. Volume I, 16–170. Chicago: University of Chicago Press, 1967.

Crane, R.S., et al. *Critics and Criticism: Ancient and Modern.* Chicago: University of Chicago Press, 1952.

Crowley, Sharon. "Invention in Nineteenth-Century Rhetoric." *CCC* 36, 1 (1985): 51–60.

——. "Method in Nineteenth-Century American Rhetoric." In *Visions of Rhetoric: History, Theory, and Criticism,* ed. Charles Kneupper. Arlington, Tex.: Rhetoric Society of America, 1987.

Dallmayr, Fred. *Polis and Praxis: Exercises in Contemporary Political Theory.* Cambridge: MIT Press, 1984.

——. *Twilight of Subjectivity: Contributions to a Post-Individualist Theory of Politics.* Amherst: University of Massachusetts Press, 1981.

Davies, J. K. *Democracy and Classical Greece.* Atlantic Highlands, N.J.: Humanities, 1978.

Deleuze, Gilles, and Félix Guattari. *Anti-Oedipus: Capitalism and Schizophrenia.* Minneapolis: University of Minnesota Press, 1983.

——. *A Thousand Plateaus: Capitalism and Schizophrenia.* Trans. Brian Massumi. Minneapolis: University of Minnesota Press, 1987.

de Rijk, L. M. "*Enkuklios Paideia*": A Study of Its Original Meaning." *Vivarium* 3 (1965): 24–93.

Derrida, Jacques. "The Age of Hegel." In *Demarcating the Disciplines,* ed. Samuel Weber, 3–34. Minneapolis: University of Minnesota Press.

——. "The Ends of Man." *Margins of Philosophy.* Trans. Alan Bass. Chicago: University of Chicago Press, 1982.

——. *Of Grammatology.* Trans. Gayatri Chakravorty Spivak. Baltimore: John Hopkins University Press, 1976.

——. "The Principle of Reason: The University in the Eyes of Its Pupils." *Diacritics* 13, 3 (1983): 1–20.

Detienne, Marcel and Jean-Pierre Vernant. *Cunning Intelligence in Greek Culture and Society.* Trans. Janet Lloyd. 1978. Reprint, Chicago: University of Chicago Press, 1991.

Dorey, T. A. "Honesty in Roman Politics." In *Cicero,* ed. T. A. Dorey, 27–45. London: Routledge, 1965.

duBois, Page. *Sowing the Body: Psychoanalysis and Ancient Representations of Women.* Chicago: University of Chicago Press, 1988.

——. *Torture and Truth.* New York: Routledge, 1991.

Edel, Abraham. *Aristotle and His Philosophy.* Chapel Hill: University of North Carolina Press, 1982.

Edmunds, Lowell. *Chance and Intelligence in Thucydides.* Cambridge: Harvard University Press, 1975.

Ehrenberg, Margaret R. *Women in Prehistory.* Norman: University of Oklahoma Press, 1989.

Ehrenberg, Victor. *From Solon to Socrates: Greek History and Civilization during the Sixth and Fifth Centuries B.C.* London: Methuen, 1968.

——. *Man, State, and Deity: Essays in Ancient History.* London: Methuen, 1974.

Eliot, Charles W. *The Conflict between Individualism and Collectivism in a Democracy.* New York: Scribner's, 1910.

Else, Gerald. "'Imitation' in the Fifth Century." *Classical Philology* 53, 2 (1958): 73–90.

Farrar, Cynthia. *The Origins of Democratic Thinking: The Invention of Politics in Classical Athens.* Cambridge: Cambridge University Press, 1988.

Farrell, Thomas. *Norms of Rhetorical Culture.* New Haven: Yale University Press, 1993.

Feinberg, Walter. *Reason and Rhetoric: The Intellectual Foundations of Twentieth-Century Liberal Educational Policy.* New York: Wiley, 1975.

Finley, M. I. *Ancient Economy.* Berkeley: University of California Press, 1973.

Fish, Stanley. "Anti-Foundationalism, Theory Hope, and the Teaching of Composition." In *The Current in Criticism,* ed. Clayton Koelb and Virgil Lokke. West Lafayette, Ind.: Purdue University Press, 1987.

——. "Consequences." In *Against Theory: Literary Studies and the New Pragmatism,* ed. W. J. T. Mitchell. Chicago: University of Chicago Press, 1985.

Fisher, N. R. E. Introduction to *Social Values in Classical Athens,* ed. N. R. E. Fisher. London: Dent, 1976.

Foucault, Michel. *The Archaeology of Knowledge and the Discourse on Language.* Trans. A. M. Sheridan Smith. New York: Pantheon, 1972.

Fromm, Erich, ed. *Socialist Humanism: An International Symposium.* Garden City, N.Y.: Doubleday, 1966.

Gagarin, Michael. "*Dikē* in Archaic Greek Thought." *Classical Philology* 69, 3 (1974): 186–97.

——. "*Dikē* in the *Works and Days.*" *Classical Philology* 68, 2 (1973): 81–94.

Gandt, Francois De. "Force et Science des Machines." In *Science and Speculation: Studies in Hellenistic Theory and Practice,* ed. Jonathan Barnes et al. Cambridge: Cambridge University Press, 1982.

Garin, Eugenio. *Italian Humanism: Philosophy and Civic Life in the Renaissance.* Trans. Peter Munz. New York: Harper, 1965.

Garver, Eugene. *Aristotle's "Rhetoric": An Art of Character.* Chicago: University of Chicago Press, 1994.

Gates, Henry Louis, Jr.. *Loose Canons: Notes on the Culture Wars.* New York: Oxford University Press, 1992.

Gebauer, Gunter, and Christoph Wulf. *Mimesis: Culture, Art, Society.* Trans. Don Reneau. Berkeley: University of California Press, 1995.

Gill, Christopher. "Personhood and Personality: The Four-Personae Theory in Cicero, *De Officiis I.*" *Oxford Studies in Ancient Philosophy* 7 (1988): 169–99.

Gilleland, Brady. "The Development of Cicero's Ideal Orator." In *Classical, Mediaeval, and Renaissance Studies in Honor of Berthold Louis Ullman,* ed. Charles Henderson. 2 vols. Rome: Edizioni di storia e letteratura, 1964.

Glendon, Mary Ann. *Rights Talk: The Impoverishment of Political Discourse.* New York: Macmillan, Free Press, 1991.

Graff, Gerald. *Professing Literature: An Institutional History.* Chicago: University of Chicago Press, 1987.

Grafton, Anthony, and Lisa Jardine. *From Humanism to the Humanities: Education and the Liberal Arts in Fifteenth- and Sixteenth-Century Europe.* London: Duckworth, 1986.

Grant, Arthur J. *Greece in the Age of Pericles.* 1893. Reprint, New York: Cooper Square, 1975.

Grassi, Ernesto. *Rhetoric as Philosophy: The Humanist Tradition.* University Park: Pennsylvania State University Press, 1980.

——. "Why Rhetoric Is Philosophy." *Philosophy and Rhetoric* 20, 2 (1987): 68–78.

Gray, Hanna. "Renaissance Humanism: The Pursuit of Eloquence." *Journal of the History of Ideas* 24 (1963): 497–514.

Griffith, Mark, ed. *Aeschylus, "Prometheus Bound."* Cambridge: Cambridge University Press, 1983.

Grimaldi, William M. A., S. J. *Aristotle, "Rhetoric" I: A Commentary.* New York: Fordham University Press, 1980.

——. *Aristotle, "Rhetoric" II: A Commentary.* New York: Fordham University Press, 1988.

——. *Studies in the Philosophy of Aristotle's "Rhetoric."* Wiesbaden: Franz Steiner Verlag GMBH, 1972.

Guthrie, W. K. C. *A History of Greek Philosophy.* Vol. 3, *The Fifth-Century Enlightenment.* Cambridge: Cambridge University Press, 1969.

——. *A History of Greek Philosophy.* Vol. 4, *Plato the Man and His Dialogues: Earlier Period.* Cambridge: Cambridge University Press, 1975.

Hadas, Moses. *Humanism: The Greek Ideal and Its Survival.* Ed. Ruth Nanda Anshen. World Perspectives, no. 24. New York: Harper, 1960.

Hammond, N. G. L. *The Classical Age of Greece.* New York: Barnes and Noble, 1975.

——. *A History of Greece to 322 B.C.* 3d ed. Oxford: Clarendon, 1986.

Hansen, Mogens Herman. "The Political Powers of the People's Court in Fourth-Century Athens." In *The Greek City: From Homer to Alexander,* ed. Oswyn Murray and Simon Price. Oxford: Clarendon, 1990.

Havelock, Eric A. *Prometheus.* Seattle: University of Washington Press, 1968.

Heidegger, Martin. *Basic Writings.* Ed. David Farrell Krell. New York: Harper and Row, 1977.

Heidel, William. "*Peri Physeōs:* A Study of the Conception of Nature among the Pre-Socratics." *Proceedings of the American Academy of Arts and Sciences.* 45, 4 (1910): 79–133.

Hicks, Robert D. Notes to *Aristotle "De Anima" with Translation, Introductions, and Notes.* 1907. Reprint, New York: Arno, 1976.

Ijsseling, Samuel. *Rhetoric and Philosophy in Conflict.* The Hague: Martinus Nijhoff, 1976.

Inwood, Brad, trans. *The Poem of Empedocles.* Toronto: University of Toronto Press, 1992.

Irwin, Terence. "Moral Science and Political Theory in Aristotle." In *Crux: Essays in Greek History Presented to G. E. M. de Ste. Croix,* ed. P. A. Cartledge and F. D. Harvey. London: Duckworth, 1985.

——. *Plato's "Ethics."* New York: Oxford University Press, 1995.

——. *Plato's Moral Theory: The Early and Middle Dialogues.* Oxford: Clarendon, 1977.

Jaeger, Werner. *Paideia: The Ideals of Greek Culture.* Trans. Gilbert Highet. 2d ed. 3 vols. New York: Oxford University Press, 1939–44.

Jarratt, Susan. *Rereading the Sophists: Classical Rhetoric Refigured.* Carbondale: Southern Illinois University Press, 1991.

Jones, Howard Mumford. *American Humanism: Its Meaning for World Survival.* World Perspectives, no. 14. New York: Harper, 1957.

Kahn, Victoria. *Machiavellian Rhetoric: From the Reformation to Milton.* Princeton: Princeton University Press, 1994.

——. *Rhetoric, Prudence, and Skepticism in the Renaissance.* Ithaca: Cornell University Press, 1985.

Kennedy, George. *The Art of Rhetoric in the Roman World.* Princeton: Princeton University Press, 1972.

——. *Classical Rhetoric and Its Christian and Secular Tradition.* Chapel Hill: University of North Carolina Press, 1980.

——. "The Rhetoric of Advocacy in Greece and Rome." *American Journal of Philology* 89 (1968): 419–36.

——, trans. *On Rhetoric: A Theory of Civic Discourse,* by Aristotle. New York: Oxford University Press, 1991.

Kerferd, G. B. "Protagoras' Doctrine of Justice and Virtue in the Protagoras of Plato." *Journal of Hellenic Studies* 73 (1953): 42–45.

——. *The Sophistic Movement.* Cambridge: Cambridge University Press, 1981.

Kimball, Bruce. *Orators and Philosophers: A History of the Idea of Liberal Education.* New York: Teachers College Press, 1986.

Kinneavy, James L. "Translating Theory into Practice in Teaching Composition: A Historical View and a Contemporary View." In *Essays on Classical Rhetoric and Modern Discourse,* ed. Robert J.Connors, Lisa S. Ede, and Andrea A. Lunsford. Carbondale: Southern Illinois University Press, 1984.

Kirk, G. S., J. E. Raven, and Malcolm Schofield. *The Presocratic Philosophers: A Critical History with a Selection of Texts.* 2d ed. Cambridge: Cambridge University Press, 1983.

Kohl, Benjamin G. *Renaissance Humanism, 1300–1550.* New York: Garland Press, 1985.

Kosko, Bart. *Fuzzy Thinking: The New Science of Fuzzy Logic.* New York: Hyperion, 1993.

Kramer, Matthew. *Legal Theory, Political Theory, and Deconstruction.* Bloomington: Indiana University Press, 1991.

Kristeller, Paul Oskar. *Renaissance Thought and Its Sources.* Ed. Michael Mooney. New York: Columbia University Press, 1979.

Kristeva, Julia. *Revolution in Poetic Language.* New York: Columbia University Press, 1984.

Kudlein, Fridolf. "Medicine as a 'Liberal Art' and the Question of the Physician's Income." *Journal of the History of Medicine and Allied Sciences* 31 (1976): 448–459.

Kuhn, Thomas S. *The Structure of Scientific Revolutions.* 2d. ed. Chicago: University of Chicago Press, 1970.

Laclau, Ernesto, and Chantal Mouffe. *Hegemony and Socialist Strategy: Towards a Radical Democratic Politics.* London: Verso, 1985.

Laín Entralgo, Pedro. *The Therapy of the Word in Classical Antiquity.* New Haven: Yale University Press, 1970.

Lanham, Richard. "The Extraordinary Convergence: Democracy, Technology, Theory, and the University Curriculum." In *The Politics of Liberal Education,* ed. Darryl J. Gless and Barbara Herrnstein. Durham: Duke University Press, 1992.

Larson, Magali Sarfatti. *The Rise of Professionalism: A Sociological Analysis.* Berkeley: University of California Press, 1977.

Lauer, Janice M. "Issues in Rhetorical Invention." In *Essays on Classical Rhetoric and Modern Discourse,* ed. Robert J. Connors, Lisa S. Ede, and Andrea A. Lunsford. Carbondale: Southern Illinois University Press, 1984.

——. "Persuasive Writing on Public Issues." In *Composition in Context: Essays in Honor of Donald C. Stewart,* ed. Ross Winterowd and V. Gillespie. Carbondale: Southern Illinois University Press, 1994.

——."Rhetoric and Composition Studies: A Multi-Modal Discipline." In *Toward Defining the New Rhetoric,.* ed. Theresa Enos and Stuart Brown. Newbury Park, Calif.: Sage Publications, 1992.

Lauer, Janice M., and Richard Enos. "The Meaning of *Heuristic* in Aristotle's *Rhetoric* and Its Implications for Contemporary Rhetorical Theory." In *A Rhetoric of Doing: Essays on Written Discourse in Honor of James L. Kinneavy,* ed. Stephen Witte, Roger Cherry, and Neil Nakodate. Newbury Park, Calif.: Sage Publications, 1992.

Leff, Michael. "Genre and Paradigm in the Second Book of *De Oratore.*" *Southern Speech Communications Journal* 51 (1986): 308–25.

——. "The Habitation of Rhetoric." In *Argument and Critical Practice: Proceedings of the Fifth AFA/SCA Conference on Argumentation,* ed. Joe Wenzel. Annandale, Va.: Speech Communication Association, 1987.

——. "The Topics of Argumentative Invention in Latin Rhetorical Theory from Cicero to Boethius." *Rhetorica* 1 (1983): 23–43.

Lefort, Claude. *Democracy and Political Theory.* Trans. David Macey. Cambridge: Polity, 1988.

Lewis, Charlton T., and Charles Short. *Oxford Latin Dictionary.* Oxford: Clarendon, 1975.

Liddell, Henry George, Robert Scott, and Henry Stuart Jones. *A Greek-English*

Lexicon. Rev. ed., 1940. Reprint with Supplement, Oxford: Clarendon Press, 1968.

Lloyd, G. E. R. *Early Greek Science: Thales to Aristotle.* New York: W. W. Norton, 1970.

——. *Science, Folklore, and Ideology.* Cambridge: Cambridge University Press, 1983.

——. "Who Is Attacked in *On Ancient Medicine.*" In *Methods and Problems in Greek Science.* Cambridge: Cambridge University Press, 1991

Lobkowicz, Nicholas. *Theory and Practice: History of a Concept from Aristotle to Marx.* Notre Dame, Ind.: University of Notre Dame Press, 1967.

Lokke, Virgil. "The Naming of the Virgule in the Linguistic/Extra-Linguistic Binary." In *After the Future: Postmodern Times and Places,* ed. Gary Shapiro. Albany: State University of New York Press, 1990.

Long, A. A. *Hellenistic Philosophy: Stoics, Epicureans, Sceptics.* 2d ed. London: Duckworth, 1986.

Lyotard, Jean-François. *The Differend: Phrases in Dispute.* Trans. Georges Van Den Abbeele. Minneapolis: University of Minnesota Press, 1988.

——. *The Inhuman: Reflections on Time.* Trans. Geoffrey Bennington and Rachel Bowlby. Cambridge: Polity,1991.

——. *The Postmodern Condition: A Report on Knowledge.* Trans. Geoffrey Bennington and Brian Massumi. Minneapolis: University of Minnesota Press, 1985.

Maguire, Joseph P. "Protagoras . . . or Plato? II. *The Protagoras.*" *Phronesis* 22 (1977): 103–22.

Marrou, H. I. *A History of Education in Antiquity.* Trans. George Lamb. London: Sheed, 1956.

May, James. "The Rhetoric of Advocacy and Patron-Client Identification: Variation on a Theme." *Americal Journal of Philology* 102 (1981): 308–15.

——. *Trials of Character: The Eloquence of Ciceronian Ethos.* Chapel Hill: University of North Carolina Press, 1988.

McKeon, Richard. "Literary Criticism and the Concept of Imitation in Antiquity." In *Critics and Criticism: Ancient and Modern,* ed. R. S. Crane. Chicago: University of Chicago Press, 1957.

——. "The Uses of Rhetoric in a Technological Age: Architectonic Productive Arts." In *Essays in Invention and Discovery,* ed. Mark Backman. Woodbridge, Conn.: Ox Bow Press, 1987.

McNeal, Richard A. "Protagoras the Historian." *History and Theory* 25 (1986): 299–318.

Merry, W. Walter, and James Riddell. Notes to *Homer's "Odyssey."* Vol. 1. 2d. ed. Oxford: Clarendon, 1886.

Mill, John Stuart. *A System of Logic.* Vol. 2. 3d. ed. London: John W. Parker, 1851.

Miller, Harold W. "*On Ancient Medicine* and the Origin of Medicine." *Transactions of the American Philological Association* 80 (1949): 187–202.

——. "*Technē* and Discovery in *On Ancient Medicine.*" *Transactions of the American Philological Association* 86 (1955): 51–62.

Minar, Edwin. *Early Pythagorean Politics in Practice and Theory.* Baltimore: Waverly, 1942.

Mitchell, W. J. T., ed. *Against Theory: Literary Studies and the New Pragmatism.* Chicago: University of Chicago Press, 1985.

Moore, Stanley. "Democracy and Commodity Exchange: Protagoras versus Plato." *History of Philosophy Quarterly* 5 (1988): 357–68.

Morrison, J. S. "The Place of Protagoras in Athenian Public Life." *Classical Quarterly* 35 (1941): 1–16.

"Mr. Sobols's Planet." *New Republic,* 15 and 22 July 1991, 5–6.

Mumford, Lewis. *Technics and Civilization.* New York: Harcourt, Brace, 1934.

Murphy, James. *Rhetoric in the Middle Ages: A History of Rhetorical Theory from St. Augustine to the Renaissance.* Berkeley: University of California Press, 1974.

Murray, Oswyn. *Early Greece.* Stanford: Stanford University Press, 1983.

Murray, Oswyn, and Simon Price. *The Greek City: From Homer to Alexander.* Oxford: Clarendon, 1990.

Nehamas, Alexander. "Eristic, Antilogic, Sophistic, Dialectic: Plato's Demarcation of Philosophy from Sophistry." *History of Philosophy Quarterly* 7 (1990): 3–16.

North, Helen. *Sophrosyne: Self-Knowledge and Self-Restraint in Greek Literature.* Ithaca: Cornell University Press, 1966.

Nussbaum, Martha C. *The Fragility of Goodness.* Cambridge: Cambridge University Press, 1986.

Ober, Josiah. *Mass and Elite in Democratic Athens: Rhetoric, Ideology, and the Power of the People.* Princeton: Princeton University Press, 1989.

Ong, Walter J., S. J. *Ramus, Method, and the Decay of Dialogue.* Cambridge: Harvard University Press, 1983.

Osborne, Catherine. *Rethinking Early Greek Philosophy.* Ithaca: Cornell University Press, 1987.

Osborne, Robin. *Demos: The Discovery of Classical Attika.* Cambridge: Cambridge University Press, 1985.

Owen, G. E. L. "*Tithenai ta phainomena.*" In *Logic, Science, and Dialectic,* ed. Martha Nussbaum. Ithaca: Cornell University Press, 1986.

Oxford Classical Dictionary. Ed. N. G. L. Hammond and H. H. Scullard. 2d ed. Oxford: Clarendon, 1970.

Podlecki, Anthony J. *The Political Background of Aeschylean Tragedy.* Ann Arbor: University of Michigan Press, 1966.

Pratt, Mary Louise. "Humanities for the Future: Reflections on the Western Culture Debate at Stanford." In *The Politics of Liberal Education,* ed. Darryl J. Gless and Barbara Herrnstein Smith. Durham, N.C.: Duke University Press, 1992.

Rabil, Albert. "The Significance of 'Civic Humanism' in the Interpretation of the Italian Renaissance." In *Humanism in Italy,* 141–74. Vol. 1 of *Renaissance Humanism: Foundations, Forms, and Legacy,* ed. Albert Rabil. 3 vols. Philadelphia: University of Pennsylvania Press, 1988.

Randall, John Herman, Jr. "Which Are the Liberating Arts?" *American Scholar* 13 (1944): 133–48.

Rhodes, P. J. *A Commentary on the Aristotelian "Athenaion Politeia."* Oxford: Clarendon, 1981.

Romilly, Jacqueline de. *Magic and Rhetoric in Ancient Greece.* Cambridge: Harvard University Press, 1975.

Rorty, Amelie Oksenberg, ed. *Essays on Aristotle's "Ethics."* Berkeley: University of California Press, 1980.

Rorty, Richard. *Philosophy and the Mirror of Nature.* Princeton: Princeton University Press, 1979.

Rose, Peter. *Sons of the Gods, Children of Earth: Ideology and Literary Form in Ancient Greece.* Ithaca: Cornell University Press, 1992.

Roseman, Norman. "Protagoras and the Foundations of His Educational Thought." *Paedagogica Historica* 11 (1971): 75–89.

Rosen, Stanley. *Plato's "Sophist."* New Haven: Yale University Press, 1983

Ross, W. David. Introduction and Commentary to *Aristotle "De Anima" Edited with Introduction and Commentary.* Oxford: Clarendon, 1961.

——. Introduction and Commentary to *Aristotle "Metaphysics" A Revised Text with Introduction and Commentary.* 2 vols. Oxford: Clarendon, 1958.

Said, Edward. *Orientalism.* New York: Pantheon, 1978.

——. *The World, the Text, and the Critic.* Cambridge: Harvard University Press, 1983.

Sandel, Michael J. *Liberalism and the Limits of Justice.* Cambridge: Cambridge University Press, 1982.

Sattler, William. "Conceptions of *Ethos* in Ancient Rhetoric." *Speech Monographs* 14 (1947): 55–65.

Schiappa, Edward. "Did Plato Coin *Rhētorikē*?" *American Journal of Philology* 111 (1990): 460–73.

——. *Protagoras and Logos: A Study in Greek Philosophy and Rhetoric.* Columbia: University of South Carolina Press, 1991.

——. "*Rhētorikē:* What's in a Name? Toward a Revised History of Early Greek Rhetorical Theory." *Quarterly Journal of Speech* 78 (1992): 1–15.

Schrag, Calvin O. *Communicative Praxis and the Space of Subjectivity.* Bloomington: Indiana University Press, 1986.

——."Rhetoric Resituated at the End of Philosophy." *Quarterly Journal of Speech* 71 (1985): 164–74.

Seigel, J. E. "'Civic Humanism' or 'Ciceronian Rhetoric'?" *Past and Present* 34 (1966): 3–48.

——. *Rhetoric and Philosophy in Renaissance Humanism: The Union of Eloquence and Wisdom, Petrarch to Valla.* Princeton: Princeton University Press, 1968.

Sher, Gerson S., ed. *Marxist Humanism and Praxis.* Buffalo, N.Y.: Prometheus, 1978.

Shorey, Paul, trans. Plato, *The Republic.* 2 vols. Loeb Classical Library, 1930. Reprint, Cambridge: Harvard University Press, 1946.

Sinclair, R. K. *Democracy and Participation in Athens.* Cambridge: Cambridge University Press, 1988.

Smith, Barbara Herrnstein. *Contingencies of Value.* Cambridge: Harvard University Press, 1988.

Smith, Paul. *Discerning the Subject.* Minneapolis: University of Minnesota Press, 1988.

Solmsen, Friedrich. *Hesiod and Aeschylus.* Ithaca: Cornell University Press, 1949.

Soper, Kate. *Humanism and Anti-Humanism.* La Salle, Ill. : Open Court, 1986.

Spivak, Gayatri Chakravorty. *In Other Worlds: Essays in Cultural Politics.* New York: Routledge, 1988.

Strauss, Leo. *Liberalism Ancient and Modern.* New York: Basic, 1968.

Struever, Nancy S. *The Language of History in the Renaissance: Rhetorical and Historical Consciousness in Florentine Humanism.* Princeton: Princeton University Press, 1970.

Sutton, Jane. "The Death of Rhetoric and Its Rebirth in Philosophy." *Rhetorica* 4 (1986): 203–26.

Swearingen, C. Jan. "The Rhetor as Eiron: Plato's Defense of Dialogue." *Pre/Text* 3, 4 (1982).

Tandy, David. *Warriors into Traders: The Power of the Market in Early Greece.* Berkeley: University of California Press, 1997.

Tandy, David, and Walter C. Neale. *Hesiod's "Works and Days."* Berkeley: University of California Press, 1996.

Taylor, M. M. *Men versus the State: Herbert Spencer and Late Victorian Individualism.* Oxford Historical Monographs. Oxford: Clarendon, 1992.

Thomson, George. *Aeschylus and Athens.* New York: Haskell House, 1967.

——. *The First Philosophers.* 1st American ed. Vol. 2 of *Studies in Ancient Greek Society.* New York: Citadel, 1965.

——. *The Prehistoric Aegean.* 2d ed. Vol.1 of *Studies in Ancient Greek Society.* 1961. Reprint, New York: Citadel, 1977.

Trinkaus, Charles. *In Our Image and Likeness: Humanity and Divinity in Italian Renaissance Thought.* 2 vols. Chicago: University of Chicago Press, 1970.

——. "Protagoras in the Renaissance: An Exploration." In *Philosophy and Humanism: Renaissance Essays in Honor of Paul Oskar Kristeller,* ed. Edward P. Mahoney, 190–213. New York: Columbia University Press, 1976.

——. *The Scope of Renaissance Humanism.* Ann Arbor: University of Michigan Press, 1983.

Untersteiner, Mario. *The Sophists.* Trans. Kathleen Freeman. Oxford: Blackwell, 1954.

Vernant, Jean-Pierre. *Myth and Society in Ancient Greece.* Trans. Janet Lloyd. Atlantic Highlands, N.J.: Humanities Press, 1980.

——. *Myth and Thought among the Greeks.* London: Routledge and Kegan Paul, 1983.

——. *The Origins of Greek Thought.* Ithaca: Cornell University Press, 1982.

Vernant, Jean-Pierre, and Pierre Vidal-Naquet. *Tragedy and Myth in Ancient Greece.* Trans. Janet Lloyd. Atlantic Highlands, N.J.: Humanities Press, 1981.

Versenyi, Laszlo. *Man's Measure.* Albany: State University of New York Press, 1974.

Vidal-Naquet, Pierre. *The Black Hunter.* Trans. Andrew Szegedy-Maszak. Baltimore: Johns Hopkins University Press, 1986.

Vitanza, Victor. *Negation, Subjectivity, and the History of Rhetoric.* Albany: State University of New York Press, 1997.

Vlastos, Gregory. "Equality and Justice in Early Greek Cosmologies." *Classical Philology* 42 (July 1947): 156–78.

——."Isonomia." *American Journal of Philology* 74, 4 (1953): 337–66.

——. "*Isonomia Politikē.*" In *Isonomia: Studien zur Gleichheitsvorstellung im griechiscen Denken,* ed. Jurgen Mau and Ernst Gunther Schmidt. Amsterdam: Hakkert, 1971.

——. "On the Pre-History in Diodorus." *American Journal of Philology* 67 (1946): 51–59.

——. "Solonian Justice." *Classical Philology* 41 (1946): 65–83.

Ward, John O. "Magic and Rhetoric from Antiquity to the Renaissance: Some Ruminations." *Rhetorica* 6 (1988): 57–118.

Weber, Samuel. *Institution and Interpretation.* Theory and History of Literature, no. 31. Minneapolis: University of Minnesota Press, 1987.

West, Cornel. *Keeping Faith: Philosophy and Race in America.* New York: Routledge, 1993.

——. *Race Matters.* Boston: Beacon Press, 1993.

West, M. L. Prolegomena and Commentary to Hesiod, *Theogony.* Ed. and trans. West. Oxford: Clarendon 1966.

——. Prolegomena and Commentary to Hesiod, *Works and Days.* Ed and trans. West. Oxford: Clarendon: 1978.

Wilhoit (Hawhee), Debra." Kairos Revisited: The Rhetorical Situation and the Art of Becoming a Rhetor." Master's thesis, University of Tennessee, 1994.

Wilson, John R. "*Kairos* as 'Profit.'" *Classical Quarterly* 31 (1981): 418–20.

Winterbottom, Michael. "Quintilian and the *Vir Bonus.*" *Journal of Roman Studies* 54 (1964): 90–97.

Wirszubski, Chaim. "Cicero's *Cum Dignitate Otium:* A Reconsideration." *Journal of Roman Studies* 44 (1954): 1–13.

Wisse, Jacob. *Ethos and Pathos from Aristotle to Cicero.* Amsterdam: Hakkert, 1988.

Wood, Ellen Meiksins, and Neal Wood. *Class Ideology and Ancient Political Theory: Socrates, Plato, and Aristotle in Social Context.* Oxford: Basil Blackwell, 1978.

Woods, William. "Nineteenth-Century Psychology and the Teaching of Writing." *CCC* 36, 1 (1985): 20–41.

Wright, Handel Kashope. "(Re)conceptualising Pedagogy as Cultural Praxis." *Education and Society* 13, 1 (1995): 67–81.

Wright, M. R., trans. *Empedocles: The Extant Fragments.* New Haven: Yale University Press, 1981.

Young, Iris Marion. *Justice and the Politics of Difference.* Princeton: Princeton University Press, 1990.

Young, Richard. "Arts, Crafts, Gifts, and Knacks: Some Disharmonies in the New Rhetoric." In *Reinventing the Rhetorical Tradition,* ed. Ian Pringle and Aviva Freedman. Conway, Ark.: L and S Books, 1981.

Index